COMPOSERS FOR THE AMERICAN MUSICAL THEATRE

Also by David Ewen

COMPOSERS FOR THE AMERICAN MUSICAL THEATRE

By DAVID EWEN

Illustrated with photographs

DODD, MEAD & COMPANY
NEW YORK

FOR PHIL AND EVELYN SPITALNEY

"A friend is in prosperity a pleasure, a solace in adversity, in grief a comfort, in joy a merry companion, at all times another I."

John Lyly in *Euphues*

Library of Congress Catalog Card Number: 68-23095

Printed in the United States of America
by The Cornwall Press, Inc., Cornwall, N. Y.

INTRODUCTION

THE MOST SIGNIFICANT cultural exportation America has been making during the past two decades or so has been its musical theatre. There is hardly a place in the civilized world that has not been invaded and conquered by America's successful musical comedies and musical plays.

This continual flow from Broadway to the great stages of the world is a belated act of reciprocity. In its beginnings, the American musical theatre was made up entirely of foreign importations. In the closing decades of the nineteenth century, operettas and comic operas from France, England, Austria, and Germany dominated the American musical theatre.

The first musical production in the American colonies was *Flora,* produced in a courthouse in Charleston, South Carolina, on February 8, 1735. This was an English ballad opera, given without the benefit of scenery, staging, costumes, footlights, or limelight. A genre that had come into existence in London in 1728 with the historic *The Beggar's Opera,* the ballad opera continued to be seen in the Colonies up to the time of the Revolution and for a number of years after that.

In 1828, a new form of musical theatre became popular in

America. This was the travesty (then known as "burlesque," though it should not be confused with burlesque shows of a later era), parodies of famous stage plays and performers. The first successful one was a satirical treatment of Shakespeare's *Hamlet*. For a number of decades, musical travesties continued presenting hilarious caricatures on the American stage, most of which came out of England.

Slowly a new kind of musical theatre began evolving and crystallizing in New York to become our first native stage-musical product. This was the minstrel show, in which performers appeared in blackface to present Negro songs, dances, and humor. The minstrel show was born on February 6, 1843, at the Bowery Amphitheatre, when four performers who called themselves the Virginia Minstrels appeared for the first time in public as part of a program that otherwise consisted mostly of circus acts. Then on March 7, 1843, in Boston, the Virginia Minstrels appeared for the first time in an entire evening of Negro entertainment. On this occasion they were dressed in swallow-tailed coats, striped calico shirts, and white pantaloons. The leading performer and director of this group was Dan Emmett, who also wrote songs for his productions. Emmett was the first important composer produced by the American musical stage. Many of his songs (all of them written for and introduced in minstrel shows) became classics. They include "Old Dan Tucker," "Jim Crack Corn," and most significantly "Dixie," which became the great war song of the South during the Civil War.

The format of the minstrel show, adhered to for the rest of the nineteenth century, was developed by the greatest minstrel of them all, Ed Christy. He seated his minstrels in a semicircle with the "Interlocutor" in the middle, Mr. Bones at one end and Mr. Tambo at the other. This seating arrangement became traditional. The Interlocutor asked questions to which either Mr. Bones (so called because he performed on a set of "bones" or clappers) or Mr. Tambo (who performed on a tambourine) gave quick, humorous responses. Christy was also the one who divided the evening's entertainment into three parts, something which once again became a standard practice. The first part was the "olio," or general entertainment, dominated by the exchanges of banter between Mr. Interlocutor and his end men. The second part was the "fantasia," where individual performers strutted their stuff in song and dance. The final part was the "burlesque," in which earlier procedures were satirized.

It was for the Ed Christy Minstrels that Stephen Foster, the foremost American composer of his generation, wrote his first classics about the Negro and the Southland, including the immortal "Old Folks at Home." Our first native form of stage entertainment, the minstrel show, then, produced our first important popular composers.

While the minstrel show was flourishing throughout the United States (and it continued to flourish up to the end of the nineteenth century) another form of musical entertainment came into being, the spectacle or extravaganza. This first became prominent with *The Black Crook,* which came to Niblo's Gardens in New York on September 12, 1866. *The Black Crook* had a slight story thread to tie the whole together into a single package: a pact made by the "black Crook" with the devil to deliver to him one human being a year. The emphasis was not on story nor on songs but upon spellbinding production numbers, scenes, ballets, and stage effects. Nothing quite like it had ever been seen in the American theatre. *The Black Crook* became the most successful musical produced in America up to that time, its initial run of four hundred performances and its profit of one million dollars being without precedent. It was seen more than two thousand times in various revivals by the time the nineteenth century ended.

There are many historians who look upon *The Black Crook* as the first important ancestor of the American musical comedy. This is because the chorus girl, dressed in tights, was one of its attractions; and the chorus line later became a basic ingredient of musical comedies. *The Black Crook,* as the ancestor of musical comedy, was one of the earliest "book" shows, a "book" show being one that had a story line on which to hang songs, dances, comedy numbers, production numbers, and so forth. And *The Black Crook* was one of the first "book" shows out of which came a successful popular song: "You Naughty, Naughty Men," sung by one of the stars of the show, Mily Cavendish.

The term "musical comedy" was used for the first time in 1874 in connection with *Evangeline,* text and music by E. E. Rice. *Evangeline* has another reason to be remembered. It is the first American musical stage production for which an original musical score was created. The one used for *The Black Crook* was made up mostly of interpolations and adaptations of familiar tunes and instrumental numbers.

The stepping-stones on which the American musical theatre progressed now become increasingly numerous. *The Brook,* in 1879—a musical farce about a picnic in the country, with book and lyrics by Nate Salsbury—was one of the first attempts to create a unified concept out of plot, characters, songs, and humor. After that came a series of farces, or burlesques, produced between 1879 and 1885, that introduced into the musical theatre portraits of life in New York among ethnic groups, notably Irish, German, and Negro. This series of shows came to be known as the "Mulligan Guard" burlesque-extravaganzas. Its stars were Ed Harrigan and Tony Hart, who also wrote the texts. All of the music was written expressly for these productions by David Braham. This was one of the first instances in which ordinary Americans in everyday situations populated the American musical stage. The dialogue, rich with an Irish brogue or German accent, was as true to life as the people and the situations. The songs were similarly in harmony with the situations from which they developed or the characters who sang them.

Harrigan and Hart stimulated the writing and production of many other burlesque-extravaganzas. The most successful was *A Trip to Chinatown* in 1893. Charlie Hoyt's text placed recognizable American characters in a San Francisco setting, while following their activities through topical problems and everyday happenings with broad humor. Its run of 650 performances was the longest any American musical had had up to this time; but this is just one way in which *A Trip to Chinatown* made stage history. It also became the first American musical to earn immense profits from the sheet-music publication of hit songs, the work of Percy Gaunt; two of these, as a matter of fact, are still remembered, "The Bowery" and "Reuben and Cynthia." *A Trip to Chinatown* was also the first musical in which an interpolated song (that is a song by a composer other than the one who wrote the basic score) became a giant success. After *A Trip to Chinatown* had opened, Charles K. Harris's sentimental ballad, "After the Ball," was placed in the show, sung by J. Aldrich Libby. It became a sensation, beginning a success story that ended up in the sale of over five million copies of sheet music and earning several million dollars for its composer.

After *A Trip to Chinatown,* the most successful burlesque-extravaganzas were those produced by Weber and Fields at their Music Hall in New York. Here Joe Weber and Lew Fields (two of the most famous dialect comedians of their time) were the stars. Their first production was *The Art of*

Maryland on September 5, 1896. It was filled with the same kind of farcical situations, parodies on current plays, take-offs of famous stage stars, dialect humor, rowdy horseplay, and offbeat stunts that would characterize all later Weber and Fields productions. Many a great star first came to prominence in those shows, including Lillian Russell, perhaps the most glamorous stage personality of her time. And many a song was introduced in Weber and Fields productions to become national hits, all of them written by John Stromberg, the official composer for the Music Hall; the most celebrated of these songs were "Dinah" (sometimes also known as "Kiss Me, Honey Do"), "Ma Blushin' Rosie," and a number which Lillian Russell introduced and made her trademark, "Come Down Ma Evenin' Star."

The last Weber and Fields burlesque was *Whoop-Dee-Doo* in 1903. With it a musical stage tradition passed out of existence. We are now at the dawn of a new century, and with it arrived new stage media to take over the limelight, such as the American operetta and musical comedy. The ancestors of our present-day musical theatre may go back many years, but its immediate parents were the operettas and musical comedies that became popular in the early 1900s. And this is where our story of the most significant composers of the American musical theatre begins.

CONTENTS

PHOTOGRAPHIC SUPPLEMENT

ASCAP

VICTOR HERBERT

ASCAP

RUDOLF FRIML

ASCAP

SIGMUND ROMBERG

ASCAP

GEORGE M. COHAN

JEROME KERN

ASCAP

IRVING BERLIN

ASCAP

ASCAP

GEORGE GERSHWIN

COLE PORTER

ASCAP

KURT WEILL

ASCAP

Halsman

RICHARD RODGERS

FREDERICK LOEWE

ASCAP

FRANK LOESSER

JERRY BOCK, RIGHT, WITH SHELDON HARNICK

Friedman-Abeles

LEONARD BERNSTEIN

ASCAP

I

VICTOR HERBERT

(1859-1924)

THE MODERN AMERICAN musical theatre came into being with the operetta.

The operetta was a foreign importation, having been born in German-speaking countries in the second half of the nineteenth century. Operetta is a musical production in which sentimentality and romance are the basic ingredients. Love proves ever triumphant and evil must meet its just due. The operetta conjures up a make-believe world or an exotic setting inhabited by kings, princes, princesses, and handsomely attired officers (call the place Graustark, if you will, or Ruritania). Staging, costuming, and song are all calculated to enchant the senses.

Franz von Suppé is often singled out as the creator of the operetta form. He was a Dalmatian composer, born in 1819, and his most famous works are *Fatinitza* (1876), *Boccaccio* (1879), and *Donna Juanita* (1880). These are not only the first successful operettas ever written but also operettas in which a tradition was established. In Suppé's operettas romantic interest predominates in the text, while the waltz became the spine and backbone of the musical score, usually the pivot upon which the big scene of the production spins.

The operetta moved from Dalmatia (which was then under Austrian rule) to Vienna where it achieved its heyday with Johann Strauss II, the waltz king, the composer of such stage classics as *The Bat* (*Die Fledermaus*) in 1874 and *Zigeunerbaron* (*Gypsy Baron*) in 1885. The effervescence, the gaiety, the glamour, the sentimentality with which operetta would henceforth be identified are found in these two Strauss masterworks. They were the inspiration for a school of operetta composers, in both Germany and Austria, headed by Franz Lehár, composer of *The Merry Widow* (one of the most celebrated operettas ever written), and Oscar Straus (no relation to Johann), composer of *A Waltz Dream* and *The Chocolate Soldier*.

Comic opera is the English equivalent, and opéra-bouffe the French equivalent, of the Austrian and German operetta —but with a difference. In comic opera and opéra-bouffe, comedy takes precedence over romance and sentimentality, but otherwise the two forms are blood relatives to the operetta in their partiality for mythical or exotic kingdoms, glamorous and high-born or legendary characters, and plots in which virtue triumphs over evil. Jacques Offenbach, composer of *Orpheus in the Underworld* (1858), *La Belle Hélène* (1864), and *La Périchole* (1868), was the genius of opéra-bouffe. Gilbert and Sullivan were the geniuses of comic operas, the most famous of which are *H.M.S. Pinafore* (1878), *The Pirates of Penzance* (1879), and *The Mikado* (1885).

Operetta and comic opera took hold in American theatres during the closing decades of the nineteenth century. The Casino Theatre, home of lavish musical productions for several decades, opened its doors in 1882 with Johann Strauss's *The Queen's Necklace*. Foreign operettas and comic operas immediately found a ready, waiting, and enthusiastic audience not only in New York but also throughout the United States. In the single year of 1894–1895, fourteen companies were touring America in presentations of these foreign musical productions. America became enchanted with not only the works of Johann Strauss II and Suppé, but also those of Offenbach and of Gilbert and Sullivan. The comic operas of the last pair became particular favorites. The first Gilbert and Sullivan production performed in America was *H.M.S. Pinafore* at the Boston Museum on November 15, 1878. It created a furor. In short order, ninety different companies were presenting *Pinafore* throughout the United States; in New York, five different companies (including one in Yiddish) were giving the opera simultaneously. After that, one after another of the Gilbert and Sullivan comic operas came to and conquered America. In fact, one of them, *The Pirates of Penzance,* received its world première in New York, in 1879, with Gilbert and Sullivan both present for the occasion; while another, *Iolanthe,* shared its world première on November 25, 1882, between New York and London.

Stimulated by the vogue for foreign operettas and comic operas, and seeking success through imitation, American popular composers began throwing covetous eyes toward the stage. The first successful American composer of comic opera was Willard Spencer. *The Little Tycoon,* obviously in imitation of *The Mikado,* was a huge success in both Philadelphia and New York in 1885 and 1886. John Philip Sousa, later to become the march king, first invaded the musical theatre with a Gilbert and Sullivan kind of comic opera of his own, *The Smugglers* in 1879; Sousa's greatest success in comic opera came in 1896 with *El Capitan.* More significant still was Reginald de Koven, composer of *Robin Hood,* produced in 1890. This is the first American comic opera from which we get a popular song that has become a "standard"—that is, a song that has survived. "Oh, Promise Me" has become something of a musical fixture at American weddings.

Victor Herbert became the first great composer of American operettas and comic operas. Those who had preceded him were minor talents; he was a major one. He was the first composer whose most important stage works are remembered fondly and are still occasionally revived on stage and screen and whose finest songs have become a basic part of our popular-song repertory.

Victor Herbert was born in Dublin on February 1, 1859; his father was a lawyer, and his mother, a talented amateur pianist. Family legend has it that shortly after Victor was born a gypsy fortune teller predicted the child would someday become his country's greatest composer. Be this fact or fancy, the child Victor was early trained in music. This education took place not in Dublin but in Sevenoaks, a little town outside London, in the cottage of his maternal grandfather, Samuel Lover. Father Herbert had died when Victor was still an infant, and the mother had taken her son to England to live with her own father.

This change of home and country proved providential for Victor's musical development. The grandfather, Samuel Lover, was a highly cultured gentleman. He was a poet, painter, the composer of songs, and the author of several famous novels, including *Handy Andy.* He spent the autumnal years of his life at his cottage, "The Vine," which he made into a setting attracting the cultural elite of London.

Herbert had left Dublin too young to carry away memories of his native land, but all his life he remained nostalgic and sentimental about his Irish birth. However, impressions gathered at Sevenoaks remained indelible. One evening, one of the most famous cellists of the time, Alfredo Carlo Piatti, gave a concerto at "The Vine." The child Herbert listened entranced. Later in life he described this experience: "Ah, his music was the supreme thing for me! Nobody in all the universe seemed quite as wonderful as he. Nothing quite so glorious as his cello. I don't suppose I said much about it at the time. But the longing to play a cello was lodged then and there in my soul. It took root and awaited its time."

His mother gave Victor his first music lessons at the piano. The child's response was quick and intuitive; both mother and grandfather had to take note that here was a born musician. Such being the case, both agreed that a thorough training was in order. Once again a change of home and country proved fortuitous for the boy.

When Victor was about six, his mother paid a visit to London where she fell in love with and married a German physician, Wilhelm Schmid. The couple established residence in Stuttgart, Germany, taking Victor with them. In Germany, far more than at Sevenoaks, Herbert could find the kind of instruction and environment he needed for his musical growth. Together with piano study, Victor was given lessons on the flute and piccolo; he played the last-named instrument in his school orchestra. Then he arrived at the instrument closest to his heart, the cello. From this point on his progress grew by leaps and bounds.

Upon leaving high school when he was fifteen, Victor ended his academic schooling to concentrate on music. For about two years, between 1874 and 1876, he studied the cello privately in Baden-Baden with Bernhard Cossmann, one of Germany's most distinguished cello virtuosos and teachers. This period of instruction, together with the listening experiences that musical Germany afforded, transformed Herbert from a student to a trained musician.

His professional career began as a cellist in various European orchestras. Performing under the direction of such masters as Anton Rubinstein, Saint-Saëns, and Brahms gave Herbert an all-important initiation into symphonic literature and into the art and science of conducting. This knowledge would serve him well years later when he became a symphonic conductor himself. In Vienna he played for a year in an orchestra led by Eduard Strauss. Eduard was the brother of Vienna's waltz king, Johann Strauss II. The Eduard Strauss orchestra carried on the family tradition by performing waltzes, polkas, quadrilles, and other examples of popular and semiclassical music. Here Herbert gathered that necessary background which would nurture him when he himself became a composer of popular and semiclassical music, and especially a composer of waltzes.

His apprenticeship as orchestral musician ended, Herbert returned to Stuttgart to become first cellist of the Royal Orchestra. Its conductor, Max Seyfritz, took Herbert in hand and taught him composition, harmony, and orchestration. This equipped Herbert to write a concerto and a suite, both of them for cello and orchestra. He himself introduced both works with the Royal Orchestra, Seyfritz conducting. As a cellist and as a composer, then, Herbert was beginning to make his mark.

He was very much of a ladies' man, too. One of the young women who fell in love with him, and to whom he responded in kind, was Theresa Förster, leading prima donna of the Stuttgart Royal Opera. Slim, dainty, elegant, she was as attractive to the eye as to the ear. Victor Herbert had often heard her sing. From his seat in the opera house he experienced the first stirrings of emotional interest in the woman as distinguished from the famous prima donna. In an attempt to establish contact with her, he wrote offering to be her piano accompanist and vocal coach. She declined, maintaining she already had the services of an accomplished musician. It took her first personal meeting with Herbert to get her to change her mind. The romance bloomed. On August 14, 1886, Herbert and Theresa Förster were married in Vienna.

Just before her marriage, Theresa Förster had been engaged to appear as a leading soprano of the Metropolitan Opera in New York. She signed the contract on the condition that Herbert be hired to play the cello in the opera house orchestra. Thus, when husband and wife arrived in New York on October 24, 1886, both had commitments to work at America's leading opera house—Mme. Herbert-Förster, a major commitment as prima donna, and Victor Herbert, a minor one as orchestral cellist.

Mme. Herbert-Förster made her American debut on the opening night of the Metropolitan Opera season, in Carl Goldmark's *The Queen of Sheba.* She was acclaimed. She stayed in the company for a full season, accumulating successes. Then she returned for a single appearance one season later. After that, her operatic appearances, both in America and in Europe, became less and less frequent until she retired permanently. There had been no decline in either her singing or her popularity to bring about her retirement. But as Herbert's career began to progress in high gear, as he began to achieve his first successes in American music, Theresa decided, with tact and wisdom, to dedicate herself exclusively to home and to husband, and to turn the spotlight over to him.

Herbert's first successes came in serious music. He appeared as cello soloist with major orchestras, frequently in performances of his own compositions. He formed and conducted an orchestra in New York, where he also founded and played in a string quartet. For a while he taught the cello at the National Conservatory. In 1893 he became the conductor of the 22nd Regiment Band, inheriting its baton from Patrick Sarsfield Gilmore, one of America's most distinguished bandmasters. Gilmore had been responsible for bringing national fame to the 22nd Regiment Band, and the organization continued to flourish under Herbert.

Herbert, then, was becoming a person of consequence in America's musical life, and he was held in high esteem by some of America's major critics and musicians. It was, therefore, neither failure nor frustration that soon led him to invade the province of popular music. The truth was that Herbert felt a compelling need to find a proper channel into which to direct the flow of the many delightful light tunes that kept running through his head and which simply had no place in a symphony nor an opera.

In short, Herbert began thinking of writing for the popular musical stage. He had had a first taste of the theatre in 1893. This was the year in which he was commissioned to write music for a spectacular production about Christopher Columbus planned for the World's Fair in Chicago. This stage project never materialized, and Herbert's music was never heard. But this initial experience of writing for a text stirred an appetite that now had to be satisfied. As he told his wife firmly: "I *must* write for the theatre."

He got an opportunity to do so from Lillian Russell. She was one of the most glamorous and most adulated singing stars of the American musical theatre; her appearances in operettas at the Casino Theatre helped smash one box-office record after another. When Lillian Russell asked Herbert to write an operetta for her, he complied with *La Vivandière* in 1893. But for some reason never explained, Lillian Russell lost interest in it, and Herbert's operetta was never produced; in fact, the score was lost and has never been retrieved.

Herbert's first produced operetta was *Prince Ananias,* contracted for by The Bostonians, the company that had introduced De Koven's *Robin Hood*. *Prince Ananias* opened in Boston on November 20, 1894. The critics attacked the libretto, but found many words of praise for Herbert's music. The song "Amaryllis" received special attention—the first proof Herbert gave that he was not out of place in the popular theatre. *Prince Ananias* had a moderately successful run in Boston. The company took it on tour to several American cities, then retained it in its repertory in Boston for several seasons after that.

And so, Herbert's career in the theatre was launched. He remained indefatigable in writing light music for the stage. Facile, prolific, well schooled, he often completed a full operetta or comic opera in a single month, down to the details of harmonization and orchestration. He could work on two, three, even four projects simultaneously. In 1899, he had three of his operettas produced in a two-month period.

It is true that much of what he wrote was perfunctory, hastily contrived, third-rate. But it is also true that when he was at his best, which was often, he created pure, shining gems. The love ballads, waltzes, light comic tunes, marches, choral episodes, instrumental entr'actes that he poured so plentifully into his stage scores are a vast storehouse of some of the most endearing melodies by an American. To Deems Taylor, Herbert's greatest songs are "as pure in outline as the melodies of Schubert or Mozart." Herbert was a king of melody. He had the gift to voice sentiment without becoming cloying and to express warmly felt emotions without yielding to clichés. He also boasted a solid technique, the product of his sound Germanic training. His best music was a marriage of the charm and sentiment of his Irish heritage with the science and skill of his Germanic education. This is what made him such a unique and individual composer for the popular American musical theatre in the closing 1890s and the early 1900s.

Immediately after *Prince Ananias* came *The Wizard of the Nile,* in 1895. Harry B. Smith (who would collaborate with Herbert frequently from now on) fashioned his libretto in such a way as to provide Frank Daniels, a popular comedian of that day, ample opportunity to exhibit his talent. His role was that of Kibosh, a fake Persian magician of ancient times. When Egypt suffers a searing drought, Kibosh is called upon to use his powers to relieve the stricken country. Wise Kibosh knows that a storm is imminent, and that the Nile would soon overflow. At the proper moment he utters his mumbo-jumbo. The Nile overflows, Egypt is saved, and Kibosh becomes a hero. But the storms and tides refuse to subside. With Egypt now threatened by the disaster of floods, poor Kibosh is robbed of his brief glory. The king of Egypt sentences him to die in a sealed tomb. Providentially, the king is accidentally left in the tomb with Kibosh. When the king is saved, he is so grateful that he finds it in his heart to forgive Kibosh.

Only one melody from this score became popular. It was "Star Light, Star Bright," the first one of Herbert's long string of distinguished waltzes.

Before the nineteenth century ended, Herbert had contributed the music to two more successful operettas: *The Serenade,* in 1897, and *The Fortune Teller,* in 1898. In the first, Harry B. Smith's plot concentrated on the love affair between Dolores, the ward of a duke, and Carlos Alvarado, a tenor of the Madrid Opera. The duke and a ballet dancer in love with Carlos contribute the complications to this romance, but in true operetta tradition, love triumphs in the end.

"It is all a farrago of nonsense," wrote Edward N. Waters, Herbert's biographer, "but for it Herbert supplied music brilliantly picturesque, clever, adroit, and extremely melodious." The high spot of the score was a serenade, "I Love Thee, I

Adore Thee." This is a melody that courses throughout the play, emerging in various disguises. It is heard as a chant by monks, an opera aria, a song of brigands. But its true personality—that of an ardent, romantic effusion—appears in the second act when hero and heroine recall how first they met and fell in love.

One of the reasons why *The Serenade* was so successful was the performance of its star, Alice Neilsen. She was unknown and comparatively inexperienced when Herbert plucked her out of the regular company, where she had been a member of the chorus, to sing the important role of Yvonne. By the time *The Serenade* ended its run, Alice Neilsen was so solidly established as a box-office attraction that H. B. Smith and Victor Herbert wrote *The Fortune Teller* just to set off her talent to best advantage. She was given a dual role in a Hungarian background: as Musette, a gypsy fortune teller, and as Irma, a ballet student at the Budapest Opera. Musette and Irma look so much alike that they can easily fill one another's shoes. They do so to straighten out Irma's love problems. In unraveling Irma's complications, Musette finds her own true love in Sandor, the gypsy musician.

Herbert's versatility in adapting his creativity to many different national styles—however remote those styles may be from his Irish birth and German upbringing—was demonstrated in this lovable operetta. Much of its music is a dish spiced richly with Hungarian paprika. Certainly Sandor's "The Gypsy Love Song" (or, as it is sometimes named, "Slumber On, My Little Gypsy Sweetheart") is the kind of sensual, throbbing music for which the Magyars have long been famous. Just as certainly it is a Herbert masterpiece.

There was a hiatus in Herbert's creative output in the first years of the new century. This was because he was throwing his energies into directing orchestral concerts, having become the principal conductor of the Pittsburgh Symphony in 1898. For six years Herbert rehearsed and led symphony concerts with all his customary energy and dedication. But when, in 1903, Herbert retired from conducting, he returned to operetta. He made that return with best foot forward—the extravaganza, *Babes in Toyland.*

In conceiving this operetta, he and his librettist (this time, Glen MacDonough) were out to write a second *The Wizard of Oz.* The latter, of course, was the juvenile classic which F. L. Baum wrote in 1900 (using the title *The Wonderful Wizard of Oz*) and which was made into a stage spectacle starring Fred Stone and David Montgomery, produced early in 1903.

In *Babes in Toyland,* Little Jane and Alan run away from home to escape the tyranny of their miserly uncle, Barnaby. At the same time they desert the cruel world of reality for storybook realms. After a shipwreck they arrive at the garden of Contrary Mary to meet up with characters out of Mother Goose. They pass through the Spider's forest and the floral palace of the Moth Queen before finally coming to Toyland. Toyland is ruled by Toymaker, a wicked magician able to bring inanimate toys to life. Once these toys become animate they rebel against the Toymaker, bringing about his doom and effecting their own liberation. Following the revolt of the toys Little Jane and Alan finally return home. There they frustrate the evil plans of their wicked uncle, and are again able to lead normal happy lives in a real world.

This story was constructed so loosely that it was often difficult to follow the thread of what was happening. But that story had an important function: It was the excuse and reason for several arresting, eye-filling stage spectacles. One was "The Legend of the Castle"; another, a ballet of butterflies; a third, a march of toys. For the last of these Herbert wrote a piquant march tune; and for the children in the play he produced such delectable tunes as "I Can't Do the Sum" (which the children sing while accompanying themselves with the rhythm of tapping chalk on black slates) and "Toyland." All this, the spectacle and the music, provided a source of enchantment for young and old alike.

During the next decade Herbert completed twenty operettas. Some were failures. Many were nondescript and deserve to be forgotten. A few, however, are numbered with the best that the American musical stage of that period had to offer.

If today we remember *Mlle. Modiste*—which came in 1905—it is because here we get the most famous of all Herbert's waltzes, "Kiss Me Again." Many legends have sprung up to explain how Herbert came to write this love song. One tells how, on opening night of Herbert's operetta *Babette* in 1904, he kissed its leading lady, Fritzi Scheff. "Kiss me again," sighed Miss Scheff—and the idea for the song was born. Another story would have it that Herbert overheard this phrase, "kiss me again," in the gardens of the Grand Union Hotel in Saratoga Springs, New York.

Neither story has any basis in fact. But in some respects truth is stranger than fiction. For one thing, Herbert did not write "Kiss Me Again" for *Mlle. Modiste*. The melody was born two years earlier. Finding no place for it at the time, Herbert put it away in his well-stocked trunk of musical ideas for use at some future date. More unusual still is the fact that, as it was heard in *Mlle. Modiste* on opening night, "Kiss Me Again" was not intended to be a love ballad, but an amusing parody of waltzes and love songs. The reason for this is that it was part of a larger sequence, "If I Were on the Stage," in which the heroine tries to prove her versatility as a singer by performing different types of songs—a polka, gavotte, waltz, and so forth; each of these types was intended to have comic appeal as a travesty. But something unforeseen happened on opening night. After the waltz part was sung, the audience went into an uproar, indicating to Herbert that he had a solid hit song in the making. Experienced showman and songwriter that he was, Herbert went to work to lift the waltz from "If I Were on the Stage" and to develop it as the principal song of the whole production. At the same time he slowed up the tempo and sentimentalized the melody, transforming the whole into a haunting waltz.

The heroine of *Mlle. Modiste* is Fifi, a salesgirl in a Parisian shop. She falls in love with and is courted by Captain Étienne de Bouvray, but their different stations in life make marriage unthinkable. After she breaks with her beloved, Fifi gains the interest and support of an American millionaire, who finances her career as a singer. As Mme. Bellini, Fifi becomes a celebrated prima donna, and as such she is invited to perform at the De Bouvray estate. Her beauty, charm, and art break down the onetime solid resistance of Father De Bouvray. Since Fifi and Étienne are still deeply in love, in spite of the passage of years, their marriage becomes a foregone conclusion.

Playing the part of Fifi was a real opera singer, Fritzi Scheff, formerly a member of the Metropolitan Opera company. In 1904, Herbert had induced her to leave the operatic stage and become the star of his operetta *Babette,* a failure. He had her in mind when he wrote the music for Fifi. As long as she lived (she died in New York in 1954), Fritzi Scheff was identified with that role, and particularly with the waltz she had introduced and made famous. Rarely could she make an appearance—be it in vaudeville, at concerts, and later over radio and television—without singing "Kiss Me Again."

Writing operettas for a specific performer, or performers—making leading roles tailor-trim to their specific talents—

brought into being two other highly successful Herbert operettas. They were *The Red Mill* in 1906 and *Naughty Marietta* in 1910.

The Red Mill was intended for Fred Stone and David Montgomery, the two comedians who achieved their first major success on Broadway in *The Wizard of Oz.* As Con Kidder and Kid Conner, two Americans wandering footloose in Europe, they arrive at a little town in Holland. There they involve themselves with Gretchen's romance with Captain Doris van Damm, a romance obstructed by the fact that Gretchen's father wants her to marry the Governor of Zeeland. The two Americans do everything they can to thwart the impending marriage, even to the point of invading the wedding ceremony and disrupting the proceedings by appearing in various disguises. When the news is spread that Captain Doris van Damm is heir to a fortune, Gretchen's father is ready to bless the marriage of the lovers.

Since this is an operetta written specifically for two comedians, comic episodes are emphasized. These are found abundantly in the wedding scene where our two Americans appear disguised as Sherlock Holmes and Dr. Watson, as two Italian organ grinders, and so forth. But the surpassing appeal of this operetta lies, as might be expected, in Herbert's melodies: the poignant and romantic ballads "Moonbeams" and "The Isle of Our Dreams"; the nostalgic number used for the closing scene, "The Streets of New York"; the breezy and humorous "Every Day Is Ladies' Day for Me."

Naughty Marietta (like *Mlle. Modiste* before it) was planned for an opera singer, its star being Emma Trentini, formerly a member of Oscar Hammerstein's Manhattan Opera company. Miss Trentini was Marietta to the manner born —Marietta being a lady of noble birth who fled from an undesirable marriage in her native Naples to find a new home in

New Orleans. All this takes place in the late eighteenth century, when New Orleans was swarming with adventurers, pirates, Spanish rulers, French officers, quadroons, casquette girls. The operetta abounds with colorful characters. The hero is Captain Dick, who falls in love with Marietta. Marietta has heard the fragment of a wonderful melody in a dream. She promises to marry any man who can finish for her the rest of this song. One of those who is in the running for Marietta's heart is Étienne Grandet, son of the lieutenant-governor. At the zero hour, Captain Dick wins Marietta, since it is he who can finish her song.

Herbert could well be expected to find a melody worthy of the pivotal position it had to occupy in a stage work. The one Marietta heard in her dream, and which Captain Dick finishes, is the heart of the entire operetta; and for it Herbert conceived one of his most celebrated songs, "Ah, Sweet Mystery of Life." Good as this number is, it has a serious rival in another rapturous love song, "I'm Falling in Love with Someone," in which Captain Dick first realizes how much Marietta has come to mean to him. Other delightful musical episodes in this score include a vigorous march tune ("Tramp, Tramp, Tramp"), Marietta's poignant recollection of her native Naples ("Italian Street Song"), and a radiant romance (" 'Neath the Southern Moon").

Indeed, *Naughty Marietta* has more successful songs in it than any other Herbert operetta, which is the reason it will always be remembered. It represents the apex of Herbert's career in the Broadway theatre; after that came a steady decline in his popularity. His best operettas after *Naughty Marietta* were *Sweethearts* in 1913, *Princess Pat* in 1915, and *Eileen* in 1917. None of these by any stretch of the imagination is another *Naughty Marietta.* His best songs after 1910 were "Sweethearts" and "The Angelus" from *Sweethearts,*

"Thine Alone" from *Eileen,* and "A Kiss in the Dark" from *Orange Blossoms* in 1922. "Thine Alone" must be included with Herbert's greatest love songs, but other songs by Herbert after 1910 are of comparatively inferior invention.

It is not difficult to explain why Herbert's popularity began to slip after 1910. The social, political, economic climate of America was beginning to undergo a radical transformation. Popular music kept step with these changes. Syncopation and ragtime had become a vogue in 1911, with Irving Berlin as their king. Then, as the 1910s began to slip into the 1920s, the dynamic rhythms of jazz began to dominate popular music. The pulse, the accentuations, the vitality of the American song reflected an age become increasingly high tensioned. People no longer danced the one-step and the waltz. They preferred the fox-trot, the Charleston, the Black Bottom. The American dance, like the American popular song, was acquiring more and more of a distinctly American personality.

This was a new day, in which the sad sweet waltzes and love songs which Herbert spun with such sensitive threads were out of place. They were foreign in style and content. They gave voice to a culture and a social ambience that were dying rapidly.

The sad truth was that Victor Herbert remained in his stage music part Irish and part German, although in all other ways as man and musician he had become thoroughly American. Having become an American citizen in 1902 he immediately identified himself completely with his adopted country. As a bandmaster he always crowded his programs with numbers of American origin and interest. As a serious composer, some of his most ambitious efforts were authentically American: for example, his opera *Natoma,* introduced in Philadelphia on February 25, 1911, its text and music of American-Indian background and interest. So satisfied had Herbert become with America as his permanent home that in 1902 he became a citizen and between 1887 and 1914 he did not pay a single return visit to Europe; the only reason he went abroad in 1914 was because he expected to have his opera *Madeleine* mounted at the Paris Opéra.

But in his popular music Herbert never really broke his ties to Europe. This goes a long way toward explaining why so many of his later efforts made so little of an impression; why so many of his later operettas were failures both commercially and artistically; why so few of his later songs became hits or have survived. Nobody realized more strongly than Herbert himself that the times had moved too swiftly for him; that they had left him behind while lifting new songwriters to fame and fortune. He often lamented to his friends that his public was forgetting him. And as the years passed, his lament grew in intensity.

Victor Herbert died convinced that posterity would forget him completely. He was the victim of a heart attack in New York City on May 26, 1924, soon after finishing his lunch at the Lambs Club. On May 28, he was buried with impressive ceremonies, his funeral attended by the many colleagues, collaborators, fellow musicians, and admirers he had made into staunch friends through a lifetime of openhearted generosity, warmth of feeling, kindness, and tolerance. They mourned him as good friends. They also mourned him because he had enriched the American theatre and American popular music. "My idea of heaven," once remarked Andrew Carnegie, the industrialist, "is to be able to sit and listen to the music of Victor Herbert all I want to." This was a posthumous tribute. It was a tribute that several generations of American music lovers have echoed.

Victor Herbert has not been forgotten. His best songs have endured. His best operettas have been continually revived both on the stage and on the screen. *The Red Mill* returned to Broadway in 1945 to accumulate a run of over five hundred performances, and *Sweethearts,* in 1947, lasted more than three hundred performances. *Babes in Toyland* was made into a successful motion picture (and for the second time) as late as 1961, in a Walt Disney production starring Ray Bolger and Ed Wynn. In addition to all this, his life story was told in the motion-picture musical *The Great Victor Herbert,* released in 1939, with Walter Connolly as the composer. Its score was a veritable cornucopia of Victor Herbert song treasures.

Victor Herbert was the first significant composer that our American musical theatre has produced. And this is the main reason he will always be remembered.

II

RUDOLF FRIML

(1879-)

BUT FOR A DISAGREEABLE episode at one of the performances of Victor Herbert's *Naughty Marietta,* Rudolf Friml might never have become a composer of operettas. That performance took place in New York in April of 1912. Since it had been planned as a sort of gala occasion, Victor Herbert himself conducted that evening. Emma Trentini, the prima donna in the title role, had by 1912 become a star of stars in the popular theatre. As a star of stars she was now indulging herself in whims and dictatorial ways. On this gala evening, she inspired a thunderous ovation for a particularly brilliant presentation of "Italian Street Song." From his conductor's stand, Herbert signaled for her to sing the number again as an encore. She haughtily ignored the request and stalked off the stage. Herbert grew so furious that he called on an assistant conductor to take over his baton for the rest of the performance. He stormed backstage, erupted into a violent temper, and vowed that never again would he work with Mme. Trentini.

He kept his word—even though he had been signed to

write a new operetta for her for the 1912–1913 season. With Herbert bowed out of the picture, Arthur Hammerstein (the producer who had Mme. Trentini under contract) had to look around for another composer. He consulted several leading publishers. Two of them—Max Dreyfus of Harms and Rudolph Schirmer of G. Schirmer—came up with a novel, daring suggestion. The house of G. Schirmer had recently published a number of art songs by an unknown composer named Rudolf Friml. Both Schirmer and Dreyfus felt that these songs revealed a sure instinct for vocal writing as well as a gift for pleasing melodies. Such a talent, they insisted, could well be harnassed for operetta. Both Schirmer and Dreyfus were convinced that Friml deserved a chance to step into Herbert's shoes, even though Friml had never written popular music and had never been affiliated with the theatre. Out of desperation (since time was of the essence), and out of respect for his advisers, Hammerstein accepted the suggestion. To hire an unknown, inexperienced composer for a major Broadway operetta starring an Emma Trentini represented a bold, even reckless gamble. How well that gamble paid off can be measured by the result: The operetta Friml wrote for Hammerstein was *The Firefly,* one of the greatest successes American operetta has known.

Rudolf Friml came from Bohemia (now Czechoslovakia), having been born in the capital city of Prague on September 7, 1879. His father was a baker, who enjoyed leisure hours playing the accordion and zither. He awakened Rudolf's latent interest in music. Having begun to study the piano at an early age, young Rudolf soon revealed an uncommon interest in composition. One of his pieces, a barcarole for the piano, was published when he was only ten.

His talent attracted the support of several friends and relatives who created a fund to send him to the Prague Conservatory. Under the direction of Antonín Dvořák, Bohemia's leading composer, this Conservatory was one of the best schools in eastern Europe. Friml, then fourteen, was required to take entrance examinations. He passed them so brilliantly that not only was he admitted but he was also permitted to skip the first two years of formal instruction. At the Conservatory, Friml was an outstanding student, both in piano (with Josef Juranek) and in composition (with Josef Foerster). He completed the usual six-year course in three years.

Upon leaving the Conservatory in 1898, Friml entered upon a professional career by becoming piano accompanist to Jan Kubelik, a fellow graduate from the Conservatory. Kubelik was a fiery violin virtuoso with a dazzling technique and a colorful personality. In 1898 he was at the beginning of a career soon to make him world famous. In that journey to success, Friml was his piano partner, not only accompanying him in his performances but also often sharing the program with him by playing piano solos.

Having toured Europe successfully between 1898 and 1900 with Friml's help, Kubelik was ready to conquer a new world. In 1901 he made his first tour of the United States, appearing in eighty concerts. The accompanist Kubelik engaged for this tour had fallen ill even before it had begun, and Friml was hurriedly recruited to fill the breach.

The next time Friml appeared in the United States was as a concert artist in his own right, and as a serious composer. This happened in Carnegie Hall in New York, on November 17, 1904, when he made his American concert debut in a program including the première of his Piano Concerto in B-flat major. When the concert ended, Friml offered a novelty, henceforth to become a tour de force at all of his concerts: spontaneously creating a series of variations on a theme provided him by somebody in the audience. At this American debut, the theme requested by the audience was the Austrian national anthem. "His improvisation evinced great cleverness," remarked Richard Aldrich in *The New York Times.*

His success led to the decision to further his own career as pianist and composer by planting his roots permanently in American soil. He made his home in a New York apartment, and began earning his living as a piano teacher, a piano virtuoso, and a serious composer of songs and piano pieces. In 1906 he appeared as a soloist with the New York Symphony Society, conducted by Walter Damrosch, in the first performance of his piano concerto with an orchestra. After that he concertized throughout the United States. He also found a publisher for his compositions in G. Schirmer. He could hardly have anticipated that these modest publications would change his destiny as a composer and bring him giant successes in the theatre. But this is what actually happened—because two influential publishers had the instincts and the vision to realize that the writer of this music had a flair for the stage.

The operetta Friml wrote for Miss Trentini immediately gave him an important place in the American theatre. *The Firefly* opened in New York on December 2, 1912, where it enjoyed a successful and prosperous run before going on tour. The text was the work of Otto Harbach, already famous as a librettist and lyricist, with an even richer future still ahead of him. Harbach's libretto cast Miss Trentini as Nina, an Italian street singer who falls in love with a wealthy playboy, Jack Travers. Discovering that Jack is a guest on Mrs. Vandare's yacht bound for Bermuda, Nina disguises herself as a cabin boy and becomes a stowaway. Though Nina gains the affection, and then the financial support, of Mrs. Vandare, she is thoroughly frustrated in attracting Jack's interest. From this point on the story sounds as if it came from Victor Herbert's *Mlle. Modiste.* Nina becomes a famous prima donna and is invited to sing at Mrs. Vandare's garden party. Jack is also a guest. With her beauty and her singing Nina now captures Jack's love.

Although the text might very well sound like an operetta by Victor Herbert, Friml's music (which he completed in less than a month) has an identity all its own. His sensual melodies, vital rhythmic pulse, and rich harmonies and orchestration all possess a Slavic personality. Three of the most important songs were written for Miss Trentini: "Giannina Mia," "Love Is Like a Firefly," and "When a Maid Comes Knocking." A fourth number, "Sympathy," was sung by two subsidiary characters. All four songs were resounding successes in 1912 and have become standards since. (Another now popular number from *The Firefly* was not heard in the 1912 stage production but was written for the motion-picture adaptation in 1937. For this movie, Friml adapted one of his early piano pieces and called it "The Donkey Serenade." Allan Jones introduced it, then popularized it in a recording that sold about a million discs.)

The success of *The Firefly* gave Friml important status on Broadway; and with status came assignments. *The Firefly* was succeeded in 1913 by *High Jinks,* whose most successful musical number was "Something Seems Tingle-ingleing." After that, Friml operettas came to Broadway and left. But not until 1924 was he able to achieve a success equal to, actually even surpassing, that of *The Firefly.*

That success came with *Rose-Marie,* book and lyrics here being a collaborative effort of Otto Harbach and Oscar Hammerstein II. Much of the appeal of *Rose-Marie* lay in its unusual setting, never before used in the musical theatre: the Canadian Rockies, home of the famed Royal Mounted Police, who figure prominently in the story.

But if the setting is unusual, the story follows operetta tradition. Rose-Marie and Jim Kenyon are in love. Jim is falsely accused of murder. To save her beloved, Rose-Marie is willing to marry Edward Hawley. The Royal Mounted Police find the real murderer, clear Jim's name, and enable him and Rose-Marie to follow their happy destiny together.

The program carried a significant note. It read: "The musical numbers of this play are such an integral part of the action that we do not think we should list them as separate episodes." This represents the earliest use of the word "integral" in the American musical theatre. "Integration" of text and music was a much later development—and one of no small importance; it led the way to the musical play as opposed to musical comedy and operetta. However, for all its expressed aim, *Rose-Marie* was not yet an "integrated" musical—in other words, a musical in which melody and spoken word are woven into a single and inextricable texture. In *Rose-Marie* individual numbers are still more important than the sum of all the parts. These individual numbers include the title song; the ballad "The Door of My Dreams"; the rousing chorus of the Canadian Mounted Police, "Song of the Mounties"; the music for "Totem Tom-Tom," a stunning production number; and surely the most celebrated number of them all, the most durable survivor from this enduring score, the love duet, "Indian Love Call." Vocal highlights such as these led Charles Belmont-Davis to say in the New York *Tribune* that *Rose-Marie* boasted "the most entrancing music it has been our privilege to hear."

In the 1920s, three hundred performances represented a successful run for a musical. *Rose-Marie* had an initial run of 557 performances; then it returned to Broadway for a short revival. Four road companies toured the rest of the country. Since then, revivals have been springing up all over the country from time to time. *Rose-Marie* was made into a motion picture three times—in 1928, 1936, and 1954. In each of these screen versions, it was Friml's music, more than any other single element, that made the film successful. As Frank S. Nugent said in *The New York Times* in reviewing the 1936 adaptation: "Here the song—and its singers—are the thing."

Before the 1920s ended, two more Friml operettas enchanted Broadway. Both went back into the historic past for their plots and both used France as the locale.

The Vagabond King, in 1925, lifted the dashing, colorful personality of François Villon out of the fifteenth century. He was the vagabond poet whose adventurous, picaresque career as a criminal and wastrel did not keep him from writing ballads and poems that made him one of the earliest of France's great poets. Out of *If I Were King,* a popular romance by J. H. McCarthy, librettists Brian Hooker and W. H. Post concocted episodes for Villon hardly more dramatic or preposterous than those the poet had actually experienced. Louis XI, ruler of France, makes Villon "king for a day." That day proves highly eventful, since Villon not only makes love to Katherine de Vaucelles, but also becomes the hero in a battle that saves the French throne from seizure by the Burgundians. At a sacrifice of her own life, Villon's peasant sweetheart, Huguette, saves Villon. By royal decree, Villon is given a place at court and assigned Lady Anne as wife.

For such an action-filled romance, Friml produced a score in kind—ranging from the ringing tones of the "Song of the Vagabonds" with which Villon's followers go off to battle, to the tender sentiments of "Only a Rose," "Some Day," and "Huguette Waltz." These melodies have through the years become as familiar to moviegoers as to lovers of operetta, since, like *Rose-Marie, The Vagabond King* was transferred to the screen three times, most recently in 1956 in a production starring Kathryn Grayson and Oreste.

The Three Musketeers, in 1928, was Friml's last successful operetta. This one, of course, was an adaptation of the famous romance of the same name by Alexandre Dumas. Dennis King (who had just achieved one of the greatest triumphs of a long and brilliant stage career as Villon in *The Vagabond King*) appeared as D'Artagnan. Coming to Paris, D'Artagnan falls in love with Constance Bonacieux, and joins up with three other musketeers—Athos, Porthos, and Aramis—to embark on a number of swashbuckling missions and escapades. In this score, as in others by Friml, vigor alternates with sentiment. The best of the rousing numbers were "The March of the Musketeers" and "With Red Wine," while the most popular song in a sentimental vein was D'Artagnan's song of love, "Ma Belle."

By 1930, the American operetta was beginning to lose its audience, which was now far more interested in musical comedies. Friml, like Victor Herbert before him, was not able to make the transition from operetta to musical comedy. The two musicals he wrote and had produced in the early 1930s were both dismal failures.

He deserted Broadway for good, establishing residence in Hollywood where he began working for the movies. He helped adapt his operettas, and on occasion he wrote some new songs for various other productions. But the old Friml magic, which once had enlivened the New York stage, was gone. In Hollywood as on Broadway, Friml was a voice out of tune with the chorus of his times.

Nevertheless, he has remained active through the years, up into old age. Year after year, he produces a huge mass of music, popular and serious. He also has toured the world as pianist and conductor in performances of the established

Friml operetta favorites. The drawing power of those old Friml tunes still proves potent; Friml concerts are usually sold out wherever they are given.

But Friml is not a man to live exclusively on memories of the past. In his extra-musical interests and in his activities and pastimes he is of the vibrant present. Although an old man, he continues to concertize vigorously, and he continues to pursue his lifelong passion for travel. He is particularly in love with the Orient, to which he has made many trips; and he has written a number of musical works of Oriental interest. This affinity with the East may be the reason why he chose Kay Ling, an American of Chinese birth, to be his secretary. It is also probably the reason why he fell in love with her and why, in 1952, he decided to marry her, after spending half a lifetime as a bachelor following his divorce from his first wife in 1915.

But his music has not kept pace with the man. Today Friml writes in the same style as he did yesterday, and this is the reason he was unable to extend the skein of his stage and song successes beyond 1930. But make no mistake about it! —those old Friml tunes continue to survive as a charming, nostalgic recollection of sedate and graceful years now gone forever. As long as those songs live, the operettas for which they were intended will continue to get heard—however old-fashioned, contrived or synthetic their texts may appear to the sophisticated audiences of our present day.

III

SIGMUND ROMBERG

(1887-1951)

SIGMUND ROMBERG was the third member of the triumvirate, including Victor Herbert and Rudolf Friml, that for a generation ruled American operetta when it was in its full glory. Where Herbert's melodic orientation was basically Irish, and Friml's Slavic, Romberg's was essentially Viennese. In that now-vanished world of glamour and charm that was Habsburg Austria, Romberg fit as naturally as if he were a character from one of his own operettas. He was born, however, not in Austria but in Hungary, in the little town of Nagykaniza, on July 29, 1887. Both of his parents were highly cultured people. His mother, Clara Fels Romberg, was a distinguished poet and short-story writer. Although his father, Adam, earned his living as a manager of factories, he was a discriminating dilettante, a lover of books, and an excellent amateur musician.

Sigmund began studying the violin when he was six years old. Two years after that he received lessons on the piano. Music absorbed him completely, particularly Hungarian gypsy tunes and Viennese waltzes, for which he was never to lose his passion. His parents, however, did not look with favor on the way music dominated him, since they were eager to see him prepare for some practical profession. They directed him to intensive academic study. For five years Sigmund attended public school, after which he went on to two preparatory schools as a preface to studies in engineering. All this time he played the violin in school orchestras and occasionally the organ at church services. He also wrote music, including a violin sonata.

The study of engineering took place in Vienna, at the Polytechnic High School. He supplemented school with music, in a city that was then the musical capital of the world. Whenever he could find the price for a seat in the balcony he attended concerts and opera performances. When money was lacking, he would watch rehearsals and performances of Viennese operettas backstage—first as an onlooker, through the intercession of a friend who worked in the theatre, and then as assistant stage manager (without pay). He spent many a Sunday evening at the salon of Alfred Grünfeld where musicians gathered to make and talk about music. He also took some advanced instruction in harmony and composition from Victor Heuberger.

Despite this deep involvement with music, Romberg managed to get a degree in engineering. Military service now called to him. This was required of all young men in the Austro-Hungarian Empire. Romberg joined the 19th Hungarian Infantry Regiment, stationed in Vienna. After a year and a half of military life, he stood ready to return to his former civilian status. His mind was now made up to forget all about engineering and to become a musician. He had also arrived at the wise decision of advancing himself in music in a comparatively young and unsophisticated country like the United States rather than in a flourishing musical center like Vienna where the standards were lofty and the competition both keen and formidable.

Romberg arrived in New York in 1909. Since he realized that his capital of three hundred dollars would not last indefinitely, he soon found a job in a factory, for seven dollars a week, assembling pencils into packages. He did not stay there long. He induced the manager of the Café Continental, a restaurant on Second Avenue in downtown New York, to hire him as a pianist for fifteen dollars a week. One week later he was holding down another position, as pianist with an orchestra appearing at the Pabst-Harlem Restaurant. By the fall of 1912 he was leading an orchestra of his own in salon music (most of it of the Viennese variety) at one of the most famous restaurants in New York, Bustanoby's at Broadway and 39th Street. There he inaugurated the practice of including on his programs popular dance music, an innovation that proved so successful that before many months passed Romberg was drawing $150 a week.

Performing popular American music soon encouraged him to write pieces in a similar vein. His first creative attempts were a turkey-trot, "Leg o' Mutton," and a one-step, "Some Smoke." Both were published in 1913 by the Tin Pan Alley firm of Joseph W. Stern and Company, and both achieved a modest popularity. These numbers came to the attention of J. J. Shubert who, with his brother Lee, was an influential producer of musical shows on Broadway. Season after season, the Shubert brothers mounted revues, musicals, and extravaganzas, the scores for which were generally provided by a staff composer. Louis Hirsch held this position until 1913, then resigned. The Shuberts, therefore, were on the lookout for Hirsch's replacement. Meeting and talking to Romberg convinced J.J. that this was his man.

Romberg's first assignment was music for a lavish revue

for the Winter Garden, home of the Shuberts's most ambitious and spectacular productions. That revue, *The Whirl of the World,* starring the comedians Willie and Eugene Howard, with the Dolly Sisters, opened on January 10, 1914. All of its twenty-four musical numbers were by Romberg, and they served the production well. On the strength of this achievement, the Shuberts stood ready to turn over to Romberg the assignment of writing the music for four productions a year.

In less than two years' time, Romberg's music was heard in fifteen musicals produced by the Shuberts, almost two hundred and fifty numbers in all. All his material was neatly tailored to the varied needs of productions and stars. But none achieved any measure of popularity, and none has survived. The best that can be said of his work during this active period is that it was no worse than the standards achieved at the time by many other Broadway composers.

There was one score during this period, however, which was an exception to the prevailing level of mediocrity Romberg was maintaining consistently. This one score proved an exception because for the first time in his career as a composer Romberg had an opportunity to be more Viennese than American, and consequently the opportunity to write from the heart rather than from the mind.

The Shuberts had acquired American rights for *The Blue Paradise,* a successful Viennese operetta. Although the Shuberts planned to retain most of the Viennese written music (the work of Edmund Eysler), they also believed that the addition of several new numbers by an American might contribute interest for American audiences. Romberg was called upon to produce those numbers, eight in all. *The Blue Paradise* turned out to be his first major success in the American musical theatre. It also was responsible for the writing of the first of his enchanting Viennese waltzes, and the first of his songs to be remembered, "Auf Wiedersehen."

"The Blue Paradise" is the name of a Viennese garden restaurant where Mizzi is employed as flower girl. She is in love with Rudolf, a student about to leave for America. The young lovers says good-bye to the tender strains of "Auf Wiedersehen." Twenty-five years elapse. Rudolf, now a wealthy American, returns to Vienna for a brief visit. He finds that the restaurant, "The Blue Paradise," no longer exists, replaced by a house occupied by one of his friends. To welcome Rudolf back to Vienna, his cronies decide to restore the garden in the back of this house into a replica of the old restaurant. A huge party takes place there during which Gaby, who is Mizzi's daughter, appears in the same dress her mother had worn a quarter of a century earlier. And she sings "Auf Wiedersehen" as a poignant reminder to Rudolf of an evening long ago when he and his beloved Mizzi had parted for good.

As Romberg's first operetta, and as the one in which his first song classic is found, *The Blue Paradise* has earned an honorable place in American stage history. But it must also be remembered as the show in which Vivienne Segal made her stage debut, in the part of Mizzi. She was a Romberg discovery. When the operetta was first tried out, the leading lady was found unsatisfactory. For a time it seemed that the production would have to be scrapped or postponed. Then Romberg was informed about a young attractive voice student in Philadelphia. Auditioning her in that city he was won over so completely to her singing and her appearance that then and there he had her signed for the starring role—this despite the fact that she had not had any stage experience whatsoever. Vivienne Segal became a star in *The Blue Paradise* at the Casino Theatre on August 15, 1915. She remained a Broadway star for the next quarter of a century.

For several years after *The Blue Paradise,* Romberg continued producing functional music for Shubert shows. It was not in this work that his heart lay. He wanted to write another operetta; *The Blue Paradise* had demonstrated to him where his real strength as a composer could be found.

His next opportunity to write music for an operetta came in 1917 with *Maytime.* This musical had also originated abroad in the German language. But Rida Johnson Young, distinguished American librettist and lyricist, overhauled the text to place the setting in New York's Washington Square section and the time in the nineteenth century. The play opens in 1840 and finds Ottilie and Richard in love. Although they pledge to belong to one another, their love affair is frustrated when Ottilie is forced by her father to marry a worthless gambler. The gambler's death leaves her penniless. But the happiness denied to Ottilie and Richard comes in the end to their grandchildren, through the union of Ottilie's granddaughter and Richard's grandson.

In *The Blue Paradise,* a waltz not only was used here as a recurrent melody throughout the play but went on to become the hit song. In *Maytime,* the waltz was "Will You Remember?," first heard as the love song of Otillie and Richard, then serving the grandchildren as their own song of love at the end of the operetta.

So successful was *Maytime* that before its first year ended at the Shubert Theatre, a second company was organized to perform it simultaneously across the street, at the 44th Street Theatre. This was the first time in stage history that any stage production had two companies playing at the same time on Broadway. Both companies then toured the United States for several years, each able to boast truthfully that it was the "original Broadway production."

Four years passed before Romberg returned to operetta.

When he did, he had another stage triumph to his credit. The new musical once again had a Viennese setting, though Vienna of another era. The Shuberts had purchased the American rights to *Das Dreimaederlhaus,* which had enjoyed extradordinary success in Vienna where it had opened in 1916; a year later it was produced in the German language in New York. This musical romanticized the later life of Franz Schubert, one of Vienna's greatest composers of songs, symphonies, sonatas, and string quartets. Heinrich Berté, in writing the music for *Das Dreimaederlhaus,* borrowed all of his melodic material from Schubert's music.

In making the transfer into English for New York, Dorothy Donnelly, the adaptor, made extensive revisions in plot and dialogue. At the same time, Romberg was called in to prepare an entirely new score. He decided to follow Berté's example by using Schubert's melodies for all of his songs, but treated in the Romberg manner.

Donnelly's text made no pretense at adhering to biographical truth. In fact, the entire romantic story was pure fabrication. Entitled *Blossom Time,* it involved Franz Schubert in a frustrating love affair with Mitzi, a fictitious character. To express his feelings for her he wrote "Song of Love." Too shy to advance his own interests, he begs his best friend, Schober, to sing for him his love song to Mitzi. Schober does so, but in the process he and Mitzi fall in love. Schubert's heartbreak at this development destroys his health and his will to compose. He is even incapable of finishing the symphony upon which he is at work—and unfinished it had to remain. When that symphony is first performed, Schubert is too sick to attend the concert. He is dying. Almost with his last breaths he creates his immortal song, "Ave Maria."

For the "Song of Love," which plays such a significant role in unfolding the frustrated love of Schubert for Mitzi, Romberg took the beautiful main melody from the first movement of the *Unfinished Symphony* (translating it into three-quarter waltz time). In the sensitive opening theme of the second movement from the same symphony Romberg found the melody for "Tell Me Daisy." The delightful ballet music from *Rosamunde* was used for "Three Little Maids," while the melody of the famous song "Serenade" was borrowed for the popular love song, also named "Serenade."

Blossom Time was a giant money-maker. It had an initial Broadway run of almost six hundred performances, beginning on September 29, 1921. Four companies toured nationally. Since the early 1920s, it has often been revived throughout the United States. Romberg is believed to have earned close to a million dollars in royalties from *Blossom Time* alone. It is ironic to contrast Romberg's financial return with that of Schubert, from whom he took all his melodies. For a lifetime of productivity as one of the world's greatest composers, Schubert earned in all about five hundred dollars!

Greater success still lay ahead for Romberg. On December 2, 1924, the operetta generally conceded to be his masterwork opened at the Jolson Theatre, *The Student Prince in Heidelberg.* It stayed on for over six hundred performances, had nine companies touring the United States, and has since become a classic of the American musical theatre by virtue of hundreds of revivals. Its motion-picture adaptation in 1954 (with Mario Lanza singing the beloved Romberg melodies on the soundtrack) became the most successful screen production to use Romberg's music. And the sheet-music sale of its main hit songs proved so prodigious that its publishers, M. Witmark and Sons, after facing bankruptcy in 1923, had a sudden new lease on life and prosperity.

Like so many earlier Romberg operettas, *The Student Prince* had originated and been successful in Europe. The old university town of Heidelberg, in the middle 1800s, is the picturesque background for another tale of frustrated love. Prince Karl Franz, heir to the throne of the mythical kingdom of Karlsberg, comes incognito to Heidelberg with his tutor, Doctor Engel. At The Golden Apple, a beer and wine restaurant where students congregated, Karl meets Kathi, daughter of the innkeeper. Romance develops, but has to come to a sudden stop when Karl receives the news that the king of Karlsberg is dead and that he must come home to ascend the throne and marry Princess Margaret. In Karlsberg, the new king is unable to forget Kathi. He decides to revisit Heidelberg. But the two lovers know well that now they are worlds apart and that the two worlds could never possibly meet. They separate for the last time.

Never before had Romberg brought to his writing the kind of high purpose and ambitious scope he brought to the music of *The Student Prince*. And never before had he been so intransigent about the way his music should be presented. In the planning and execution of his score, Romberg always gave preference to artistic and theatrical values over commercial ones—much to the rapidly mounting fears of the producer and director, who felt that the show they were putting on might be too artistic to be commercially successful. Romberg insisted upon a large-sized male chorus of forty well-trained voices to sing such rousing numbers as his "Drinking Song" (with which the university students toast romance at The Golden Apple) or the "Students' Marching Song." He dispensed with an eye-appealing chorus line, and he refused to permit pretentious dance sequences to be used. He was hypercritical in selecting the leads, more concerned with the quality of their voices and the range of their musicianship than with their box-office appeal. Romberg subjected these principals to the most rigorous rehearsals so that his melodies might be sung exactly as he had written them, correct in every detail of tempo and rhythm. Romberg was convinced that into this score he had brought three of his most wonderful melodies. Two were love songs for Kathi and the Prince ("Deep in My Heart, Dear" and "Serenade") and the other a haunting, nostalgic melody with which the tutor recalls his days of youth at the Heidelberg University ("Golden Days").

There is perhaps good reason why both "Serenade" and "Deep in My Heart, Dear" should be two of Romberg's most eloquent love songs. In writing them he was writing his own love music—for he was deeply in love. He had met Lillian Harris at Saranac Lake in the Adirondack Mountains, in New York, where he had come to work with Al Jolson on a Winter Garden extravaganza. Lillian was a guest at a nearby inn, and she and several others had been invited by Jolson to a party. When she arrived—pert, trim, delicate—she brought into the room the freshness of a mountain breeze. The romance started that evening. She became a powerful stimulus to Romberg during the writing of *The Student Prince.* Although her only connection with the theatre was a seat in the auditorium, she had discriminating tastes as well as an idealism that did not have to be diluted with commercialism. She was convinced that Romberg's native talent should be poised on a level considerably higher than that of the revues and extravaganzas which the Shuberts were presenting at the Winter Garden. She had been enchanted with *Blossom Time* long before she became acquainted with the composer. Now that they were in love with each other, she did what she could to convince him to keep his creative sights as high as possible, without a single concern for expedience. She gave him the courage and the will he needed to refuse to make any concessions of any kind in the writing and the producing of *The Student Prince.*

Lillian Harris and Romberg were married in a private

ceremony in Paterson, New Jersey, on March 20, 1925, with the Mayor of the city officiating.

Romberg's wife wanted him to concentrate exclusively on operetta, now that *The Student Prince* had proved the wisdom of this course. And this is what he did. Offers to write new operettas were coming thick and fast. The income he was drawing from his produced operettas had made him a wealthy man. There was no further necessity for him to expend time and effort on routine assignments.

Not all of the operettas Romberg wrote after *The Student Prince* were either good *or* successful. But he always aimed high. And when he hit his mark, he got the bull's-eye. He created two more landmarks in the American operetta theatre. One was *The Desert Song,* in 1926, and the other, *The New Moon,* in 1928.

With *The Desert Song,* Romberg found a new valuable collaborator in the person of Oscar Hammerstein II, already at that time a creative figure of no little importance in the musical theatre. In fashioning book and lyrics for *The Desert Song,* however, Hammerstein was not alone; he was joined by Frank Mandel and Otto Harbach.

When it tried out in Wilmington, Delaware, *The Desert Song* suffered a number of unfortunate accidents. A fuse blew out, throwing the performance into total blacknes for a few minutes. Hardly had the audience recovered from its fright when a ceiling beam collapsed on the stage, sending the scenery down in a crash. After that there was an unplanned, unrehearsed comic episode when a mule, in the final scene, insisted upon accompanying the music with his loud braying. In spite of all these disturbing incidents the performance went well, and the audience responded warmly after the final curtain.

Then on November 30, *The Desert Song* arrived in New

York. It looked for a while as if the accidents of Wilmington were just the omens for future box-office disaster. Some of the critics damned the libretto in no uncertain terms. Richard Watts, Jr., remarked in the *Herald-Tribune:* "The question of how simple minded the book of a musical comedy can be was debated . . . last night and the verdict arrived at was 'no end.'" Immediately after the première the demand for tickets was sluggish; for a while it looked as if *The Desert Song* would have to fold its tents silently and disappear. Then suddenly business began to pick up; a few weeks more, and capacity business became the rule. What had happened to bring about this change of fortune is that Romberg's music had begun to gain circulation and had been acquiring such popularity that curiosity was aroused about the operetta itself. *The Desert Song* had a run of almost five hundred performances, then was produced in major American capitals, as well as in London and Australia. Like the earlier Romberg masterworks, it has often been revived. Three movies were made out of it—the first in 1929, the second in 1943, and the third (starring Kathryn Grayson and Gordon MacRae) in 1953.

In writing his score Romberg traveled as far afield from the Vienna of *Blossom Time* and the Heidelberg of *The Student Prince* as French Morocco. The idea for this operetta came to the librettists from reading a newspaper account of a revolt by the French Riffs against the French protectorate in Morocco. Here, the authors realized, was a new exciting background for operetta treatment, in front of which could move such picturesque characters as Riffs, bandits, harem girls, and French officers.

A story, following traditional operetta patterns, was not hard to manufacture. A bandit who calls himself the Red Shadow is in love with Margot; Margot prefers Pierre, son of the Governor of Morocco. The bandit abducts her to the harem of Ali ben Ali where he uses his charm and sex appeal to win her love. When she insists that her heart belongs elsewhere, the Red Shadow recognizes defeat, and magnanimously offers to take her back to Pierre. But now Margot is becoming more interested in the bandit than in Pierre. The Governor of Morocco and his troops arrive to rescue Margot. When the Governor himself attacks the Red Shadow, the bandit refuses to offer any resistance, which his own men regard as an act of cowardice. But this strange behavior on the part of the bandit is soon explained. He is actually Pierre, the Governor's son in disguise. Once this mystery is cleared, Margot can have both Pierre and the bandit, since they are one and the same person.

When *The Desert Song* had tried out in Wilmington, Romberg had expressed dissatisfaction with his title number. He scrapped it, and in two days' time came up with an altogether new melody. This replacement became one of the main reasons why *The Desert Song* was transformed from failure to success: a waltz become famous under its alternate title of "Blue Heaven" as well as under its original name, "The Desert Song." This became the principal love song of the operetta. A second romantic ballad, "One Alone," sung by the Red Shadow, is hardly less memorable. By way of contrast the score provided two stirring, red-blooded numbers, "Riff Song" and "French Military Marching Song."

In *The New Moon,* the librettists (Oscar Hammerstein II and Frank Mandel this time, supplemented by Laurence Schwab) found another fresh, attractive setting for a romantic story—New Orleans in 1788. Its hero is a character lifted out of a history book. He was Robert Mission, a French aristocrat come to New Orleans disguised as Monsieur Beaunoir's bondservant. In New Orleans, Robert falls in love with his master's daughter, Marianne. "The New Moon" is a ship which subsequently arrives at the port, bearing Captain Paul Duval, come to arrest Mission for his past revolutionary activities in France. Robert manages to elude his pursuer until the fugitive invades a gala ball for the purpose of stealing a kiss from Marianne. There he is apprehended. After Robert and Marianne vow that their love for each other is eternal, Robert is dragged off to "The New Moon" for his return to France. Aboard ship, mutiny breaks out. This enables the prisoner and his followers to escape. They set up a new government on an island off the coast of Florida, where Robert is soon joined by his beloved.

During a two-week tryout in Philadelphia, in December of 1927, *The New Moon* met with such resistance from both audiences and critics that the producers had to invoke emergency measures. The text was drastically rewritten; Romberg's score was scrapped and a completely new one was prepared; the casting underwent a radical overhauling. In fact, the production became a new show. After these measures had been consummated, *The New Moon* came to Broadway on September 19, 1928, to receive an ecstatic response from the critics. Percy Hammond was completely won over to "the beauty of its tailoring, the seductiveness of its score, the spryness of its dancers, and the solemnity of its plot." Brooks Atkinson described it as "an unusually pleasing musical comedy." Gilbert W. Gabriel considered it "certainly and superlatively as good as they come." St. John Ervine, a visiting English critic working for the New York *World,* described it as "the most charming and fragrant entertainment of its sort that I have seen for a long time."

They had good reason to be so enthusiastic, and the best reason of all was the wealth of its musical material. No other Romberg operetta had so many songs that first became hits and then standards. There was not one but four outstanding romantic numbers: "Lover, Come Back to Me," "Softly, as in a Morning Sunrise," "One Kiss," and "Wanting You." There were also several songs with muscle and sinew, including the now classic "Stouthearted Men."

Box-office prosperity was assured. When the operetta was sold to the movies in 1929 it commanded the highest price thus far given for a Broadway musical. A second motion-picture adaptation came in 1940, starring Jeanette MacDonald and Nelson Eddy.

The New Moon was Romberg's last triumphant operetta, but it was not his last operetta. The ones he wrote and had produced in the 1930s became fatal casualties because Broadway audiences were tired of operettas and preferred spending their money on musical comedies. One box-office disaster after another gave Romberg disheartening evidence that *his* kind of musical theatre was becoming for the most part passé. *Nina Rosa,* in 1930, lasted 137 performances; *East Wind,* in 1931, 23 performances; *Melody,* in 1933, 79 performances; *Forbidden Melody,* in 1936, 32 performances; *Sunny River,* in 1941, 36 performances. The only Romberg musical capable of passing 200 performances—a number that then represented success—was not an operetta at all but an attempt at "musical-play" writing. This was *May Wine,* in 1935, where the setting once again was Vienna but the plot represented a realistic treatment of a contemporary subject. The theme was psychiatry, a subject beginning to receive attention in the 1930s, which had already been used in several musical comedies, and which Moss Hart and Kurt Weill would use with extraordinary effect in 1941 in *Lady in the Dark.*

Romberg took stock of himself. Nobody had to tell him what was wrong. Like the works of Victor Herbert and Rudolf Friml, his music had lived in the past; like them, he had been content to work in a stage form that was dying and in a musical style that was becoming outmoded. Even when he worked for a new medium, such as talking pictures, he remained in the same pattern. His first movie, in 1930, was called *Viennese Nights;* another movie, in 1934, was *The Night Is Young,* and this, too, was set in Vienna. Other of his movies had basically foreign backgrounds. None was intrinsically American; none reflected modern times.

One day in the mid 1930s he said to his wife: "I've got to get out of the rut I am in. I've got to get away from Vienna, for instance. That is all passé. European backgrounds! Maybe that's what is dating me. I've got myself stranded in Europe and I have to get out of it. I think I'll refuse anything from now on without an American background."

He would divorce himself from Broadway. He would even move out of New York, which had been his home for so long. In late spring of 1936 he bought a house on North Roxbury Drive in Beverly Hills, California, next door to George and Ira Gershwin. This was the first time the Rombergs ever owned a home of their own; and there they stayed for the rest of Romberg's life.

MGM, to whom Romberg was under contract, gave him his first chance to write music for an American story: David Belasco's *The Girl of the Golden West,* which, at the turn of the century, had been a successful stage play before Giacomo Puccini turned it into an opera. As a movie Western, with songs, *The Girl of the Golden West* starred Jeanette MacDonald and Nelson Eddy. It was a failure—which Romberg's songs did nothing to prevent.

This was Romberg's last complete score for the movies. He contributed a few songs to just one more screen production, *They Gave Him a Gun,* with Franchot Tone and Spencer Tracy, which was released a year after *The Girl of the Golden*

West. After this, Romberg remained creatively silent for several years. Creatively silent—but by no means idle.

With the United States engaged in World War II, Romberg helped entertain American servicemen, just as he had done in the earlier world war. He toured camps, battleships, and hospitals, playing his now famous melodies together with the popular tunes of other composers.

He also branched out in a new direction, as a conductor of his own orchestra, touring the United States in performances of light music billed as "An Evening with Sigmund Romberg." The first such tour, which began in Baltimore on October 20, 1942, failed to stir much interest and suffered severe financial losses. But the William Morris Agency, which had arranged the tour, remained convinced that there existed a large audience for the kind of music Romberg was dispensing. Second and third tours were also failures. Then the tide turned. A fourth tour, beginning with a concert at Carnegie Hall in New York on September 10, 1943, attracted capacity houses. So huge was the profit from this new venture that the deficits from the three earlier ones were wiped out. From then on, "An Evening with Sigmund Romberg" became an assured success wherever it was given. Following the end of World War II, and after a certain degree of normalcy had returned to Europe, plans were developed for an international tour. These were frustrated by Romberg's death. But in America, Romberg's career had come full circle. It ended as it had begun—with the playing of light music for the masses.

Before he died, Romberg realized his ambition to write a successful Broadway musical comedy—in an American style and tempo, with an American background. This is something which both Victor Herbert and Rudolf Friml before him had failed to do. Romberg's musical was *Up in Central Park;* it appeared on January 27, 1945 and was a huge success. It ran on Broadway for fourteen months; it enjoyed a long and prosperous national tour; it became a movie starring Deanna Durbin and Dick Haymes. Few of Romberg's past stage successes (unless it was his first operetta in 1915) gave him quite the satisfaction that this one did. For years now, the opinion prevailed both on Broadway and in Hollywood that Romberg was through; that, like Herbert and Friml, he just could not adapt himself to the new themes posed by the musical theatre of the 1940s or satisfy the new tastes of the audiences of this period. Since 1939, Romberg had failed to get a single Hollywood assignment. His last appearance on Broadway—with *Sunny River* in 1941—had been a disaster.

The new challenges which the libretto and lyrics of Herbert and Dorothy Fields posed for him in *Up in Central Park* were fully met. His musical speech betrayed few traces of an operetta accent. On the contrary, it was thoroughly in musical comedy idiom: for example, the main love song, "Close as Pages in a Book," or the ballad "It Doesn't Cost You Anything to Dream," or the nostalgic "Carousel in the Park," or the atmospheric background music for the ice-skating ballet in which the staging and costumes simulated a Currier and Ives lithograph and the choreography was by Helen Tamiris.

The plot of *Up in Central Park* had to do with graft perpetrated by the infamous Tweed Ring in New York politics in the 1870s. John Matthews, a reporter, is investigating the suspect political machine headed by Boss Tweed, and graft involved in the building of Central Park. During this investigation, John meets and falls in love with Rosie Moore, daughter of one of Boss Tweed's ward heelers. Rose has dreams of becoming a singer. When one of Tweed's lieutenants offers to finance her career, she deserts John to marry her sponsor. Largely as a result of John's revelations, the Tweed machine is destroyed. At the same time, Rosie's husband is killed while escaping from the home of his mistress. Rosie and John happen to meet again in Central Park where their long interrupted romance is revived.

Sigmund Romberg died suddenly in New York on November 10, 1951. He had been working on a new musical comedy, once again a period piece with a New York background. *The Girl in Pink Tights* described the circumstances surrounding the production of *The Black Crook,* the sensational musical extravaganza produced in New York in 1866. *The Girl in Pink Tights* was seen on Broadway three and a half years after Romberg's death, on March 5, 1954. It would be pleasant, indeed, to be able to record that Romberg's posthumous presence on Broadway was successful, that he had ended his long career in the Broadway musical theatre on a note of triumph. Regrettably this was not the case. *The Girl in Pink Tights* was received apathetically. It barely limped beyond one hundred performances before expiring.

On the other hand, two important screen events—both taking place three years or so after Romberg's death—proved that Romberg's finest music had not died with him. One was the motion-picture adaptation of his classic operetta, *The Student Prince,* in which Edmund Purdom and Ann Blyth starred, with Mario Lanza singing Romberg's songs on the sound track. "This bright-faced, wide-screen production of the old Romberg romance . . . is a cheerfully and thoroughly uninhibited outpouring of synthetic German schmaltz, as bubbly as boiling maple syrup and as tuneful as a crowded Yorkville *Stube.*" So wrote Bosley Crowther in *The New York Times.* He added: "More so, in fact—and since music is the best thing *The Student Prince* can boast, it is welcome to find that the music in this case is very good."

Later the same year (1954), Romberg's screen biography,

Deep in My Heart, came to the Radio City Music Hall. José Ferrer played the role of the composer. As is so often the case with screen biographies of famous popular composers, a thin story line (which is rarely faithful to biographical truth) is the string on which to bead gems of melody. In *Deep in My Heart* these gems were plentiful, indeed: old songs like "Leg o' Mutton," Romberg's first publication; lesser songs like "I Love to Go Swimmin' with Wimen," "It," and "Mr. and Mrs."; treasures like "One Alone," "Auf Wiedersehen," "Lover Come Back to Me," "When I Grow Too Old to Dream" (introduced in the movie *The Night Is Young*), and "Softly, as in a Morning Sunrise." This was surely a song feast to satiate even the most ample of musical appetites! Audiences enjoyed this feast to the full in the movie theatre and on records in a best-selling soundtrack release by MGM.

IV

GEORGE M. COHAN

(1878-1942)

In the 1930s the operetta was beginning to go out of fashion. Occasionally, in the years that followed, it returned to enjoy a brief day of glory on the Broadway stage. This happened, for example, in 1944 with *The Song of Norway,* an operetta based on the life and music of Edvard Grieg. It happened again in 1953 with *Kismet,* where the music was a popular adaptation of melodies by Alexander Borodin. In both cases the operettas were major successes. But these were exceptions to the rule. By the time the 1940s arrived, operetta was a stage form that had basically lost its validity, its *raison d'être*—and, by the same token, its audience. It had been replaced by musical comedy.

For the most part, musical comedy was American in concept, materials, and spirit. Where the operetta had inhabited a make-believe world with make-believe people, musical comedy generally aspired toward modern and comparatively realistic contexts. Recognizable American characters were frequently called upon to undergo American experiences within American settings. Where operetta was leisurely and sedate in both text and music, musical comedy moved with an accelerated tempo and an energetic stride, in line with the growing dynamism, enthusiasm, and initiative that characterized the beginning of the twentieth century.

Musical comedy came into existence at just about the time that the operetta had begun to capture the hearts of American theatregoers. Its father was George M. Cohan. He was a theatrical jack-of-all-trades: composer, lyricist, librettist, actor, director, producer. In all these capacities he was the shrill voice of the America of his times. His American characters were invariably a stereotype of his own brash, cocksure personality. The complications in which they were enmeshed were those familiar to Americans everywhere, just as their backgrounds could be recognized. These characters talked the way Americans talked, often in the vernacular. They sang, not the sentimental, nostalgic waltzes of the operetta, but the kind of lively or sentimental tunes which were obviously American made. Cohan filled his musicals with his own fiery brand of patriotism and homespun philosophy which struck a responsive chord because they articulated what most Americans then felt and thought.

The plots of his musicals might be contrived and synthetic. His characters might be one-dimensional. His dialogue might be cluttered with clichés. His songs might make few if any demands on musical or poetical sophistication. All this is true. It is impossible to conceive of reviving a George M. Cohan musical comedy today, because those musicals are so old-fashioned that they would appear as antiques. Nevertheless, the importance of Cohan's musicals transcends the simple pleasures they once brought their audiences. More than anybody before him, Cohan helped to inject a new, brisk energetic timing to our musical stage, a tempo characteristic of America at a time when, through the development of the

One of the best

automobile and the airplane, it was growing increasingly interested in movement and speed. The slow-paced graceful operetta was like the horse-drawn surrey with the fringe on the top—locomotion for a slow-moving era. Cohan's musicals were, by comparison, a high-powered limousine, a new kind of transportation for a new era. He helped to create a new kind of theatre for a new audience. Others who followed him carried into the theatre greater inventiveness, originality, and sophistication than Cohan was ever capable of. But they could hardly have accomplished what they did if Cohan had not set the stage for them.

Before he became the first significant creator of musical comedies, Cohan had been successful in vaudeville as a performer, writer of vaudeville sketches, and creator of popular songs.

He was born in Providence, Rhode Island, on July 3, 1878 (*not* July 4 as some reference books maintain). His parents were vaudevillians. As an infant, George made his stage debut by appearing as a human prop in their vaudeville act. Later he attended the lower grades in public school and took some lessons on the violin; this was the extent of his formal education. After that the theatre was his whole world. Whatever he knew came from the theatre and was about the theatre; and all of it came from firsthand experiences. When he was nine he had a speaking part in his parents' act which, beginning with 1888, was billed as "The Four Cohans." The Four Cohans included George's sister, Josephine, as well as George and his parents. Year after year, George's part in the act was extended until he became both its leading performer and the author of most of its material.

He wrote and had his first song published when he was sixteen. It was "Why Did Nellie Leave Home?" and it was a failure. His second song, "Hot Tamale Alley," did better, since it was introduced by a dynamic and popular vaudevillian, May Irwin. Then in 1898, with "I Guess I'll Have to Telegraph My Baby," Cohan had his first hit song. Ethel Levey caused a sensation with it when she introduced it in vaudeville. Soon after that, in 1899, she became Cohan's first wife.

Beginning with 1900, the "Four Cohans" was a vaudeville headline act drawing the then impressive pay of $1,000 a week. (Actually there were five Cohans in the act, since Cohan's wife, Ethel Levey, had joined it.) George M. Cohan was its star, having taken away the limelight completely from his parents. He wrote the songs and the sketches and in addition was the business manager. But all this activity did not satisfy a young man of his irrepressible energies and driving ambitions. He began writing songs and sketches for other vaudevillians, too. Even so he felt the compulsive need to conquer other worlds. He was thinking of one world in particular, that of the Broadway musical theatre.

He expanded one of his vaudeville sketches into a three-act play with songs, *The Governor's Son,* opening on Broadway on February 25, 1901, with a cast headed by the five Cohans. It failed to make an impression on Broadway, though on the road it did quite well. Cohan's second invasion of Broadway was hardly more successful—*Running for Office,* in 1903. Once again it was an expansion of one of his old vaudeville sketches.

In 1904, Cohan entered into a producing partnership with Sam H. Harris. They needed a show for their maiden producing effort—and, to be sure, Cohan had every intention of writing it. This time, however, he avoided the temptation of reheating an old dish and reworking his vaudeville material. Instead he wrote a new play, fitted it out with new songs, and developed the main character to point up his own strength as a performer so that he might be starred. This production was *Little Johnny Jones*, which opened at the Liberty Theatre on November 7, 1904. Four of the five Cohans were in the cast (sister Josephine had withdrawn), and George M. was featured in the title role. Musical comedy as we know it today came into existence with *Little Johnny Jones*.

From his beginnings in the Broadway musical theatre, Cohan made it a practice to base some of his characters on real persons. Some of those in *The Governor's Son* and *Running for Office* were the stage counterparts of Cohan's political friends in New York. Johnny Jones was Tod Sloan, a famous American jockey, much in the news because in 1903 he went to England to ride in the Derby. As the hero of Cohan's new musical, Johnny Jones is also an American jockey in the English Derby. There he is approached by a gambler to throw the race. Johnny, of course, turns a deaf ear. But when he loses the race, some of his English fans are sure he has been dishonest. Determined to prove his innocence, Johnny stays behind in England, hiring a detective to get the evidence that would clear him. When Johnny's friends, and the professional gambler, all set sail for America, the detective goes along hoping to find the evidence he needs to prove Johnny's innocence. The detective and Johnny have worked out a scheme whereby the detective can signal Johnny if he is successful in his quest: the discharge of fireworks from the deck of the ship, while visible to Johnny on the Southampton dock. This is how Johnny learns that he has been proved innocent. He is now able to pursue his romance with his American girl friend which had been disrupted when his integrity had been in question.

The musical opens with one of its best songs: "The Yankee Doodle Boy," with which Johnny makes his entrance and breezily introduces himself to his fans as "a real live nephew of Uncle Sam's, born on the fourth of July." Without preliminaries, character and performer become one and the same man. This may have been the reason that that opening scene made such a powerful impact, for George M. Cohan was a "Yankee doodle dandy" in his own right—even though he had come into the world just one day too soon to have been born on America's Independence Day.

Another important George M. Cohan song arrives at a climactic point in the play. Johnny Jones is at Southampton to bid bon voyage to his friends and to the detective he has hired. He tells them farewell with one of the most celebrated songs about New York, a song since become an unofficial theme for New York's Main Street, "Give My Regards to Broadway."

Besides these two hit songs, *Little Johnny Jones* boasted a flag-waving routine and a monologue, "Life's a Funny Proposition." Singing the praises of country, as he strutted up and down the stage with a flag draped around his body, was a routine that Cohan would use again and again with extraordinary effect in later musicals. Another of his trademarks was to deliver little philosophical speeches, while pointing an eloquent forefinger at his audience, of which "Life's a Funny Proposition" was the first.

With songs like "The Yankee Doodle Boy" and "Give My Regards to Broadway," with a characterization like that of Johnny Jones whose American identity was revealed in every move and gesture and line of dialogue, and with his flag-waving routine, Cohan helped to establish a recognizable American profile for the theatre which once and for all set musical comedy sharply apart from the operetta.

This profile was emphasized more strongly still in Cohan's next musical comedy, also a success—*Forty-Five Minutes from Broadway,* in 1906. The title refers to the community of New

Rochelle, a suburb of New York, whose natives are described by one of the Cohan songs as "Reubens" with "whiskers like hay." Tom Bennett comes to this little suburb, forty-five minutes from Broadway to claim a fortune left by a distant relative. With him is his secretary, Flora, and a companion, Kid Burns, a chronic gambler and horseplayer. Burns meets and falls in love with Mary Jane, who had been employed as a housemaid by the dead relative for many years. She is believed to have been chosen by the deceased as his heir, but no will could be found to substantiate this. Kid Burns finally finds the document in an old suit. This discovery throws him into despair, since he is sure that as an heiress Mary Jane will surely lose interest in him. But Mary Jane chooses love over wealth: She tears up the will.

Forty-Five Minutes from Broadway brought two new stars to the Broadway musical stage. One was Fay Templeton, a veteran from burlesque, who appeared as Mary Jane. The other was Victor Moore, a young comedian, cast as Kid Burns; for the next thirty years and more he would occupy a place of rare honor in the American theatre. Fay Templeton sang one of the hit numbers from this show, "Mary's a Grand Old Name"; Victor, sang another, the title number. A third standout in the score was "So Long, Mary."

Absent from the cast of *Forty-Five Minutes from Broadway* was George M. Cohan himself. He lost no time in filling this gap by writing for himself a fat part in his very next musical—*George Washington, Jr.,* also produced early in 1906. Here our hero is the son of an American senator whose snobbish social attitudes make him glorify all things English to the denigration of his own country. He very much wants his son to marry the daughter of an English nobleman. But young George is so much of an American patriot that he assumes the name of the first President of the United States. He goes on to prove that both the English nobleman and his daughter are phonies through and through. This leads the father to forget his passion for English ways and people and to become an American patriot like his son. He is now completely sympathetic to having his son George marry the American girl with whom the boy had long been in love.

Among the outstanding songs of this score were "I Was Born in Virginia," "If Washington Should Come to Life," and a patriotic number for a flag-waving routine, "You're a Grand Old Flag." When this last-named song was heard for the first time, on opening night, it had the title of "You're a Grand Old Rag." This was a description of the American flag heard by Cohan from the lips of a Civil War veteran. The day after the première of the musical, a number of patriotic societies condemned the song as an insult to the American banner because it had been referred to as a "rag." Cohan assuaged their feelings by changing the controversial word to "flag."

An out-of-town presentation of *George Washington, Jr.* was the last time that Cohan's wife, Ethel, appeared in a Cohan production, in Cleveland during the winter of 1906. Cohan and Ethel had come to the parting of ways, not only as theatrical performers but also as life partners. They were divorced the following February, and on June 29, 1907, he married Agnes Nolan, a young actress who remained his devoted wife as long as he lived.

The subject of social-climbing Americans interested in getting their children to marry foreign nobility continued to interest Cohan. He returned to this theme in *The Yankee Prince* in 1908. Other of his musicals sought sources of stimulation from American settings: the town of Norfield, Massachusetts (where Cohan and Agnes liked to spend their summers), which the composer used as the background for *Fifty*

Miles from Boston in 1908. This show is remembered mainly for its song "Harrigan." In *The Talk of New York,* in 1907, Cohan traveled from one familiar setting in New York to another: the race track, the lobby at the Hotel Astor, the Claremont Inn on Riverside Drive, and so on. For this show Cohan revived the lovable character of Kid Burns for Victor Moore; here, too, we encounter two still familiar Cohan songs, "When a Fellow's on the Level with a Girl That's on the Square" and "When We Are M-a-double-r-i-e-d."

Although Cohan continued writing musical comedies, as well as revues, after 1910 his greatest successes came with non-musical shows—*Get Rich Quick Wallingford* in 1910 and *Seven Keys to Baldpate* in 1913. As for his songwriting efforts, the greatest of Cohan's song successes after 1910—indeed, the greatest song success of his whole career—came with a number not intended for any musical production whatsoever, but inspired by America's declaration of war against Germany in 1917. He wrote "Over There" in a white heat of excitement and inspiration early one morning at his home in Great Neck, Long Island, after seeing the newspaper headline that America was at war. Soon after it was written, the song was introduced by Charles King at a Red Cross benefit at the Hippodrome Theatre, and before long it was interpolated by Nora Bayes into her vaudeville act. "Over There" went on to sell about two million copies of sheet music and one million records. It was sung, heard, and played throughout the war, to become the one musical number above all others identified with that conflict. President Wilson considered it one of the most significant builders of home-front and war-front morale. Nearly a quarter of a century later, President Roosevelt still recognized its importance as patriotic music by bestowing on Cohan the Medal of Honor.

The years following World War I saw a decline of Cohan's

prestige and influence in the musical theatre. New librettists like George S. Kaufman and Morrie Ryskind, new composers like George Gershwin, new lyricists like Lorenz Hart and Ira Gershwin, were introducing into the musical theatre a slickness, smartness, brilliance of technique, wit, and overall sophistication against which Cohan could not compete. Those flag-waving routines, those little homilies and practical philosophy speeches, those old-fashioned songs about country, girl, mother, Ireland, or Broadway—all those Cohan trademarks, in short—began to sound trite in the jazz era of the 1920s. *Billie,* Cohan's last musical, was a failure in 1928. A number of nonmusical plays by Cohan in the early 1930s were received just as badly. Cohan's last play, *The Return of the Vagabond,* in 1940, ran only seven performances.

Beyond deficits at the box office and rejection by the critics, Cohan suffered two major setbacks to his pride and influence after World War I. In 1919 he allied himself with a losing cause when, as a producer, he fought bitterly against a strike imposed on the theatre by Actors Equity Association. The complete victory of Actors Equity left him so bitter that for a time he thought of abandoning Broadway for good. As a matter of fact, he did close down the successful producing firm of Cohan and Harris. Although he returned to the Broadway stage both as a performer and as a writer, he seemed to have lost much of his onetime zest and exuberance for his work, particularly when he saw how the critics and the audiences were beginning to turn away from his plays, musicals, and songs.

He suffered another serious setback a decade later, this time in Hollywood. Soon after the screen erupted into sound, Cohan contracted to go to Hollywood and appear in his first talking picture—*The Phantom President,* with songs by Rodgers and Hart. Cohan expected to be welcomed to the movie capital with the fanfare due one of Broadway's immortals. Instead he learned to his amazement that there were some in Hollywood who did not know who he was, while others had such vague recollections of what he had accomplished that they treated him high-handedly. His suggestions for improving the picture were rudely rejected. The director tried teaching him how to deliver a song—he who had delivered perhaps a thousand songs in vaudeville and the musical theatre. The director even tried showing him how to perform the kind of flag routine that Cohan himself had devised and had made so famous. The whole movie experience was a shattering one for him. He left Hollywood vowing that never again would he appear in a movie.

Fortunately, he lived long enough to see Hollywood make handsome amends for the way it had treated him: through the production in 1942 of his life story in one of the most successful screen musicals ever made, *Yankee Doodle Dandy,* starring James Cagney as Cohan in a performance that won the Academy Award. Cohan was deeply touched by this picture, which gave him a full measure of recognition and which presented his most famous routines and songs with authenticity and devotion. One of Cohan's last acts, while he was fatally sick, was to take a quick trip to Broadway and slip into the darkened theatre and watch for the last time a few moments of his picture.

Cohan also lived long enough to gather new triumphs on the Broadway stage—though this time only as a performer. In 1933 he was starred in *Ah, Wilderness!,* a nonmusical comedy by Eugene O'Neill that won the Pulitzer Prize. Cohan's endearing portrayal of the father of a sensitive adolescent in New England at the turn of the twentieth century won the hearts of the critics uncompromisingly. "The fine art of the evening," said the critic of the New York *Sun,* "remains that of Mr. Cohan."

Four years later Cohan was starred as President Franklin D. Roosevelt in the political musical satire *I'd Rather Be Right,* with songs by Rodgers and Hart. Once again his acting inspired hosannas of praise. "Mr. Cohan has never been in better form," reported Brooks Atkinson. "The audience was his, and lovingly his, all last evening." For Cohan these tastes of success on the living stage were bitter as gall—for he was speaking somebody else's lines and singing somebody else's songs.

He continued to gather honors, such as the Medal of Honor from the hands of President Roosevelt in 1941, and the triumphant opening of his screen biography, *Yankee Doodle Dandy,* on May 30, 1942. The latter event led the Mayor of New York to proclaim Cohan's birthday that year as George M. Cohan Day.

When Cohan died at his home in New York City on November 5, 1942, he was eulogized as few men of the theatre have been. Gene Buck, former president of ASCAP and a distinguished lyricist, said that Cohan "was the greatest single figure the American theatre ever produced."

He was also one of America's great songwriters. However sentimental, corny, or naive some of these songs may be, they have not lost an irresistible nostalgic appeal even to present-day sophisticates. This became apparent in April of 1968 when *George M!,* a stage musical based on Cohan's life, came to Broadway. Though the libretto was sub-standard—a loosely knit fabric made up of random episodes—and while both dialogue and characterizations were generally synthetic, *George M!* (with Joel Gray playing the part of Cohan magnificently) became a hit. And it became a hit because Cohan's songs sent audiences out of the theatre humming.

V

JEROME KERN

(1885-1943)

MUSICAL COMEDY found a creative talent of the first order in Jerome Kern. He was an aristocratic melodist, but he was much more than that. He was a composer whose use of subtle changes of rhythm, unexpected intrusion of new ideas, and novel enharmonic changes brought to his writing a continual freshness and eloquent expressiveness.

But the writing of some of the greatest and most successful songs to come out of American musical comedy represents only one facet of Kern's achievements. Another facet was the changes he brought about in musical comedy. If George M. Cohan was its father, then Kern was the first to bring to it a significance that had both dramatic and musical importance. A profound student of the theatre, as well as a remarkable composer, Kern was able during his long and fruitful career to revolutionize musical comedy not once but twice—extending its horizon, enriching its aesthetics, opening up for it a new world. This is why such other later giant figures in musical comedy—people like George Gershwin and Richard Rodgers—looked upon Kern as one who had influenced them profoundly. This is also why an editorial writer of the New York *Herald-Tribune* could say when Kern died: "Genius is surely not too extravagant a word for him."

He was born to a cultured middle-class family in New York City on January 27, 1885. His father was a prosperous businessman, owner of an organization that had the concession to sprinkle city streets with water and a successful investor in real estate. His mother, a woman of considerable cultural attainments, was an excellent amateur pianist.

Jerome revealed a gift for music when, at the age of five, he began taking piano lessons with his mother. From then on he was continually found at the piano where he was making excellent progress. At ten he could play by ear songs from Victor Herbert's *The Wizard of the Nile* after attending a performance of that operetta—the first time, incidentally, he ever saw a Broadway show. As a student at a high school in Newark, New Jersey (the city where his family had opened a new business and to which the Kern family had moved in 1895), Kern's musical talent was recognized and appreciated. He was often called upon to play the piano and organ at assemblies and to write the music for school productions. His teachers there often referred to him as "the little genius."

During the summer of 1902, after graduating from high school, he worked for his father, now the owner of a merchandizing house. The father hoped Jerome would forget all about music and think of business as a life's career. The summer job was planned as Jerome's apprenticeship. But it did not take the father long to become disenchanted with the boy's business potential. One day, Jerome was sent to New York to purchase two pianos from an Italian dealer. With characteristic Latin hospitality and expansiveness, the dealer invited Jerome to drink some wine. The wine turned Jerome's head and warped his perspective. When Kern discovered that the

Italian had two hundred pianos in his warehouse he purchased the entire lot. This deal almost sent his father's merchandizing establishment into bankruptcy. The father saved the situation by conceiving an installment plan whereby the two hundred pianos could be disposed of. The whole affair spelled doom for Jerome Kern's career in business, which, as far as the boy himself was concerned, was just as well, since business held no interest for him whatsoever, and he wanted very much to continue his music study.

That fall he enrolled in the New York College of Music where, for about a year, he was trained in piano and harmony. On September 5, 1902, he made his debut as composer when a piece for the piano, "At the Casino," was published in Tin Pan Alley.

Having completed a year at the College of Music, Kern left for Europe in 1903 for some additional study in Heidelberg, Germany. His travels finally brought him to London where he established temporary residence. At that time, Charles K. Frohman, an American producer, was putting on musical shows in London. Since audiences came habitually late to these shows, Frohman made it a practice to hire young composers to write songs and other musical material which could be sung and played at the beginning of the production—filler material until the audience had arrived and the main songs and performers could be presented. Frohman engaged Kern to create such material at a salary of ten dollars a week. This is how Kern made his bow in the musical theatre, specifically with the song "My Little Canoe," which Billie Burke sang in *The School Girl* at the Pavilion Music Hall during the winter of 1903. (At that time Miss Burke was seventeen, making her first appearance as a singer on any stage. In later years she became a star of the American stage and screen and was the wife of Florenz Ziegfeld.)

For several months Kern continued writing functional songs for Frohman. One became successful. This was a topical number, "Mr. Chamberlain." The "Mr. Chamberlain" in this song was a distinguished English statesman of the early twentieth century who became the father of Neville, England's Prime Minister just before World War II. The writing of "Mr. Chamberlain" is an important event in Kern's early career not only because it is his first success but also because it was the beginning of his collaboration with P. G. Wodehouse, who wrote the lyrics. Some years later, Wodehouse would become famous for his whimsical stories in which a butler named Jeeves is the main character. In 1903 he was a young man at the dawn of his literary career, serving as a columnist for the London *Globe* and selling poems and stories to various magazines. An English actor, Seymour Hicks, introduced Kern to Wodehouse so that they might write a song for his use. Hicks presented that song—"Mr. Chamberlain"—in the London musical *The Beauty and the Bath* in 1903. A dozen years later, Wodehouse would once again collaborate with Kern, this time in the United States, to achieve not only hit songs but a new era for American musical comedy.

By the time Kern returned to the United States in 1904 he knew what he wanted to do. His ambition was to write popular songs and place them in the theatre. To get a start, even if at the bottom, he went to work in Tin Pan Alley at the Lyceum Publishing Company (the firm that had issued his "At the Casino" two years earlier). His job was to make out bills and invoices in the office. Before long, Kern left Lyceum to become a song plugger for Shapiro-Remick, whose songs he demonstrated in five-and-ten-cent stores.

While thus employed he was hired in 1904 to adapt for Broadway the score of an English musical, *Mr. Wix of Wickham.* This was a comedy with an Australian setting, though the principal character was a shopkeeper from England. Kern's job was to give some of the English-written songs an American flavor and to contribute a few numbers of his own. Those Kern songs (especially one called "Waiting for You") made at least one New York critic sit up and take notice. He was Alan Dale, who in his review inquired: "Who is this Jerome Kern whose music towers in an Eiffel way above the average primitive hurdy-gurdy accompaniment of the present-day musical comedy?"

In 1905, Kern went to work for Max Dreyfus, the head of the Tin Pan Alley publishing house of Harms. Kern was hired as a salesman to market sheet music in shops along Hudson Valley in New York; he was also required from time to time to plug the songs of Harms in various stores in New York City. Dreyfus had an extraordinary gift for recognizing talent in the raw. He sensed that in Kern he had found a talent worth developing. But first he wanted Kern to learn the hard way what made a song successful with the public, by having him work as a salesman and a song plugger. At the same time he encouraged Kern to write his own songs, offering to publish those he considered worthwhile. One of the first Dreyfus published proved a hit. From then on, until the end of the composer's life, Dreyfus remained Kern's publisher —and one of his closest friends.

The hit song Harms published was "How'd You Like to Spoon with Me?," with lyrics by Edward Laska. Kern and Laska marched into the offices of the Shuberts, creating the fiction that Reginald de Koven had sent them. Through this ruse the composer and lyricist were able to perform their number for the powerful producers, who instantly liked it so much that they decided to place it in the very next Shubert production, *The Earl and the Girl,* opening at the Casino Theatre on November 4, 1905. The song was used for a big production number during which six chorus girls soared on flower-decorated swings from the stage to the audience. The song proved a standout, as the New York *Dramatic Mirror* reported; it was even used soon afterward in a London musical.

"How'd You Like to Spoon with Me?" was interpolated into *The Earl and the Girl.* The rest of the music for this show was the work of another composer (in this case, Ivan Caryll). This practice of interpolation, having individual songs placed into various shows for which other composers did the basic scores, continued to gain a hearing for Kern during the next seven years. In fact, almost a hundred of his songs were heard this way, in approximately thirty musicals. A few of these songs were better than average, and some were mediocre or poor. None has survived. Nevertheless, this was not a period of wasted motion for Kern. On the contrary, this apprenticeship prepared him for giant tasks and achievements that lay before him. It taught him a good deal about the inner workings of the musical theatre. Kern learned from firsthand experiences what made a song "tick" in a production and what made it fail.

During this period, on October 25, 1910, Kern married Eva Leale. She was an English girl, the daughter of the manager of a hotel in Walton-on-Thames. Kern had met her there one summer. They were married in a simple church ceremony in Walton, after which Kern brought his bride back with him to the bachelor quarters he was then occupying on West 68th Street in New York. Their only child, Betty, was born eight years later.

Kern's first complete score for a Broadway musical was for *The Red Petticoat,* produced on November 13, 1912. This was somewhat of an offbeat kind of musical about miners in Nevada in which the star of the show, Gracie Fields, played the part of a lady barber. The show missed its mark, however, and was a failure. So was *Oh, I Say!* in 1913, Kern's second attempt to write a complete score. The main point of interest in this music lay not in any single song but in the fact that in his orchestration Kern used saxophones, something then still rare in popular-music scoring.

At long last, Kern hit the bull's-eye, with *The Girl from Utah,* on August 24, 1914. This is the musical comedy that first lifted Kern to that lofty station in American theatre and American popular music from which he was never again to descend. *The Girl from Utah* was an adaptation of an English musical for which Paul Rubens and Sidney Jones had provided the score. When this musical was brought to the Casino Theatre in New York with Julia Sanderson in the title role, Kern was asked to contribute several new songs. He complied with eight numbers. Two had special interest and charm. One was his first masterpiece.

In *The Girl from Utah,* the heroine fled from her native town in the United States to come to London. She was running away from a prospective marriage with a Utah Mormon, who already had a number of wives. The Mormon followed her to England. But our heroine is helped in eluding him by the hero of the musical, with whom she finally finds romance and happiness.

The two numbers that stood out prominently in this, Kern's first successful Broadway musical, were "Why Don't They Dance the Polka Anymore?" and "I'd Like to Wander with Alice in Wonderland." The number that was an unqualified masterpiece was "They Didn't Believe Me," a ballad presented hauntingly by Julia Sanderson, whose voice and delivery were very much in Kern's mind when he wrote it for her. "They Didn't Believe Me" inspired ovations at the Casino Theatre and went on from there to achieve a fabulous success throughout the country. It sold two million copies of sheet music (Kern had never before had a song that sold over two hundred thousand copies). This triumph was achieved in spite of the fact that the song was most unusual in its melodic structure, in its modulations, and in its harmonic language. In fact, this is the first song in which Kern revealed the creative powers he was capable of.

At the time that *The Girl from Utah* was throwing the spotlight on Jerome Kern's remarkable talent, there existed in the Broadway sector a little theatre called The Princess which had a seating capacity of only three hundred. So small a house inevitably had a hard time finding enough attractions to keep it open all year. This problem disturbed Elizabeth Marbury, an agent-producer who was co-manager of that theatre with F. Ray Comstock. Miss Marbury soon came to the conclusion that the solution lay in having special shows with a small overhead cost written for the theatre. She asked Jerome Kern and Guy Bolton, the latter a young English librettist and lyricist, to create a show for her that would not cost more than $7,500 to mount.

Kern and Bolton came up with *Nobody Home*—an adaptation of an English musical, *Mr. Popple of Ippleton*—which was produced at the Princess Theatre on April 20, 1915. It described the amusing experiences of an Englishman in New York who falls in love with an American showgirl. There were no stars in the cast, no fancy sets or elaborate costumes, no large groups for production numbers. Everything was scaled down to miniature, from the eight girls in the chorus to the ten instrumentalists in the orchestra. The show boasted an intimate quality which led one critic to describe it as a "kitchenette production." There was not much here to hold the eye fascinated or to stun the senses. There were only two simple sets, and no big scenes whatsoever. This musical comedy counted upon content rather than outward dress to interest its audiences—upon wit, sparkling dialogue and lyrics, unusual situations and turns of plot, and effervescent songs like "You Know and I Know" and "The Magic Melody."

And so, what soon came to be known as the "Princess Theatre Show" came into existence with *Nobody Home*. And with it a new era of the American musical theatre was ushered in.

Nobody Home just about paid its way during a run of 135 performances. This, and the fact that the critics seemed to like it, convinced Miss Marbury to try again, and once again she recruited Kern and Bolton to do the job. This time they adapted a stage farce by Philip Bartholomae, *Over Night*, with Kern contributing fifteen musical numbers. They called their musical *Very Good, Eddie*. With a cast headed by Oscar Shaw, Ernest Truex, and Alice Dovey it opened on December 23, 1915.

In this script, two honeymoon couples are about to take a trip on the Hudson River Day Line in New York City. In the confusion of sailing time, one couple is left behind while the other gets on board. The only trouble is that the pair are mismated: the couple aboard ship consists of the bridegroom of one couple and the bride of the other. What follows is a hilarious attempt on the part of this mismated pair to appear like real newlyweds rather than inspire suspicion and gossip.

The whole escapade had about it an infectious air of frivolity, heightened and intensified by the lightness of touch which each of the principal performers brought to their parts. "Scarcely any previous musical comedy," Cecil Smith wrote in *Musical Comedy in America*, "had been favored with a plot and dialogue so coherent, so neatly related to those of well-written plays. . . . The intimate musical comedy became established as a suitable and successful genre."

Kern's musical touch could also be light and gay—in, for example, the title number and "When You Wear a Thirteen

Collar." But the noble melody of which Kern was now a recognized master was also represented, most notably in the songs "Nodding Roses" and "Babes in the Wood."

In the 1910s, Broadway shows did not have the kind of runs they do today. With the comparatively low production costs prevailing at that time, if a musical ran 200 performances it brought in a handsome profit, while a 300-performance run represented a box-office bonanza. *Very Good, Eddie* lasted 341 performances. And its immediate successor at the Princess Theatre—*Oh, Boy!* in 1917—accumulated 463 performances.

For the writing of *Oh, Boy!*, a third collaborator was added to the team of Kern and Bolton. He was P. G. Wodehouse, the same man who had written lyrics for Kern back in London in 1903. Wodehouse, now a famous writer, had come to New York to write dramatic reviews for the magazine *Vanity Fair*. On opening night of *Very Good, Eddie,* Kern suggested to Wodehouse that he write the lyrics for the next Princess Theatre Show, which Wodehouse consented to do.

Up to the middle 1910s, the song lyric had been the sadly neglected stepchild of both the song industry and American musical comedy. Too often, at that time, lyricists were content with awkward prosody, clichés, mawkish sentiments, stilted rhymes and rhythms and childish turns of phrase. Wodehouse was one of the first to do for the lyric what Kern was doing for the music—bringing an adult intelligence and a sure-handed technique, together with a freshness of viewpoint and self-expression, to his work. Later lyricists who helped make an art out of song versification—men, say, like Ira Gershwin and Lorenz Hart—freely confessed how much guidance and stimulation they had derived from Wodehouse's lyrics.

Wodehouse, then, became the new member in the writing

partnership creating the Princess Theatre Shows. It proved a strong addition. The Princess Theatre Shows became more scintillating than ever. This fact was recognized by an unidentified versifier in a New York column when he wrote:

"This is the trio of musical fame,
  Bolton and Wodehouse and Kern;
Better than anyone else you can name.
  Bolton and Wodehouse and Kern.
Nobody knows what on earth they've been bitten by,
All I can say is I mean to get lit an' buy,
Orchestra seats for the next one that's written by
  Bolton and Wodehouse and Kern."

Oh, Boy! had a college-town setting. George, temporarily separated from his newly married wife who had gone to visit her sick mother, seeks diversion at the college inn. There a young, attractive girl, Jackie, becomes involved in a rumpus. To keep out of the hands of the police, she finds a haven in George's apartment. When different people come to visit George, Jackie assumes various disguises and impersonations. But George's wife, who makes a precipitous return home, is not fooled. However, she becomes appeased upon learning that the only reason George has been secreting Jackie is to save the reputation of his father-in-law, who had been Jackie's escort that evening.

The whole production placed tongue square in cheek—an attitude maintained by Kern in a song, "Nesting Time in Flatbush," which parodied a ballad popular in the 1910s, and the still remembered, "When It's Apple Blossom Time in Normandy." The best ballad in the Kern score was "Till the Clouds Roll By," a song that became so popular in the Kern repertory that its title was used as the name of Kern's screen biography in 1946.

The next Princess Theatre Show as *Oh, Lady! Lady!* in 1918. This was also a smash box-office success—in fact so much so that to accommodate the immense overflow at the Princess Theatre a second company was formed to play at the nearby Casino Theatre. Here we find the action on Long Island. A playboy, on the eve of his marriage, becomes entangled with an old girl friend. The ways in which he tries to elude her, and the complications contributed by a reformed crook and a woman shoplifter employed as valet and lady's maid, form the basis of the lively goings-on. Dorothy Parker (in later years a renowned wit, poet, and short-story writer, but in 1918 a drama reviewer) wrote: "Well, Bolton, Wodehouse and Kern have done it again. If you ask me, I will look you fearlessly in the eye and tell you in low, throbbing tones that it has it over any other musical in town. . . . I like the way the action slides casually into the songs. I like the deft rhyming of the songs. . . . And oh, how I do like Jerome Kern's music." The best of this music could be found in the songs "Before I Met You" and "You Found Me."

Actually, still another wonderful song had been intended for *Oh, Lady! Lady!;* had it been allowed to remain in the score it would have been the cream of the crop. It was a ballad called "Bill." Vivienne Segal, star of *Oh, Lady! Lady!,* insisted that "Bill" was not suited for her kind of voice, and the song had to be withdrawn. Kern kept it on ice until he could find the proper spot for it. He found that spot when he wrote *Show Boat*—but that is another and later story.

There was only one more Princess Theatre Show after that: *Oh, My Dear,* in 1918. But for this production Louis Hirsch and not Jerome Kern wrote the music.

The Princess Theatre Show had introduced a new note in the musical theatre: a stronger accent than ever on American people, places, and things; a greater concern for logical plots, sprightly situations, smart dialogue and lyrics, sophisticated songs. The remarkable musical comedies written by Rodgers and Hart, and the intimate revues that sprang up on and off Broadway in the early 1920s, all owed their existence to the stimulation provided by the Princess Theatre productions.

Though the Princess Theatre Show represented a sharp break with the more elaborate, the expensively mounted, the star-studded kind of musicals then being put on by producers like the Shuberts and Ziegfeld, those grandiose productions had by no means lost their popularity. Nor was Kern to ignore this kind of theatre; in fact he was involved with it even while he was helping to create the Princess Theatre musicals. In 1917, with Bolton and Wodehouse, he wrote *Leave It to Jane*. Here, too, a college town is the setting. The heroine is the daughter of the college president. When the college is in danger of losing its star football player to a rival institution, Jane uses her wiles as a siren to get him to stay. He stays, of course—and she falls in love with him.

The music by Kern was the main attraction of *Leave It to Jane* in 1917. This was also the case when *Leave It to Jane* was revived in 1959 in an off-Broadway production (a revival that ran for several years). As Richard Watts, Jr., said about the revival: "I have remembered the Kern score with delight, recalling five of the songs in particular. And hearing them again last night, I was happy to find that, not only was the score as a whole as charming and freshly tuneful as memory has made it, but my quintet came off easily as the best of a gloriously melodious lot. . . ." *Leave It to Jane* must stand on its unforgettable melodies, which include the title number, the languorous "The Siren's Song," and an outstanding comedy number, "Cleopatterer."

One of the most lavishly mounted and costumed of Kern's musical comedies was *Sally* in 1920, with a book by Guy Bolton. Since Florenz Ziegfeld was the producer—and, as the creator of the *Follies,* Ziegfeld spared no expense to make his show the most splendiferous on Broadway—*Sally* was the last word in grandiose staging. All this magnificence was planned as the frame for one of the most glamorous musical comedy stars of her generation. She was Marilyn Miller—exquisite, delicate, with the fragile quality of precious chinaware. Her voice was small, but it wooed and captured the listener. When she danced she had lightness and airy grace. But she did not need to sing or dance or even speak to flood the stage with radiance. All she had to do was have the limelight focus its beam on her. "Marilyn gave to the play a curious enchantment," recalled Guy Bolton and P. G. Wodehouse, "that no reproduction in other lands or other mediums ever captures."

As Sally, Marilyn Miller was a dishwashing waif at an American inn. She finds a protector in a waiter, a former Balkan prince. He arranges for Sally to appear as a Russian ballerina at a garden party on Long Island. Her dancing captures the hearts of one and all—most of all, that of the wealthy socialite, Blair. Sally goes on to pursue her career as dancer until she becomes a star of the Ziegfeld *Follies.* Thus she wins not only fame but even Blair himself.

Perhaps the most magical moment in the entire show came at that wonderful crossroad at which a great star and a great song become one—when Marilyn Miller introduced Kern's "Look for the Silver Lining." She sang it early in the production: a dirty-faced, abused waif trying to forget her sordid existence in the contemplation of a more hopeful future. So completely did Marilyn Miller and "Look for the Silver Lining" become associated with one another that when Miss Miller's screen biography was filmed it assumed the name of this song for its title.

Kern (with the collaboration of Otto Harbach and Oscar Hammerstein II) produced a second musical for Marilyn Miller, *Sunny,* five years after *Sally.* Here the star was seen as a circus horseback rider in England who falls in love with an American. She is, however, forced to marry the owner of the circus, a marriage that ends in divorce. Sunny stows away on the same ship bound for America aboard which her beloved American is sailing. They are reunited, this time permanently.

The big song of this production was "Who?" Kern always stood ready to concede that the main reason this song became so successful was because Oscar Hammerstein II, as lyricist, had happily come upon the provocative word "who" to link to the single note sustained through the first nine beats of the refrain. Any other word but that one, Kern always insisted, would have spelled failure.

Kern wrote scores for a dozen or so musicals in the first half of the 1920s. There was rarely one that did not boast at least one Kern number to flood the theatre with enchantment. Even in such successes as *Sally* and *Sunny,* however, there was nothing to suggest an attempt to free musical comedy from routines and methods that were now becoming shopworn. But Kern was not a man to remain long satisfied with the status quo. He had made a break with the musical theatre of the 1910s with the Princess Theatre Shows. He made an even more dramatic break with the musical theatre of the 1920s with *Show Boat.*

Show Boat was a best-selling novel by Edna Ferber published in 1926. Reading it, Kern was deeply stirred, for here Miss Ferber had brought to fiction a slice of Americana about which little had been known up to then: the fascinating people performing on showboats at the close of the nineteenth century; they traveled up and down the Mississippi providing stage entertainment to towns along the way. This was a background appealing to Kern's partiality for a pronounced Americanism in musicals. These showboat people, he felt, brought fresh, new characterizations into musical comedy. The social implications in a story that had a Negro girl suffer racial prejudice because she was married to a white man would endow the up-to-now escapist musical theatre with a new immediacy and dimension. Kern became convinced of this.

When first he approached Miss Ferber with his idea to make *Show Boat* into a musical, she was stunned. Thinking in terms of *Sally* and *Sunny* she could hardly conceive of her novel as a showcase for chorus girls, tap dances, comedians, and the other paraphernalia with which musical comedy was then cluttered. Kern dismissed her fears by insisting he was thinking of a *new* kind of musical theatre which would respect her own concern for plot structure, character, social problems, and local color.

After he had won Miss Ferber's consent, Kern discussed the project with Oscar Hammerstein II who became thoroughly enchanted with the whole idea. Hammerstein consented to write both the text and the lyrics. Almost immediately, both Hammerstein and Kern agreed that in making the transfer from novel to stage, every element of the musical theatre had to spring naturally from background, plot, and characters; that nothing would be superimposed upon the overall structure merely because it had good audience appeal. "We had fallen in love with it," Hammerstein later explained. "We couldn't keep our hands off it. We acted out the scenes together and planned the actual direction. We sang to each other. We had ourselves swooning."

Their musical was set partly aboard the showboat *Cotton Blossom* that cruised the Mississippi, and partly in Chicago at the Midway Plaisance during the World's Fair. Magnolia, daughter of Cap'n Andy (owner of *Cotton Blossom*) falls in love with Gaylord Ravenal, an irresponsible gambler. Magnolia and Ravenal take over the leading parts in the showboat production when its star, Julie, and her husband, Steve, are kept by the Natchez sheriff from appearing because Julie is black and Steve is white. When the evening show ends, Gaylord and Magnolia are made fully aware of how much they are now in love with each other. Gaylord proposes and is accepted. Several years now pass. Gaylord and Magnolia have moved to Chicago, where a daughter, Kim, was born to them. Gaylord's chronic gambling habits and irresponsibility have dripped poison into the marriage. Gaylord, in fact, has disappeared. To support herself and her daughter, Magnolia tries to get a singing job at the Trocadero. Its star performer is none other than Julie. Upon learning of Magnolia's need, Julie magnanimously gives up her position so that Magnolia might be hired in her place. Magnolia is an immense success—a success witnessed by her father, Cap'n Andy, come to Chicago to take her and Kim back to his showboat. Upon returning there, Magnolia and Kim find Gaylord waiting for them, now determined to mend his way and be a better husband and father than he has been up to now.

The colorful backgrounds, the tender and logically drawn story line with its powerful dramatic interest, the always believable characters—all this proved a powerful stimulant in lifting both Kern and Hammerstein to creative heights new even for them. Up to now satisfied for the most part to be just a functional librettist, Hammerstein here becomes a dramatist; up to now content to make his verses take a back seat to the melody and serve it in all humility, Hammerstein here becomes a poet whose words are music's equal partner. Hammerstein's text had truth, dignity, strength. His dialogue and lyrics were fresh and supple, often poetic. He allowed no extraneous element to intrude into the telling of his story. Every piece of stage business was an essential part of a cohesive whole. All this represented something revolutionary for the musical theatre. It marked the beginnings of the musical play.

This, too, was Kern's finest hour as a composer. Never before or since did he produce a score with such an outpouring of deathless melodies. *Show Boat* overflowed at the brim with hits, all of a richness of imagination and variety of invention with few parallels in the musical theatre: "Only Make Believe," "Why Do I Love You?," "Can't Help Lovin' Dat Man," "You Are Love," "Bill," "Ol' Man River." All of them have become standards; one, "Ol' Man River," has by today also acquired almost the status of a folk song.

Show Boat sailed into the Ziegfeld Theatre on December 27, 1927, in a breathtakingly beautiful production mounted by that master showman, Ziegfeld. Everything about the musical enraptured the critics. Richard Watts, Jr., called it a "triumph"; Robert Garland said it was "a wonder and a wow." Audiences also fell in love with it. *Show Boat* stayed on for two years and almost never played to an empty seat; then, after the production had toured the country for about a year, it came back to New York for a return successful run. Since that time *Show Boat* has proved a financial bonanza, as well as an artistic triumph. It has been seen, heard, and admired throughout the world. There is hardly a year without a revival somewhere in the United States. It was adapted for motion pictures three times and it has had numerous recordings (including a symphonic arrangement adapted by Kern himself for the concert hall). It is one of the most valuable properties in all theatre history, and it will probably stay that way for a long time to come.

Kern wrote the music for two more productions that belong in the musical play category, and three others that clung to the more traditional ways of musical comedy. The two musical plays were *The Cat and the Fiddle,* in 1931, and *Music in the Air,* one year later. *The Cat and the Fiddle* followed the lead of *Show Boat* in dispensing with a chorus girl line and overdressed production numbers. All resources of the musical theatre are once again placed at the disposal of plot and characters. In contemporary Brussels, Shirley, an American girl who dotes on jazz, falls in love with Victor, a Roumanian composer deep at work on an opera. Victor overhears Shirley sing an American tune which gives him the inspiration for the main aria of his opera. That opera becomes a success; so does the romance of the two lovers, in spite of their divergent musical interests.

The song that recurs throughout the production is a canzonetta, "The Night Was Made for Love," which leans more toward opera than toward musical comedy. This song is still remembered, and so is the delightful tune "She Didn't Say Yes." Both provide testimony that, in reaching for more serious and ambitious contexts, Kern did not lose his popular touch.

Music in the Air had all the outward appearance of being an old-fashioned operetta. It had the kind of setting operettas dote on: the picturesque old-world town of Edendorff in Bavaria. It had the kind of characters to whom operetta could be partial: an operetta star; a successful writer of operetta librettos; a young schoolmaster; a small-town girl come to the big city to find a career in the theatre. *Music in the Air* even boasted an operetta-like story. Karl, the young schoolmaster, and Sieglinde, daughter of the town music teacher, are in love. Sieglinde is interested in a career as a singer. She comes to Munich where, through the influence of Bruno, a librettist, she gets a chance to sing in operetta. For a while, Bruno and

Sieglinde get emotionally involved, while the distressed schoolmaster (who has followed Sieglinde to Munich) consoles himself by flirting with an operetta star. Sieglinde is a failure on the stage, and Bruno loses interest in her. Sieglinde and Karl return to Edendorff, realizing more than ever that they belong to one another.

In spite of surface considerations, *Music in the Air* was a musical play, because of its well-defined characterizations and because of the skillful way in which Hammerstein's dialogue and lyrics dovetailed with Kern's music. The latter was at turns romantic, atmospheric, nostalgic—but always an inevitable part of the whole texture. "Almost every minute is full . . . of mesmeric airs," wrote Percy Hammond. He was thinking particularly of "I've Told Ev'ry Little Star" and "The Song Is You," two numbers which lost none of their magic when *Music in the Air* was revived on Broadway in 1951. "The lovely Kern score," wrote Brooks Atkinson about the revival, "is still full of friendship, patience, cheerfulness and pleasure. . . . The immortal songs . . . still flow . . . like enchanted improvisations. They are part of the theatre's richest treasures."

Sweet Adeline in 1929, *Roberta* in 1933, and *Very Warm for May* in 1939 are musical comedies rather than musical plays. The first was an American period piece described in the program as "a musical romance of the Gay Nineties." It boasted two outstanding ballads, "Why Was I Born?" and "Here Am I," both of them introduced by Helen Morgan, who had risen from comparative obscurity to stardom as Julie in *Show Boat*.

Roberta was a musical stage adaptation by Otto Harbach of Alice Duer Miller's novel *Gowns by Roberta*. Here the action takes place mainly in a Parisian modiste shop, which provides an excuse for the presentation of a fashion show. The love affair in the story concerns John, an American football star, and Stephanie, a designer of fashions. Stephanie was played by Tamara, who night after night caused a storm in the second act by singing the ballad "Smoke Gets in Your Eyes." Once again with this song we are in the presence of a masterpiece. In 1958 it still revealed its potency to sell records by the millions when it was revived by The Platters in a Rock 'n Roll version. But good as it is, "Smoke Gets in Your Eyes" did not stand out in solitary splendor from the rest of the score. "Yesterdays" and "The Touch of Your Hand" are also memorable. A fourth Kern song gem, "Lovely to Look At," joined this choice company when *Roberta* was made into a motion picture for the first time in 1935, starring Fred Astaire and Ginger Rogers. A remake of *Roberta* into a movie in 1952—this time with Howard Keel and Kathryn Grayson—assumed as its title *Lovely to Look At.*

Of by no means subsidiary interest is the fact that in the cast of the first stage production of *Roberta* was a comedian then new to Broadway audiences. His name—Bob Hope. Bob Hope reassumed the role he had originated when *Roberta* was staged for television in 1958.

Very Warm for May was Kern's last musical. It was not a very good show, and it did not stay around very long. And so, Kern's rich and active career in the Broadway theatre ended with failure. Nevertheless, Kern himself emerged from this catastrophe with glory: One of his greatest and most successful songs came out of this score, "All the Things You Are."

With one phase of Kern's career ended, another went into high gear. After 1939, Kern's new songs were intended exclusively for the screen. In Hollywood, as on Broadway, Kern's song gems glistened with all their customary iridescence. He received Academy Awards on two occasions: in 1937 for "The Way You Look Tonight," which Fred Astaire and Ginger Rogers sang and danced to in *Swing Time,* and again, in 1942, for "The Last Time I Saw Paris," sung by Ann Sothern in *Lady, Be Good!*

The last-named song was written soon after the tragic event that had inspired it: the fall of Paris at the hands of the Nazis. Hammerstein wrote his lyrics as emotional release for his intense feelings upon hearing the news that Nazis troops had marched into Paris. He had no idea to what purpose he would use that lyric, or who would write the music. But once the lyric was down on paper, he asked Kern, and Kern complied. This was the only famous Kern song that was not written expressly for some stage or screen production; it was also the only famous Kern song in which lyric was written before the music. A number of famous performers made the ballad instantly popular, among them Noel Coward, Sophie Tucker, and Hildegarde. MGM acquired it for *Lady, Be Good!,* a screen version of the George and Ira Gershwin stage musical. And there, as the only song not by the Gershwins, it captured the "Oscar."

Kern's last original and complete score for the screen was written for *Centennial Summer,* released in 1946. The last song Kern wrote was "No One But You," intended for a Broadway revival of *Show Boat* in 1946. Kern came east late in 1945 to supervise this revival, and also to complete negotiations for the writing of his first new Broadway score in six years. He did not live to see *Show Boat* revived and achieve a new run of over four hundred performances. Nor did he live to write that new musical. That assignment passed on to Irving Berlin and resulted in *Annie Get Your Gun,* the greatest success of Berlin's career as composer for the theatre. Stricken by a heart attack on a street in New York, Kern was rushed to a hospital where he went into a coma from which he never recovered. He died in the hospital on November 11, 1945.

Before he died, Kern had made arrangements in Hollywood for the filming of his biography. That screen musical, named *Till the Clouds Roll By* and starring Robert Walker as the composer, was released after Kern's death, in 1946. Unfortunately, the picture did little to clarify Kern's personality, to bring to life a most extraordinary man. Kern was far more human, more scintillating, more challenging, more provocative, and more fascinating than the stereotype of a composer found in this movie. But as a panorama of Kern's creative life, *Till the Clouds Roll By* was an eloquent testament. It offered twenty-two of Kern's greatest songs from his early "How'd You Like to Spoon With Me?" to the late "Long Ago and Far Away," which he wrote to Ira Gershwin's words for the movie *Cover Girl.* As these masterpieces paraded before movie audiences in a majestic procession, most of the people surely stood ready to agree with President Truman when he said on learning of Kern's death: "His melodies will live in our voices and warm our hearts for many years to come. . . . The man who gave them to us earned a lasting place in his nation's memory."

VI

IRVING BERLIN

(1888-)

In 1910, a year or so before "Alexander's Ragtime Band" placed Irving Berlin with the most successful composers in Tin Pan Alley, he appeared in a revue, *Up and Down Broadway.* This represented his debut before the footlights. Dressed as a tennis player, and assuming the mannerisms of a man-about-town, he sang two songs which he had written in collaboration with Ted Snyder, his partner in this act, "That Beautiful Rag" and "Sweet Italian Love Song."

In the same year of 1910, Berlin placed one of his songs in the *Ziegfeld Follies,* the greatest and the most lavish of all revues then being mounted on Broadway; and in 1911 he was again a contributor of songs to the *Follies.*

Then, after "Alexander's Ragtime Band" helped to crown Berlin king of ragtime, he completed the writing of his first full score for a Broadway musical. Once again it was a revue—*Watch Your Step,* in 1914, described in the program as a "syncopated musical."

During World War I, Berlin wrote, produced, and acted in an all-soldier revue, *Yip, Yip, Yaphank.* And during World

War II, he wrote, produced, and acted in the epoch-making soldiers' revue *This Is the Army.*

In 1916, Berlin collaborated with Victor Herbert in providing music for a revue called *The Century Girl,* and in 1918 he was George M. Cohan's partner in writing the material for the *Cohan Revue of 1918.* One year after that he was the principal contributor of songs to the *Ziegfeld Follies,* for which, in 1927, he became the only composer ever contracted to provide the complete score (all other *Follies* editions up to then being the work of various composers and lyricists). Between 1921 and 1924, Berlin wrote, directed, and helped produce a series of four brilliant editions of the *Music Box Revue,* where some of his greatest songs received their first hearing. And in 1933 he provided the songs, and helped Moss Hart write the book, for a topical revue, *As Thousands Cheer,* which became one of the giant box-office successes of that period.

The revue, then, played a significant role in Irving Berlin's career as a songwriter for the musical theatre. A chapter on Irving Berlin, consequently, offers a convenient place in which to outline briefly the history and evolution of the revue up to the time that Irving Berlin became associated with it.

The revue was nothing more than vaudeville dressed up in fancy clothes. Vaudeville had come into vogue in the middle 1880s through the resourcefulness of a remarkable showman, Tony Pastor, a graduate from the minstrel show. Taking a cue from the fantasia section of the minstrel show, where different minstrels were called upon to perform various routines, Pastor came up with the idea of variety entertainment, for white-faced or black-faced performers, in a theatre all its own. He opened his first vaudeville theatre in Paterson, New Jersey, on March 21, 1865. It was a failure. But Pastor was not discouraged. He opened two more vaudeville theatres in succession in the downtown section of New York. Then, on October 24, 1881, he opened the Tony Pastor Music Hall in Union Square. It was there that vaudeville first came fully into its own.

It was not long before some other enterprising showman would come to the conclusion that vaudeville could bring in a larger revenue at the box office if it were transferred into the Broadway theatre, fitted out with more elaborate trappings, and endowed with some of the lavish accoutrements of the extravaganza. Such a showman was found in George W. Lederer, who also decided that material would have to be written expressly for such a production, and could not consist of songs and acts which the performers themselves brought in, as was the previous case with vaudeville. With all this in mind, Lederer brought *The Passing Show* into the Casino Theatre in 1894. It consisted of songs, dances, comedy, and various types of spectacles. Book, music, and lyrics were written by Ludwig Englander and Sydney Rosenberg with one eye on the performer and the other on the needs of the production.

The revue came into being with *The Passing Show*. Lederer's invention proved enough of a success to inspire competition. Before the century was over, revues like *The Merry Whirl, In Gay New York,* and so on proved prosperous investments. Then, in 1907, a supershowman entered the revue field to endow it with an altogether new glamour, magnificence, and status. He was Florenz Ziegfeld. For a quarter of a century, the *Ziegfeld Follies* was the yardstick by which all other lavish revues were measured. Year after year, the most beautiful girls in the world stepped across the stage of the New Amsterdam Theatre, home of the *Follies,* with costumes and settings the last word in magnificence. Year after year, the *Follies* offered theatregoers the greatest stars the musical stage had to offer, and along with them newcomers who, within the *Follies,* would soon become stars themselves.

With the *Follies* as their Northern Star by which to guide their own efforts, other important producers entered the revue arena in the years that followed: The Shuberts began presenting their own *Passing Shows* in 1912, and the *Greenwich Village Follies* in 1919; George White brought out the first of his *Scandals* in 1919; Irving Berlin wrote and presented the first of his *Music Box Revues* in 1921; and Earl Carroll created the first of his annual *Vanities* in 1922.

The revue became the all-important training ground where many a composer developed into importance, success, and at times greatness. One of them was Irving Berlin.

He was born Israel Baline in the small Russian town of Temun on May 11, 1888. He was four when his family, refugees from Russian persecution, came to the United States, settling in a tenement in New York's East Side. Since the father was unable to earn enough to provide for a large family of eight children, a few of them had to work in sweatshops. Irving was still a child when he sold newspapers in the street.

There was little in his childhood to suggest where his future greatness would lie. He was not involved in any musical or stage activity, nor did he seem to show any interest for it. He was a normal East Side city boy with normal city pastimes, such as playing ball, swimming in the East River, and joining his friends in wars against rival gangs. Having no interest whatsoever in school or books, he managed to survive only the first few years of public school before coming to the conclusion that he had had enough of education.

The city streets now became his home away from home, and then they became the place where he earned his living. When he was fourteen, he ran away from his family and started to support himself by singing the popular sentimental ballads of the day in the city streets and in nearby saloons. Before long he was earning about fifty cents a day from the pennies which passersby and onlookers threw at him as a reward for his performances.

He found his first full-time job in 1906 as a singing waiter in Pelham's Café, a downtown saloon. Here he performed not only the popular tunes of the day but also parodies of popular songs, writing his own words to familiar melodies. While working at Pelham's Café he changed his name from Israel Baline to Irving Berlin. This happened with the writing and the publication of his first song, "Marie from Sunny Italy," in 1907. Only the lyric was his; the music was supplied by Nick Michaelson, the pianist at the café. Berlin's total income from his first songwriting effort was thirty cents in royalties.

By 1909, Berlin had written and published a number of lyrics for moderately successful songs. More important still, he had also begun producing his own melodies, beginning with "Dorando," a song about an Italian marathon runner then much in the news. He boasted a minor hit in "That Mesmerizing Mendelssohn Tune," in which the melody of Mendelssohn's *Spring Song* received syncopated treatment. By now, Berlin was so adept at songwriting that he was given a job as staff lyricist for the Seminary Music Company, headed by Ted Snyder (to whose melodies many of Berlin's lyrics were written). Berlin had also become sufficiently known by 1910 to warrant his appearance in the Broadway theatre—as a performer singing his own songs in *Up and Down Broadway;* as a songwriter for the Ziegfeld *Follies* with "Goodbye, Becky Cohen" with which Fanny Brice made her *Follies* debut and started her ascent to stardom.

The year of 1911 was a momentous one for Berlin, for this was when he wrote and published "Alexander's Ragtime Band." Ragtime songs had been coming out of Tin Pan Alley for a number of years now, and Berlin himself had written a few of them before 1911. But no single song did more to establish ragtime as a popular-song idiom than "Alexander's Ragtime Band," and no single song did more to establish Berlin as a top man in Tin Pan Alley. When Emma Carus sang it in Chicago she brought down the house. Before long, "Alexander's Ragtime Band" became the most frequently played, sung, whistled, and danced to song throughout the country. Ragtime songs, only mildly popular up to then, became a nationwide obsession, an obsession that Berlin himself helped to keep intense and alive with such other resounding hits as "Everybody's Doin' It" and "That Mysterious Rag." He was now the acknowledged king of ragtime and was billed as such when he appeared as a headliner at the Hippodrome Theatre in London, where he introduced still another of his ragtime numbers, written expressly for this occasion, "International Rag."

But ragtime was not the sole string in his creative lyre. With the strains of "Alexander" still quivering in all parts of the country, and selling over a million copies of sheet music, Berlin proved himself a master in an entirely different song style, and one in which he was to become a master of masters, that of the ballad.

The first of his ballads came in 1913 with "When I Lost You." By selling two million copies of sheet music it represented a financial success equal to that of "Alexander." Its inspiration came from the sudden tragic death of his bride, caused by typhoid fever which she had contracted during their honeymoon in Cuba. Her death came only two weeks after the newly wedded Berlins moved into their first home, on Riverside Drive in New York. In pouring out his hurt and grief in words and music, Berlin was beginning a practice which a decade later would yield a harvest of immortal ballads

—drawing his inspiration and stimulation from the well of his own emotional experiences.

By the end of 1913, then, Berlin had established himself as one of America's most successful songwriters. This fact became fully recognized by his publisher, Ted Snyder, when he made Berlin a partner in his firm. From here on, Berlin proceeded to expand his creative activities by engaging more actively than ever in the world of the musical theatre. Up to now, he had had a number of his songs interpolated into a few musical productions. In 1914, he completed his first full stage score. This was for *Watch Your Step,* starring the dancing idols of the period, Vernon and Irene Castle. This production was conceived in such a way as to give these dancers an opportunity to perform a variety of dances, such as the polka, tango, and fox-trot; also to introduce some of their own invention, such as "The Castle Walk." Although this show had a slight plot to provide unity, it was essentially a revue, offering a program of sketches, skits, songs, comedy routines, and production numbers together with the dances by the Castles. Basically, this revue was, as the program stated, a "syncopated musical show." One of its big scenes had the great Italian master of grand opera, Giuseppe Verdi, rise from the grave to protest the way in which his arias were being syncopated; and the scene ended with his confession that perhaps syncopation did manage to breathe a new vitality into them. In line with such interest in syncopation, Berlin contributed to the dancing Castles a ragtime number in "Syncopated Walk." Berlin also had an opportunity to demonstrate his already recognized gift at writing ballads with a still-popular number, "Play a Simple Melody." Here, for his first time, Berlin combined two melodies contrapuntally—the principals in the cast singing the main melody of the chorus, while a choral ensemble provides a countermelody of its own with its own lyrics.

In 1915 Berlin was once again called upon to write all the music for a revue, *Stop, Look and Listen.* Among the fifteen or so songs found in the score is one that the composer always regarded as a favorite, "I Love a Piano." Many years later, this number was delightfully revived by Judy Garland and Fred Astaire in the motion-picture musical *Easter Parade.*

Declaration of war by America against imperial Germany put Irving Berlin in uniform. He was stationed as a private at Camp Upton, where he rose to the rank of sergeant. Camp Upton was then a temporary station for Europe-bound troops. Soldiers awaiting shipment were restless, in dire need of entertainment and a place for amusement. A new service center was needed for this purpose, and $35,000 was required to build it. Major General J. Franklin Bell, commanding officer at the post, suggested to Berlin that he produce an all-soldier show to raise the necessary funds. Berlin worked out all the material for a revue based on his own army experiences, assembled anybody at camp who could be of help, and then went about the business of producer and director to whip an amateur company into something resembling professional competence.

The revue, *Yip, Yip, Yaphank*—which the program identified as a "musical 'mess' cooked up by the boys of Camp Upton"—opened at the Century Theatre in New York on July 26, 1918. It began with a Captain instructing his men to attack to submission the enemy across the footlights, the audience, and to use as ammunition a barrage of jokes, songs, sentimental sketches, and dances. What followed was a series of swiftly moving scenes providing different pictures of a rookie's life. The climax came with a large production number in which the soldiers put on their gear and marched aboard ship for overseas duty. Berlin was one of the performers. He sat in front of a huge sack of potatoes singing in a sad and broken voice, "Poor Little Me, I'm a K.P." And he straggled from his cot at the break of dawn for reveille, with a number that became the big hit of the show, "Oh, How I Hate to Get Up in the Morning."

The show grossed $83,000 in New York and another $75,000 on tour in Boston, Philadelphia, and Washington, thus providing for Camp Upton's new service center, not the expected $35,000, but $158,000.

After the war was over, Berlin contributed several songs for the *Ziegfeld Follies of 1919*. This was one of the most expensive, one of the most handsomely mounted, and one of the most star-studded productions Ziegfeld had thus far put on. In this grandiose presentation Berlin was represented by three hit songs. One of these he lifted from *Yip, Yip, Yaphank*—"Mandy," a minstrel-show routine. In the *Follies* it was used as a first-act finale in which Marilyn Miller was dressed up to portray the famous old minstrel George Primrose. Another of the top stars at the *Follies* that year was the comedian Eddie Cantor. He introduced a delightful Berlin comedy number, "You'd Be Surprised," with which he would henceforth become identified. That song sold about 750,000 copies of sheet music in its first year and almost 150,000 piano rolls. In addition, Eddie Cantor's recording for Victor, released in 1919, was the only one he ever made to sell over a million discs.

Yet the most important Berlin song in that edition of 1919 was probably neither "Mandy" nor "You'd Be Surprised," successful though these became. That honor perhaps falls to "A Pretty Girl Is Like a Melody," which John Steel sang for a production number in which several beautiful girls paraded around the stage representing classical compositions. From

1919 on, "A Pretty Girl" became a kind of theme song for the *Follies;* it was also used extensively as theme music for fashion shows and beauty contests the world over.

Berlin, then, had no trouble maintaining his position as perhaps the Number One composer of Tin Pan Alley. This apparently was not enough for him. Beginning with 1919 he started extending both his energies and his sphere of influence beyond the area of songwriting. He founded his own publishing house, an event commemorated throughout the United States with "Irving Berlin Week." This house became one of the most powerful in Tin Pan Alley, not only because it had a monopoly of Irving Berlin copyrights, but also because it published many hit songs by other composers and lyricists. But beyond becoming his own publisher, Berlin was also his own performer. He traveled the vaudeville circuit (at a top salary of $2,000 a week) singing a program of his own songs.

The songwriter, the publisher, the vaudeville star, soon began seeking still other channels into which to direct his seemingly boundless energy. In 1921 Berlin also became a theatre owner, joining Joseph M. Schenck and Sam H. Harris in the building of the Music Box Theatre on West 45th Street. This was then one of the most costly and beautiful theatres in the Broadway sector. To open his theatre, Berlin presented the first of his *Music Box Revues,* for which he provided all of the textual as well as musical material.

The *Music Box Revue* was planned along the most extravagant lines in an undisguised effort to rival, and perhaps outdo, the *Ziegfeld Follies.* Cost was not spared: the then unprecedented sum of almost two hundred thousand dollars had been expended on the production. Many of the lavishly staged numbers had something of the golden Ziegfeld touch in the munificence of the costuming and scenery and in the proliferation of beautiful girls on the stage. "Such ravishingly beautiful tableaux," wrote Arthur Hornblow in *Theatre Magazine*, "such gorgeous costumes, such a wealth of comedy and spectacular freshness, such a piling of Pelion on Ossa of everything that is decorative, dazzling, harmonious, intoxicatingly beautiful in the theatre—all that and more was handed out in a program that seemed to have no ending."

The main song of that first edition was "Say It With Music." Berlin had written it hoping to make it the theme music of all subsequent editions of his revue. But when this song was tried out in a night club, before the revue had opened, it made such an impact that the listeners demanded numerous repetitions. To keep his song from getting worked to death before his revue had a chance to raise its first curtain, Berlin tried to curtail its circulation. In spite of this, the song continued to get heard; by the time it was presented in the revue it had become thoroughly familiar. Berlin came to believe that any further repetition in later editions could only be anticlimactic, since it had become far too popular.

That first edition offered another Berlin song gem in "Everybody Step," a syncopated number in which the now growing interest in jazz and jazz rhythms finds reflection. Important Berlin songs continued to pour out of the next three editions of the revue. In 1922 came another vigorous jazz tune in "Pack Up Your Sins," used for a production number set in "Satan's Palace." By contrast a graceful, nostalgic reminder of bygone days came with "Crinoline Days" and with the ballad "Lady of the Evening." For 1923, Berlin wrote "Climbing the Scale," a delightful melody built on the ascending notes of the major scale. (This was thirty-five years before Richard Rodgers wrote a song in a similar way, "Do Re Mi" in *The Sound of Music*.) The ballads of the 1923 edition included "The Waltz of Long Ago" and a now Berlin classic, "What'll I Do?" The latter was interpolated into the production after the show had opened and was sung by Grace Moore. She was then a young and unknown singer whom this number helped to make successful; within a few years' time she would dominate the world of opera as a glamorous prima donna. In 1924, Miss Moore sang another of Berlin's immortal ballads, "All Alone," once again a number interpolated into the show after its opening.

"All Alone" was one of several autobiographical ballads reflecting the composer's state of heart when he wrote them. He and Ellin Mackay were in love. She was the daughter of the head of Postal Telegraph, an heiress to millions, and a blue-book socialite. They were of different worlds, social stations, religions. They differed radically in cultural background, education, and upbringing. Ellin's father, Clarence H. Mackay, violently opposed their romance and did what he could to destroy it. The impact of this difficult time, often marked by painful enforced separation, reverberates in such Berlin ballads as "All Alone" and "All By Myself," just as the intensity of his love can be found in "Always" and "Remember." Ellin and Irving Berlin were secretly married at a private ceremony at City Hall in New York, on January 4, 1926. For a number of years Clarence H. Mackay was unforgiving. He disinherited Ellin and refused to have further contact with her, even after his first grandchildren were born. But a reconciliation did take place after a number of years, and in time there even developed an attachment between the two men.

Berlin wrote music for two more highly successful revues. Ziegfeld engaged him to write the complete score for the *Follies of 1927*, the first time in *Follies* history that one man wrote all the music. Eddie Cantor was one of the stars, and for him Berlin wrote "Learn to Sing a Love Song" and "You Gotta Have It." Another star was Ruth Etting, the torch singer, a famous recording star of that time. She introduced Berlin's "Shaking the Blues Away."

With the revue *As Thousands Cheer,* Berlin enjoyed his greatest box-office success before World War II. Here he wrote not only the songs but collaborated with Moss Hart on the text. After opening at the Music Box Theatre on September 30, 1933, *As Thousands Cheer* stayed on for four hundred performances. This was a "topical revue"—its songs, sketches, routines inspired by current events. Famous people of that day stepped from the front pages of the newspapers to become subjects for humor or satire. John D. Rockefeller and Mahatma Gandhi were impersonated by Clifton Webb; Helen Broderick appeared as the wife of President Hoover and as Aimee Semple MacPherson, an evangelist then very much talked about; Marilyn Miller was seen as Barbara Hutton, the heiress to the Woolworth fortune, who was then being courted by Prince Mdivani. One of the sketches laughingly detailed what happened at the White House early in 1933 with the change of administration; another showed just as humorously the consequences of having the Metropolitan Opera sponsored for radio broadcasts. A highly serious episode brought a change of pace: "Supper Time," a number poignantly presented by Ethel Waters which showed her preparing the supper table for a husband who has just been lynched. A torrid interlude arrived with the singing of a Martinique number, "Heat Wave," once again delivered by Miss Waters. The revue ended with a rousing finale in which Marilyn Miller and Clifton Webb joined the ensemble in singing "Not for All the Rice in China."

But the most celebrated number in the revue was "Easter Parade," sung by Marilyn Miller, Clifton Webb, and the ensemble in the first-act finale. For this number Berlin reached into his trunk of unused melodies, or melodies that had been failures and had been discarded. He came upon "Smile and Show Your Dimple," which he had written in 1917 and which had been ignored. The melody, dressed up with new lyrics, proved the high point of the production. And long after the production was gone and forgotten, the song lingered on to become an annual Easter favorite.

The last revue for which Berlin provided both text and music was a child of its time, a war child. Soon after the disaster at Pearl Harbor plunged America into World War II, Berlin began thinking of writing and producing another all-soldier show like the one he had done during World War I. He wanted his show to provide entertainment for American troops the world over; he wanted it to offer civilians a many-sided picture of GI life; he also wanted it to be a bountiful source of revenue for war charities. Finally given the green light by the Pentagon, Berlin returned to Camp Upton (where he had been stationed in the earlier war) to absorb at first hand camp-life experiences in 1942. He made his home and office in the regular army barracks and, though a civilian, lived the life of a regular GI.

This Is the Army, its cast made up exclusively of soldiers, was crystallized in a few months' time to open at the Broadway Theatre in New York on July 4, 1942. In the opening chorus, "This Is the Army, Mr. Jones," inductees, wearing long underwear, were briefed on what their new military status will do to their life and habits. Then the loneliness of a GI in his barracks was pointed up in the song "I'm Getting Tired So I Can Sleep," while the diversions and amusements found at service centers were carried over in "I Left My Heart at the Stage Door Canteen." Production numbers paid tribute to the Navy and Air Force, and another to the Negro in uniform. There was also a healthy dose of nostalgia in the show when it recalled from *Yip, Yip, Yaphank* "Mandy" and

"Oh, How I Hate to Get Up in the Morning." For the latter song, Berlin once again put on his old World War I uniform. Surrounded by a chorus of men similarly attired (six of whom had performed with him in *Yip, Yip, Yaphank*) he sang the lament of the sadly harassed rookie at reveille—and regularly stopped the show.

So successful was *This Is the Army* at the Broadway Theatre that a planned four-week engagement extended to twelve weeks. A national tour followed, ending up in Hollywood where Warner Brothers made it into a motion picture. After that, the stage production went on to fulfill its original aim of entertaining the armed forces. It traveled into every combat zone in Europe and the Pacific. The last performance of *This Is the Army* took place in Honolulu on October 22, 1945, after having traveled around the world for more than three years and having entertained over two and a half million men and women in uniform. It earned over ten million dollars for Army Emergency Relief and an additional $350,000 for British relief agencies. In recognition of Irving Berlin's giant achievement, General George C. Marshall presented him with the Medal of Merit.

The screen version of *This Is the Army* included the singing of a number that had not appeared in the stage version—"God Bless America." It had been written during World War I. Berlin had originally intended it for the final scene of *Yip, Yip, Yaphank*. But he then came to the conclusion that having soldiers sing a patriotic song as they marched aboard a ship bound for the European front was like "gilding the lily," as he put it. He added: "So I wrote a new song . . . which was better for the purpose and forgot all about 'God, Bless America.' "

He forgot about it until 1938 when Kate Smith asked him for a patriotic song to introduce on Armistice Day on her coast-to-coast radio program. Berlin felt that his 1917 song might serve the purpose very well. Kate Smith introduced it on November 10, 1938. With the threat of war then hanging darkly over all of Europe, America in 1938 had become inundated by a wave of patriotism and national pride. "God, Bless America" was the song capable of reflecting the spirit of the times. Kate Smith's recording was a million-disc seller. This recording was soon played in theatres and other public places of amusement all over the country. Both major political parties featured "God, Bless America" as a key song during the Presidential nominating conventions. The National Committee for Music Appreciation gave it a special citation. In time, a national poll placed it second only to "The Star-Spangled Banner" as America's most famous national anthem. There was even some talk in Congress of trying to get it to replace "The Star-Spangled Banner," a suggestion that drew a protest from Berlin himself. The financial rewards of this success were over $300,000, all of which Berlin turned over to the Boy and Girl Scouts. In gratitude, President Eisenhower bestowed on the composer a gold medal.

By the end of World War II, the revue was entering upon the limbo to which its parents—the minstrel show and vaudeville—had already been relegated. Berlin now devoted his songwriting activity to musical comedy, on the one hand, and motion pictures, on the other. He had already written songs for three musical comedies: In 1925 there was *The Cocoanuts,* a zany vehicle prepared by George S. Kaufman for the madcap antics of the Marx Brothers. In 1932 came *Face the Music,* a musical with book by Moss Hart touching amusingly on the way in which the great Depression had changed the American way of life; for this production Berlin wrote a social conscious number closely identified with the Depression, "Let's Have Another Cup o' Coffee" and a touching ballad,

"Soft Lights and Sweet Music." Then, in 1940, *Louisiana Purchase* starred Victor Moore as a hapless, bungling United States senator come to New Orleans to uncover political graft only to become enmeshed in amatory intrigues that almost destroyed him.

Of these three musicals, *Louisiana Purchase* had the longest run, 444 performances. Although this represented a thoroughly solid success, it proved just a faint whisper when compared to the thunder of *Annie Get Your Gun* in 1946, whose run of 1,147 performances represented the greatest stage success of Berlin's entire career. It was triumph well earned. *Annie Get Your Gun* is Berlin's most varied, most opulent score, a veritable cornucopia of hits; it is also one of the most brilliant scores ever conceived for musical comedy. It is altogether possible that the reason Berlin here soared so high was because he was confronted with a double challenge. His producer was Richard Rodgers, one of America's foremost composers for the theatre. Another of America's preeminent composers for the stage was Jerome Kern, who had originally been intended for the writing of this music, and whom Berlin displaced when Kern died. Carrying Jerome Kern's torch, under the vigiliant producing eye of a Richard Rodgers, was surely a situation calculated to put even an Irving Berlin on his mettle.

Ethel Merman played Annie Oakley—an illiterate, loud-voiced, gusty backwoods girl who was handy with a gun. She is the star of Buffalo Bill's Wild West Show, whose main rival is Pawnee Bill's Show, of which Frank Butler, a sentimental fellow, is the director. Frank is the man Annie finds to her taste, but trying to win him is a problem, since Annie is quicker with a trigger than with romance; and beyond this, Frank's preference in women is for sweet little girls whom he can carry around like a doll. The romance, however, comes to a happy resolution after the two Wild West shows are merged into one. But not before Annie and Frank have been able to describe themselves, their work, and their inmost and deepest sentiments in songs like "They Say It's Wonderful," "The Girl That I Marry," "Doin' What Comes Natur'ly," "I Got the Sun in the Morning" "I Got Lost in His Arms," and a number since become the theme music for the world of entertainment, "There's No Business Like Show Business."

Berlin's next musical was *Miss Liberty* in 1949. This, too, was a rich segment of Americana—the rivalry of two powerful New York newspapers in the late 1880s. The plot concerns itself mainly with the love affair of Horace, an American reporter, and Monique, a French model; also with the task of financing a base for the Statue of Liberty, recently acquired as a gift from France, and of which Monique had been fraudulently passed off as the model.

Call Me Madam, in 1950, offered Ethel Merman another boisterous, lusty role that she could interpret with all her innate exuberance—that of an American woman Ambassador to the mythical kingdom of Lichtenberg. Actually, the inspiration for the heroine was an actual person of Washington, D.C.—Mrs. Perle Mesta, famous in the nation's capital as a party giver. Washington politics, international diplomacy, foreign intrigue, as well as our heroine's romance with the Prime Minister of Lichtenberg, all are ingredients in a spicy stew in which the significant musical condiments were "You're Just in Love" (another of Berlin's delightful contrapuntal use of two melodies, each with its own lyrics), "The Best Thing for You," and a song that may very well have helped bring General Dwight D. Eisenhower into the White House, "They Like Ike."

The White House featured even more prominently in the

musical comedy, *Mr. President,* in 1962, entangling a present-day, fictitious President of the United States and his family in typical musical comedy complications.

Of the many scores contributed by Berlin to motion pictures through the years, some of the best have starred Fred Astaire or Bing Crosby, or both (*Top Hat, Holiday Inn, Blue Skies,* and *Easter Parade*); while others were merely an excuse for the presentation of a cavalcade of Irving Berlin song hits (new as well as old) in a package labeled with the title of an Irving Berlin standard (*Alexander's Ragtime Band, White Christmas, Blue Skies, There's No Business Like Show Business, Say It With Music*).

For *Top Hat,* in 1935, starring Fred Astaire and Ginger Rogers, Berlin wrote "Cheek to Cheek," one of his biggest money-makers, as well as one of his most touching love ballads. For *On the Avenue,* in 1937, starring Dick Powell and Alice Faye, he wrote "I've Got My Love to Keep Me Warm." And for *Holiday Inn,* in 1942, starring Fred Astaire and Bing Crosby, he wrote "White Christmas." The last of these is the only song by Berlin to capture an Oscar. But this, surely, is not its sole claim to immortality. During World War II, it was the song favorite of GI's everywhere, particularly in the far-flung areas of the Pacific, bringing a warm, nostalgic glow in reminding them of the holiday season at home. After World War II, "White Christmas" became possibly the most profitable song ever marketed, selling more than five million copies of sheet music, and about fifty million discs in some three hundred and fifty recorded versions; the most famous recording of all, that of Bing Crosby, sold twenty-five million records. Today, it is the number sung and played most often during the Christmas holidays, and it has become second in Yuletide popularity to the all-time Christmas classic from Austria, "Silent Night, Holy Night."

VII

GEORGE GERSHWIN

(1898-1937)

George Gershwin carried with him into the musical theatre a creative force, an originality of thought and technique, a personal identity that had the hallmark of genius. His impact on the development of theatre music was far-reaching. Nobody before him or in his own time had his brand of musicianship, his variety of style, his fabulous invention. The musical comedies and the musical plays that followed him owe him an unpayable debt. By his example, composers both of his own time and of a later day were encouraged to bring to their musical writing for the commercial theatre some of the dimensions and directions of serious music.

Most of the shows for which Gershwin wrote his treasurable music did little or nothing to change the concept of what musical comedy should be. Those Gershwin musicals pursued the traditional practice of piecing together the parts of a production like a jigsaw puzzle, but with the parts always regarded as more important than the completed picture. Those Gershwin musicals, like most other musicals of the 1920s, were intended for entertainment alone, and whatever had entertainment value had a place within the context of the production. Gershwin's songs were never intended to evolve naturally, inevitably from text, character, and setting; they were planned as functional pieces for a specific situation, performer, or piece of stage business. This is why a good deal of what Gershwin wrote for his various musical comedy productions has fallen by the wayside. Within the theatre they served a purpose, and outside of it they had little interest. But a good many other numbers have outlived the vehicles for which they were intended because they contain such a wealth of fresh melodic thought, such fascinating harmonic idioms, such an irresistibly vital rhythmic pulse, as well as freshness and spontaneity.

Two of Gershwin's musical comedies, however, rose head and shoulders above the prevailing mediocrity of the musical stage at that time to reveal a decidedly original profile. Both were satires; both arrived at a new concept of what our musical theatre could be and could become. Met with such a challenge, Gershwin's musical writing achieved new theatrical expressivity and importance, was endowed with new dimensions. Those two musicals were *Strike Up the Band* and *Of Thee I Sing*.

There was nothing in Gershwin's childhood to suggest he would become a musician, let alone one of the most celebrated in America. He was born in Brooklyn, New York, on September 28, 1898, the second of four children. George's childhood and boyhood were lived in the city streets, particularly the streets of New York's East Side, to which the Gershwin family moved when George was still an infant. There, anybody who studied a musical instrument or revealed a liking for good music was regarded as a "Maggie," the current term for "sissy." In those streets, a boy was esteemed by his friends and neighbors for his talent at playing ball, roller skating, swimming, performing in street games. George had no intention of being a "Maggie." He steered a clear course away from music, something easy for him to do since nobody in his family was musical; there was no attempt at home to give him any musical direction. George concentrated on street activities. He became the neighborhood roller-skating champion. He also distinguished himself at punchball and street hockey, two favorite boys' games at that time.

On those rare occasions when music touched him, it did make an impression he could not shrug off easily, such as hearing Anton Rubinstein's *Melody in F* on an automatic piano in a penny arcade when he was six; or listening to some jazz come from the window of a Harlem night club, which he had come upon accidentally while roller skating in that neighborhood; or overhearing from the school auditorium the strains of Dvořák's *Humoresque* on the violin. The last of these experiences, in fact, made such an impact upon him that he went out of his way to become a friend of the performer, a fellow pupil at public school by the name of Maxie Rosenzweig. (Later in life he changed his name to Max Rosen and was rather successful on the concert stage.) Maxie and George became good friends. It was from Maxie that George first learned something about the world of great music and great composers. Stimulated, George soon made a beeline for the piano whenever he visited Maxie, or for that matter whenever he found a piano in one of his friends' homes. George became fascinated trying to pick out agreeable musical sounds and sequences. One day he played for Maxie a tune he had concocted. Maxie shook his head sadly. "You haven't got it in you to become a musician, George," Maxie told him.

Despite Maxie's discouragement, George kept on making music whenever he could. When a piano finally came into the Gershwin household—brought in so that George's older brother, Ira, could take lessons—George's interest in and preoccupation with music began drawing him away from his street friends and their games. He was now continually at the piano, while Ira grew tired of lessons after a few months. Before long, George asked for and got his first teacher, a local lady who charged him fifty cents an hour and diligently led him through the pages of Beyer. Instinctively, George sensed that she was not the right teacher, and he changed her for one or two others in the neighborhood, none of whom proved any more satisfactory. At last, in Charles Hambitzer, George found a knowledgeable musician who could satisfy his insatiable hunger for musical information and training. George was fourteen years old, and from this point on his progress became remarkable. As Charles Hambitzer wrote to his sister one day: "The boy's a genius without a doubt."

The first piece of music George wrote was a popular song, "Since I Found You." It was never published. In fact the song was not even finished, since toward the end of the chorus the melody moved from G major to F and George did not know how to make the necessary transition. That his first piece of music should have been a popular song is not without significance. Although he was receiving a sound training in classical music from Hambitzer, although he was already beginning to attend concerts of serious music, his first attempt at creativity came not with a serious composition but with a popular tune. He loved the classics, especially Bach, Beethoven, and Chopin; he enjoyed listening to symphonies and concertos; he liked playing etudes and nocturnes. But from his beginnings as a composer he had no ambition to write seriously. He was far more interested in emulating Irving Berlin rather than Bach. He was crazy about popular music, and this passion was further intensified when he heard for the first time two songs by Jerome Kern, which without delay he proceeded to imitate.

He had no intention of abandoning his studies of music. He continued as Hambitzer's pupil, and then supplemented this by studying harmony and counterpoint with Edward Kilenyi. But he believed with overpowering conviction that if ever he was to become a successful popular-song composer—his crowning ambition—he would have to learn the song business at its source: Tin Pan Alley. Tin Pan Alley was 28th Street between Fifth Avenue and Broadway where some of the leading publishing houses were then concentrated. Through a friend of the family he finally managed to get a job with the publishing house of Remick as demonstration pianist and song plugger, at fifteen dollars a week. Only fifteen years old, he was the youngest such employee in Tin Pan Alley.

At Remick's he began making headway as a songwriter. Sophie Tucker, the distinguished vaudevillian, liked one of his songs, "If You Want 'Em You Can't Get 'Em," and convinced Harry von Tilzer to publish it. This was in 1916. During that same year, Gershwin showed a few of his songs to Sigmund Romberg, who was then writing the music for productions at Winter Garden. Romberg's interest in young Gershwin led him to use a Gershwin song, "The Making of a Girl," in *The Passing Show of 1916,* which opened on June 22. For the use of his song—his bow in the American musical theatre—Gershwin was paid seven dollars.

By 1917, Gershwin felt that working at Remick's had taught him as much as it could about the song business. He now wanted to advance himself as a composer for the theatre. He took on a job as a rehearsal pianist for *Miss 1917,* a revue for which Victor Herbert and Jerome Kern had written the music. This was the first time that Gershwin came face to face with Kern. One afternoon, after rehearsal, Kern heard Gershwin improvising at the piano and grew so excited that the next day he brought his wife to the theatre to hear the young pianist.

Each Sunday the cast of *Miss 1917* arranged concerts of popular songs at the Century Theatre, for which young Gershwin was recruited as piano accompanist. At one of these evenings, two of Gershwin's songs were presented by Vivienne Segal, one of which, "You-oo Just You," was published in 1918 by the firm that had so recently employed him, Remick.

But it took still another publisher to recognize Gershwin's true potential. He was Max Dreyfus, head of T. B. Harms. Dreyfus offered Gershwin a job under a novel arrangement. All Gershwin had to do to earn his weekly salary of thirty-five dollars was to keep on writing songs and showing them to Dreyfus; those that Dreyfus liked he would publish under a royalty arrangement. The first song published by Harms was "Some Wonderful Sort of Someone" in 1918. This was the beginning of a close and profitable composer-publisher association that lasted for over a decade.

Dreyfus was responsible for getting Gershwin his first assignment to write some numbers for a stage musical, a revue, *Half-Past Eight,* starring Joe Cook. The show was a disaster. It lasted only a few performances in Syracuse, New York, in 1918, where it tried out; it never came to Broadway; and the payment of $1,500 promised Gershwin for his music was never made. Painful though this experience had been, Gershwin had no time to lick his wounds. He was too busy writing other songs and getting them placed in various musical productions, including *Ladies First* where Nora Bayes, one of the great ladies of the musical theatre, was singing his numbers.

In 1919, Gershwin put both feet firmly on Broadway for

the first time. Alex A. Aarons, a young producer about to invade the Broadway scene, was so taken with some of the freshness and novelty in Gershwin's songs that he contracted the young man to write the score for a Broadway musical, *La, La, Lucille*. Beginning with May 26, 1919, it had a run of over a hundred performances. The plot was not of great consequence: a dentist can inherit two million dollars if he divorces his wife; an astute lawyer works out a way in which the dentist can get the inheritance and keep the wife by divorcing and then remarrying her. More attractive than the text were one or two of the dozen songs Gershwin contributed, most notably "Nobody But You," whose winning lyricism and tender emotion were the immediate results of the influence Jerome Kern was having upon him at the time.

One foot, then, was in the Henry Miller Theatre where *La, La, Lucille* was playing. Another foot was planted in a new motion-picture palace, the Capitol, which opened at Broadway and 51st Street on October 24, 1919. The elaborate stage show during the initial week included a Gershwin song soon to become its composer's first big hit—"Swanee." At the Capitol Theatre "Swanee" went unnoticed, in spite of an impressive presentation in a large production number. But a few weeks later it was sung by Al Jolson at a Sunday evening concert at the Winter Garden; soon after that Jolson interpolated it into the extravaganza *Sinbad,* in which he was then starring. Jolson made "Swanee." It sold a million copies of sheet music and over two million records in a year's time. With *La, La, Lucille* in one hand and "Swanee" in another, Gershwin's reputation on Broadway became solidified.

Success breeds success. An important producer of lavish revues now became interested in Gershwin: George White, onetime dancing star of the *Ziegfeld Follies,* who conceived the *Scandals* as an annual competitor to the *Follies*. The first edition of the *Scandals,* in 1919, was enough of a success to convince George White he had a winner. He now signed a contract with young Gershwin to provide all the music for the 1920 edition. Gershwin not only wrote that score but also that for four subsequent editions. Out of these revues emerged Gershwin's first song gems: "I'll Build a Stairway to Paradise," used as a production number in 1922, and "Somebody Loves Me" in 1924.

The year of 1924 was when Gershwin had his rendezvous with destiny. This is the year he completed writing *Rhapsody in Blue,* with which he appeared for the first time as a serious composer to command the respect of the world. *Rhapsody* was written for an All-American music concert performed by Paul Whiteman's orchestra at Aeolian Hall in New York on February 12, 1924. The composition caused a sensation. It went on from there to become one of the most frequently played and most highly regarded pieces of serious orchestral music by an American. It brought Gershwin wealth and world fame. Its first recording, by Paul Whiteman, sold a million discs, and the publication of the music was a best-seller. *Rhapsody* commanded unprecedented fees for performances both on stage and on the screen.

For the rest of his life Gershwin would continue producing successful works for the concert hall and opera house—including a piano concerto; the tone poem *An American in Paris;* the *Cuban Overture;* a second rhapsody for orchestra; and the folk opera *Porgy and Bess.* His contributions to serious music—however impressive and durable—cannot concern us here.

If he was making significant strides as a great creative force in American music in 1924, he was also making striking progress as one of the most talented composers our popular musical theatre has known. His career in the theatre took a giant leap forward in 1924 with *Lady, Be Good!*, a musical comedy. Guy Bolton and Fred Thompson collaborated on the text, while George's older brother, Ira, provided the lyrics for all the songs. This union of two brothers—one writing the words to the other's music—was an event of considerable moment both to George Gershwin's career and to the history of American popular music.

George and Ira Gershwin had collaborated on some random numbers before *Lady, Be Good!*—beginning with "The Real American Folk Song" in 1918, which Nora Bayes sang in *Ladies First*. After that, Ira Gershwin worked with other composers, too, most notably Vincent Youmans, with whom he wrote a successful musical comedy in 1922, *Two Little Girls in Blue*. *Lady, Be Good!* was the first show for which Ira did all of the lyrics for brother George. George and Ira remained a words-and-music partnership (and one of the best on Broadway) until George died. Ira's extraordinary talent in versification, his avoidance of clichés, his fresh approaches to song ideas, his immaculate good taste—all helped make him one of the foremost lyricists of his time. His writing talent and his powerful creative imagination were powerful factors in arousing, stimulating, and expanding George's musical tastes and methods.

The main characters of *Lady, Be Good!* are Dick and Susie Trevors, a brother-and-sister dance team come upon unhappy financial times. They are forcibly ejected from their apartment for having failed to pay the rent. The only way Dick can solve his problems is by marrying a rich girl. But sister Susie, with the aid of an unscrupulous lawyer, works out an elaborate scheme to put their hands on an inheritance. That inheritance, however, turns out to be as phony as the lawyer himself. But the problems of the dancing team are happily resolved by the time the final curtain descends, without compelling Dick to marry a girl he does not love.

Gershwin's music stood out like shining gold surrounded by brass. There was not much in the text to carry a fresh point of view or an unexpected procedure. Alan Dale, the critic, considered the score the only thing that "redeemed a quite typical musical comedy," and the critic for the *Sun* described the music as "brisk, inventive, gay, nervous, delightful." It was all that and much more. Here Gershwin brings to fulfillment promises made in the *Scandals*—particularly in songs like the title number, "Fascinating Rhythm," "So Am I," and "The Half of It Dearie, Blues." All these revealed a heightened virtuosity in the use of changing meters, dynamic rhythms, fresh harmonic colorations, and a highly personal lyricism.

Good as this score was—and it had few if any equals in the Broadway musical theatre of the early 1920s—it would have been better still had a song Gershwin originally wrote it for been allowed to remain in the production. This was "The Man I Love," now a Gershwin classic. It was sung by Adele Astaire during the Philadelphia tryouts of *Lady, Be Good!* But the producer insisted that it be dropped because he thought it slowed down the action. Gershwin did this reluctantly, and had it published as an independent number. It made a big hit in Europe before recrossing the ocean and getting a toehold in the United States. Gershwin never did find a place for it in any of his stage shows, one of his very few songs for which this was true.

Gershwin wrote the music for fourteen Broadway musicals after *Lady, Be Good!* Some did well at the box office, others did not. The most successful of the more traditional musical comedies were *Oh, Kay!* in 1926, *Funny Face* in 1927, and *Girl Crazy* in 1930.

Oh, Kay! starred Gertrude Lawrence. In 1926 she was already a luminous star of the English stage. Her American debut had taken place in 1924 in a British importation, *Charlot's Revue,* where her irresistible charm and talent completely captured the hearts of audiences and critics. American producers now scrambled over one another to sign her for a Broadway musical, and for a while it looked as if Ziegfeld would capture the prize. However, when Miss Lawrence discovered that Gershwin was writing the music for *Oh, Kay!,* this was the show she selected for her first appearance in an American-made musical comedy. As Kay she gave the first of those unforgettable performances on Broadway that carried her to the very peak of her profession and kept her there until her sudden death.

Prohibition was the unpopular law of the land in 1924, and bootlegging was a crime the public was either encouraging or ignoring. The subject of bootlegging is the spine of the plot in *Oh, Kay!* Having suffered financial reverses, Kay and her brother, an English duke, come to America and rent their yacht out for rum-running. Suspected of involvement in bootlegging by government agents, Kay and her brother seek refuge on Jimmy Winter's estate on Long Island, in whose cellar the rum-runners conceal their cache of liquor. Placed in the house as butler to watch over this precious cargo is Shorty McGee, a part in which Victor Moore once again revealed his rare gift to portray timid, confused misfits. Kay falls in love with Jimmy Winter, and marries him after she has cleared herself and her brother of involvement in the illegal goings-on.

For Gertrude Lawrence, Gershwin wrote one of his enduring love ballads, "Someone to Watch Over Me"; also a number that tripped along on a light, rhythmic toe, "Do, Do, Do." The rest of the exceptional score comprised "Clap Yo' Hands" and "Fidgety Feet," both extraordinary excursions in rhythmic virtuosity, and "Maybe," whose strength lay in its haunting lyricism.

Funny Face helped open a new theatre in the Broadway sector, the Alvin on West 52nd Street, on November 22, 1927. Like its distinguished predecessor, *Lady, Be Good!*, *Funny Face* was a starring vehicle for Fred and Adele Astaire. Fred played the part of Jimmy Reeve, the guardian of Frankie, a heroine role assumed by Adele Astaire. A cumbersome plot revolved around Frankie's efforts to retrieve a precious set of pearls from her guardian's safe, efforts complicated when two blundering thugs are out for the same loot. One of these thugs was played by Victor Moore. He stole the limelight from the Astaires, and it was he who was largely responsible for the success of this musical.

Here the main Gershwin songs included " 'S Wonderful," "Let's Kiss and Make Up," and "The Babbitt and the Bromide"—the last of these one of Ira Gershwin's most brilliant sets of satirical verses, good enough to become the only song lyric published in Louis Kronenberger's *An Anthology of Light Verse*. When *Funny Face* was made into a movie for Fred Astaire and Audrey Hepburn (thirty years after the stage première!) the story was jettisoned, which was no loss. But the best Gershwin songs remained; and this without a doubt was a powerful asset.

Among the more formal and traditional of the Gershwin stage musicals, *Girl Crazy* in 1930 is undoubtedly the one people today remember most often. This is partly because it was made into a motion picture three times (most recently in 1965, starring Connie Francis and renamed *When the Boys Meet the Girls*); partly because *Girl Crazy* was the place where both Ethel Merman and Ginger Rogers made their Broadway musical comedy debuts; and partly because it brought us some of Gershwin's greatest songs.

The action transpires on a dude ranch in Custerville, Arizona. Danny Churchill, a New York playboy, is sent west by a father overly concerned over his son's weakness for liquor, gambling, and women. But Danny brings his vices with him, even to a deserted western town. He opens a dude ranch equipped with gambling tables, featuring a well-stocked bar and chorus girls. Reformation, however, comes to Danny through his love affair with the local postmistress, Molly.

The part of Molly was assumed by Ginger Rogers in her first significant Broadway role. To her, Gershwin consigned his best love song, "Embraceable You," and a haunting ballad, "But Not for Me." Anywhere else and at any other time Miss Rogers would have captured and held the limelight, for she performed the part of the ingenue with sensitivity, poignancy, and charm; she was lovely to look at and lovely to listen to. Unfortunately for Miss Rogers, another monumental debut was taking place on the same stage, that of Ethel Merman. A spring breeze is no competition for a whirlwind.

Ethel Merman's role was that of Kate Fothergill, wife of the man who runs the gambling at the dude ranch. When she belted out her first song, "Sam and Delilah," she magnetized her audience with those shrill, piercing, trumpet-like tones. Her later numbers were more exciting still: "I Got Rhythm," where the audience held its breath while she clung to a note for sixteen measures while the orchestra kept on playing the melody, and "Boy, What Love Has Done to Me." Early the next morning, Gershwin read to her some of the rave reviews about her debut. "You're in with both feet," he told her.

Gershwin was given an opportunity to extend and enrich the scope of theatrical music in two significant productions. In both instances he rose fully to the occasion, by creating two of the most remarkable scores produced in the theatre of the 1930s. Both of these musical comedies were satires, the first one on war and international diplomacy called *Strike Up the Band.* This show was first conceived in 1927, but failed to arrive until 1930, and then in a greatly revised version. The text by George S. Kaufman and Morrie Ryskind represented something radically new for the Broadway musical theatre—being one of the first musicals to reveal a social consciousness, and the first in which the satire was so sharp and cut so deeply. In fact, *Strike Up the Band* was a musical with a message; the message was delivered without solemnity but with levity and acidulous wit. America goes to war with Switzerland over the issue of chocolates. Horace J. Fletcher is an American manufacturer of chocolates who is frustrated when the United States government refuses to raise the tariff to protect his financial interests. In his dreams, Fletcher sees himself as the general of an American army gone to war against Switzerland. The Americans destroy the enemy after capturing its secret call to arms—a yodel. Fletcher comes home a military hero. But when it is learned that Fletcher has used Grade B milk for his chocolates he falls into disrepute.

Though two of Gershwin's songs were of the hit status—the haunting ballad "Soon" and "I've Got a Crush On You"—what is particularly significant about this score is the way in which the canvas of his creativity has now been enlarged. The first-act finale (where all that had happened in the story up to this point is being reviewed) and the incidental music to two dream sequences provided Gershwin with an opportunity to achieve the kind of *Lebensraum* that his creativity needed and deserved. Another notable feature about this score is the way in which Gershwin tapped a rich vein of satire—especially in the title number, which deflates the pomposity of military marches. In details, too, Gershwin's satire has a keen edge, while he reveals a new responsibility to make music interpret text, character, or passing episodes: the way in which the spicy discords in "Entrance of the Swiss Army" betray the fact that this is just a bogus army; or the manner in which a jazz phrase for trumpet underlines the "American" in the racy number "I'm a Typical Self-Made American."

As good as it was, *Strike Up the Band* only suggested the potential as satirists of authors Kaufman and Ryskind, lyricist Ira Gershwin, and composer George Gershwin. This potential became realized even more fully in *Of Thee I Sing* in 1931. Domestic rather than international politics is the target here: the follies and foibles of governmental bureaucracy in Washington, D.C. The satiric note is accented strongly early in the musical with "Wintergreen for President," the number accompanying a torchlight parade promoting Wintergreen's Presidential campaign. Interspersed in this sprightly tune are quotations from "Hail, Hail the Gang's All Here," "Tammany," "The Stars and Stripes Forever," among other familiar songs. Wintergreen, with Throttlebottom as his running mate, campaigns on a "love" ticket; "Love Is Sweeping the Country" is their campaign song. The winner of a beauty contest in Atlantic City, New Jersey, is to become the First Lady. But Wintergreen falls in love with simple Mary Turner, who has a gift for baking corn muffins; it is to her that Wintergreen protests his love in the title number and it is she whom he marries. After Wintergreen is swept into office in a landslide, Diana Devereux threatens to sue him, since, having won the beauty contest, she is entitled to be his wife. The scandal that follows compels the Senate to consider impeaching the President. Then the news reaches the floor of the Senate that Mary, the President's wife, is about to become a mother. Since an expectant father has never yet been impeached by the Senate, Wintergreen is saved. A happy solution for the existing dilemma is found by consigning Diana to Vice-President Throttlebottom as wife.

There were few areas of national politics that escaped

annihilation at the hands of the authors. The humble and neglected state of the Vice-Presidency (at least as it was in the early 1930s) was pointed up in a characterization that is surely the high-water mark of Victor Moore's inimitable portraits of harassed little men in a hostile world. He cannot get a library card because he fails to find two references, and the only way he can see the White House is to go on a tour. He is not the only one victimized by the satirists. The Supreme Court and the Senate come in for their share of not so innocent merriment. Before the First Lady can give birth to her child, the Supreme Court must vote on its sex. And the Senate gets hotly involved in a debate over whether Jenny, Paul Revere's horse, should receive a long overdue pension; the debate ends, and the Senate rises in silent homage, when it is informed that Jenny has long been dead.

Tongue is all the time in cheek; and this is as true of George Gershwin's music as it was of text and lyrics. Viennese waltz music is used to sentimentalize the announcement of the birth of the President's child; strains of Salvation Army band music echo in "Posterity Is Just Around the Corner"; grand-opera devices are mocked in the Senate scene; the whole-tone scale is used with delightfully comic effect when a count is made of the members of the Supreme Court; and nostalgia of Southland songs is gently smiled at in Diana's musical protestation that she is "the most beautiful blossom." In addition to such episodes, Gershwin introduced all kinds of orchestral and choral sequences into his musical texture; he made extensive use of the recitative to help carry along the plot line; and he enlarged his musical structure by creating extended sections combining song, recitative, chorus, and orchestral interludes.

The happy marriage of plot, characterization, dialogue, lyrics, and melodies; the merciless and relentless way satire, and at times nonsense, lays bare our national follies; the courageous manner in which formulas and conventions are brushed aside to make room for fresh and novel procedures (such as using motion pictures to bring flashes of election returns)—all this created a new kind of musical theatre. No wonder, then, that critics called this musical a "masterwork" and a "landmark." It became the first musical every to receive the Pulitzer Prize and to have its text published in book form. Its Broadway run was the longest enjoyed by any Gershwin musical, and its national tour the most extensive and successful.

In 1933, an unhappy attempt to capitalize on the success of *Of Thee I Sing* led its authors to write a sequel, *Let 'Em Eat Cake.* The spontaneity of the earlier production was absent, and the bite and sting were blunted. *Let 'Em Eat Cake* described the further adventures of Wintergreen and Throttlebottom. They run for reelection and are defeated. Wintergreen now heads a revolutionary movement against the government, but is unsuccessful. Much of what follows is grim rather than witty, somber instead of mirthful. An excellent song, "Mine"—whose chorus boasted a countermelody sung contrapuntally—and some brilliant lyrics by Ira Gershwin in numbers like "Union Square" and "Comes the Revolution" proved unsatisfying compensations. *Let 'Em Eat Cake* was a failure. This was the last of the Gershwin stage musicals.

But it was not their last production with music. The last time the Gershwins were represented on Broadway was with their folk opera, *Porgy and Bess,* produced by the Theatre Guild. It was not a success when first seen and heard, both in its Boston tryouts and in its New York première on October 10, 1935. Nevertheless, it was Gershwin's greatest achievement in serious music—and he never wavered in his belief that he had produced a masterwork, and that time would justify his faith. The tragedy is that Gershwin did not live to see this happen. The history of *Porgy and Bess,* following Gershwin's death, would have exceeded even his wildest anticipations and hopes. Returning to New York in 1942 (five years after Gershwin died) it had the longest run of any revival in New York stage history. On that occasion it received a special award from the Music Critics Circle while some of the leading critics (who had been so harsh in their evaluations back in 1935) referred to it as a crowning masterwork, the greatest opera by an American. Between 1952 and 1956, *Porgy and Bess* was performed by a traveling Negro company throughout Europe, the Middle East, the Soviet Union, and Latin America to receive an acclaim achieved by few other operas in history; after that the opera was also performed successfully in the Orient. *Porgy and Bess* became the first opera by an American-born composer to play at the historic La Scala Opera House in Milan. In 1965 it entered the permanent repertory of the famous Volksoper in Vienna. Meanwhile, in 1959, it had been made into a motion picture—a Samuel Goldwyn production starring Sidney Poitier, Dorothy Dandridge, Diahann Carroll, and Sammy Davis, Jr.

While it is quite true that *Porgy and Bess* is an opera, a good deal in it springs from Broadway musical comedy: numbers like "It Ain't Necessarily So," "There's a Boat That's Leavin' Soon for New York," and "A Red Headed Woman Makes a Choochoo Jump Its Track." In short, *Porgy and Bess* is the final happy meeting ground of Gershwin's lifelong efforts in serious music and in popular music. The ever growing powers he had been demonstrating as a composer for musical comedies find their ultimate strength in this opera. To Gershwin, *Porgy and Bess* represented the dawn of a new day as a composer. Tragic to say, however, this was not dawn but dusk.

In 1936, George and Ira Gershwin came to Hollywood to write songs for movies. Their first assignment was *Shall We Dance,* starring Fred Astaire and Ginger Rogers. The Gershwins worked on two more films after that: *A Damsel in Distress* with Fred Astaire and Ginger Rogers, and *The Goldwyn Follies.* George Gershwin never completed the last of these scores (though he did manage to write two remarkable songs for it, "Love Is Here to Stay" and "Love Walked In"). While working on *The Goldwyn Follies,* Gershwin suffered physical collapse from which he never recovered. He was a victim of a brain tumor. An operation located a growth which, because of its position, could not be removed. He died in a hospital on the morning of July 11, 1937.

One of his deepest regrets in the closing months of his life was the fact that he had never married. He had always been attracted to women, and they to him. On many occasions he was in love. Several times he even inched close to the altar. But he always seemed to find a logical, even conclusive reason why he should not marry. His complete preoccupation with his music, career, dreams, and ideals seemed to make it impossible for him to give himself to any one woman in the way a marriage demanded. Several women loved him dearly, but felt he surrounded himself with a wall through which they could never penetrate, a wall behind which he continually sought shelter while his mind was busily piecing together new melodies and fresh serious-music projects.

The truth of the matter was that he could never marry a woman because all his life he was already married—to the most exacting mate of all, to his music.

VIII

COLE PORTER

(1891 - 1964)

WITH THE EXCEPTION of *Kiss Me, Kate,* and possibly *Anything Goes,* Cole Porter's musicals were rather conventional. They adhered to the old concept that a musical should be nothing more than a diversion for the tired businessman, should have little to tax the intelligence of the audience. It is quite true that in their time the best of Cole Porter's musicals represented enchanted evenings in the theatre. But today most of these productions have been forgotten and have little likelihood of revival.

Remaining in the memory from those old Cole Porter musicals are outstanding performances by established stars like Ethel Merman, Victor Moore, or Bert Lahr and by newly risen stars like Danny Kaye and Mary Martin. But what we remember even more strongly is the long string of remarkable songs that came out of those productions, for what was essentially new and fresh in those musicals is what came from Cole Porter's pen. As both a composer and a lyricist, he introduced to the musical stage his own brand of urbanity, wit, and culture of a kind not frequently encountered in the theatre of those days. Some of his songs proved so fresh and new, and were so much ahead of their own time, that they were ignored at first hearing and had to wait for recognition.

In fact, it took Cole Porter a long time to establish himself on Broadway. Audiences simply had to be educated to his kind of brilliance and virtuosity. When Elsa Maxwell, the famous hostess of the world's social elite, heard Porter's songs for the first time (Porter was then young and unknown), she told him: "Young man, the only reason you are a failure is because you are much too good. Your standards are too high. But, mark well my words, one day you will haul the public to your own level, and then the world will be yours." It was a long time before Cole Porter was able to raise his audiences to his own standards and they stood ready to accept him on his own terms. Then the world truly became his—the world of the American musical theatre. And it remained his for a quarter of a century.

Cole Porter was born with a silver spoon in his mouth, on a 750-acre fruit ranch in the Indiana town of Peru on June 9, 1891. The family's wealth came from his grandfather, J. O. Cole, a tycoon who had accumulated a fortune estimated at ten million dollars. He was a man of iron will and strong determination, and he ruled his family with the same inflexible strength with which he had always governed his investments.

Cole's mother, Kate, was one of two children. After she married a humble Peru druggist, Samuel Fenwick Porter, they went to live with her father. Samuel Porter was a dreamer whose passion was poetry. Kate was the doer, and it was she who exerted the greatest influence upon the child Cole. An excellent pianist, she began teaching him music when he was six. By the time he was ten he could play several musical instruments besides the piano, some of which he managed to learn by himself. He had also written words and music of his first piece of music, "The Song of the Birds." One year later, his mother paid a firm in Chicago $100 to publish Cole's piece for the piano, "The Bobolink Waltz."

The grandfather had every expectation that his grandson would eventually inherit and run his vast interests. This was the reason why he frowned upon all of Cole's music making and took little interest in the boy's all too obvious talent. He insisted that Cole prepare for his future responsibilities by receiving a thorough education and then studying law.

For four years Cole attended the Worcester Academy in Massachusetts, an exclusive private school, where he proved exceptional in language and arts, and much less so in the sciences. There he kept pursuing his favorite hobby of writing verses and melodies. In 1909 he became class valedictorian, and in the fall of the year, after a summer's holiday in Europe, he entered Yale. During his years at college, Porter led the glee club, helped produce some of the college shows, and wrote two college songs that are still remembered, "Bingo Eli Yale" and "Bulldog." One of his songs was also published commercially, "Bridget" issued by Remick's in Tin Pan Alley in 1910.

He graduated from Yale in 1913. In line with his grandfather's wishes he went on to Harvard Law School. There he spent far more time in writing songs than in studying his texts. His lack of interest in his studies, and his passion and talent for music, were recognized by the Dean of the law school, who urged him to follow his natural bent by leaving law school and enrolling in the Harvard School of Music. Porter did this eagerly, for a long time keeping his grandfather in the dark about the sudden change in his studies. He stayed at the music school for three years, receiving a thorough training in piano, theory, music history, and other musical subjects. All the while he remained steadfast in his ambition to write popular songs and to try getting them heard in the Broadway theatre. Two of his songs were actually placed in Broadway shows in 1915: "Esmeralda" in *Hands Up* and "Two Big Eyes" in *Miss Information.*

He was still attending the Harvard School of Music when he got his first important opportunity to write songs for the Broadway stage. A former fellow student at Yale, T. Lawrason Riggs, wrote the text for a musical, *See America First.* He asked Porter to do the music and lyrics. Once Porter had completed this chore, he interested Elizabeth Marbury in producing the show. Miss Marbury, having recently become so successful with the offbeat Jerome Kern musical, *Very Good, Eddie,* was tolerant to fresh ideas. She felt that the satire of Riggs's text and Porter's bright and shining music and lyrics might have the same kind of appeal that *Very Good, Eddie* had had.

See America First opened at the Maxine Elliott Theatre on March 25, 1916, with a cast headed by Clifton Webb, then making his Broadway stage debut. (He later became a star on both the stage and the screen.) The musical proved a dud and a bore. Described in the program as a "patriotic comic opera," it tried to spoof the kind of flag-waving musicals for which George M. Cohan had become so famous. The methods of librettist and composer were too obviously in imitation of Gilbert and Sullivan to be either fresh or new. *See America First* lasted only fifteen performances. "I've Got a Shooting Box in Scotland" was the best song in a nondescript score. After the show closed, the song was kept alive for a while by Fred and Adele Astaire on the vaudeville circuit.

By the fall of 1916, Porter had completed his studies at Harvard's School of Music. Partly to escape from his frustration in seeing his first musical a failure, and partly because his appetite for travel and adventure had now become keen, he joined the French Foreign Legion. If he expected to be the central figure in heroic exploits on the hot sands of Africa, he was doomed to disappointment. All that he was called upon to do was to perform for the French army various innocuous staff assignments in France. He seemed to have a good deal of free time to enjoy the delights of Paris and to write songs about his military experiences which delighted his fellow soldiers.

With America in the war, Porter was assigned to teach French gunnery to American troops. Once again he had considerable freedom. He rented an elegant apartment in Paris on Rue Gounod where he entertained his friends and worked on songs. Discharged from the army in April of 1919, he continued to linger in Paris, which he now regarded as home. He became a darling of Parisian society, which flocked to his apartment for his celebrated parties and to listen to his latest songs. He also found the time and energy to do some serious study of composition and theory—at the renowned Schola Cantorum, and mainly with Vincent d'Indy, one of France's most highly esteemed musicians.

During 1919, Porter took a brief trip home to visit his family. En route to the United States, aboard ship, he met Raymond Hitchock, a Broadway producer, for whom he played some of his numbers. Hitchcock liked them well enough to engage Porter to write the songs for a forthcoming edition of a revue he was producing each year on Broadway. There were ten Porter songs in *Hitchy-Koo of 1919*. The best were "My Cozy Little Corner in the Ritz," the first of many songs Porter would write about his beloved Paris, and "An Old-Fashioned Garden," which regularly drew an enthusiastic response in the theatre and which enjoyed a huge sheet-music sale. "It was my first hit," Porter commented many years later about "An Old-Fashioned Garden," "and it is still one of my favorites."

He was back in Paris late in 1919. There on December 18, he married Linda Lee Thomas, a former Louisville, Kentucky, belle who was in the social register. She was regarded as one of the most beautiful women in the world and one of the most gracious hostesses. Attractive, talented, elegant, and always *le dernier cri* in their dress, interests, and diversions, the Porters soon became fabled characters in a city not easily impressed. They bought a handsome house on Rue Monsieur which they decorated sumptuously and filled with treasures in paintings, porcelains, antiques, first editions, and other of *objets d'art*. Sometimes they entertained as many as several hundred guests in a single evening, representing the cream of European society, royalty, politics, culture. Two dozen footmen would greet the visitors; world-famous musicians and showpeople would help entertain. One evening the entire company of the world-famous Ballet Russe de Monte Carlo gave a performance at a Cole Porter evening at home. Sometimes the parties lasted through a weekend, and sometimes even longer than that; the Porters occasionally, at the whim of a moment, would transport guests by special train or motorcade to the Lido in Venice or to the Riviera in southern France.

During the summers, the Porters carried on their festive parties and dinners in Venice where for a number of years they rented the Palazzo Rezzonico, where the great English poet Browning had died. Here fifty gondoliers served as Porter's footmen. A hundred and fifty guests could be accommodated at a special night club built alongside the canal outside the palace. A gourmet dinner would be prepared by special chefs while a Negro jazz band or a string orchestra provided the music.

The Porters were living high, wide, and handsome. This was a postwar period which made a fetish of good times, fun, gaiety, pranks. Luxury was the meat of Porter's existence; excitement, its champagne. Life had to be lived fully and intensively, without a second thought about tomorrow. The Porters were not only the children of their times, the Roaring Twenties; they were also its symbol.

That music did not fall by the wayside in this frenetic pursuit of good times is an eloquent proof of Porter's relentless need to create. Composing songs had become a basic necessity. In 1924, Porter placed five songs in the *Greenwich Village Follies* on Broadway. But recognition of his uncommon talent was still some years off. What his talent needed most of all was a suitable showcase in which to display his songwriting gifts to best advantage.

The songs found such a showcase for the first time in 1928, in the musical comedy *Paris.* Porter had met the producer E. Ray Goetz in the playgrounds of Europe. Goetz disclosed to Porter that he was planning a Broadway musical with a Paris setting; Goetz's wife, Irene Bordoni, long a musical-stage favorite on both sides of the Atlantic, would be the star. She would play the part of a Parisian adventuress who has designs on a society boy from Boston only to be frustrated by the boy's mother. Goetz wanted the whole production to have an authentic French flavor. He invited Porter to write the songs, since Goetz was convinced nobody who did not know and love Paris the way Porter did could possibly do the job. Besides, he felt that Porter's kind of wit and sophistication with melodies and lyrics would lend themselves naturally to such an assignment. Goetz told him: "The kind of songs you sing for us at your parties is the kind of songs I'd like to see in *Paris.*

A "book" musical in which Paris is the background, and where a Parisian-born actress is the star, stimulated Porter's creative juices. He produced two songs in which his creative personality both as a composer and as a lyricist becomes fully recognizable. "Let's Do It" (made all the more fetching through Irene Bordoni's French accent) was the kind of a spicy dish theatregoers would henceforth expect from Cole Porter. So was "Let's Misbehave." Unfortunately, the latter song was dropped from *Paris* during out-of-town tryouts. Among the other Porter songs in the production when it came to Broadway on October 8, 1928, the best was "Two Little Babes in the Wood."

The success of *Paris* encouraged E. Ray Goetz to plan another musical about Paris; and once again he asked Cole Porter for the songs. *Fifty Million Frenchmen,* in 1929, told the adventures of a rich American playboy in Paris. He meets and falls in love with Looloo, an American tourist from Terre Haute. Since he does not want his wealth to influence her, he poses as a pauper. He supports himself in Paris by becoming now a guide, now a gigolo, now an Arabian magician. As the plot develops—and it is complicated when Looloo is pursued by a Grand Duke—the scene shifts from one famous Parisian haunt to another: the bar at the Ritz Hotel; Longchamps race track; the American Express Company on Rue Scribe; Montmartre; Les Halles, the markets. Looloo finally falls for the young American, who is now convinced she loves him for himself alone.

Richard Watts, Jr., described *Fifty Million Frenchmen* as "pretty much of a Cole Porter field day." He added: "Because he is a master of his profession, the show is a striking one." The significance of Cole Porter as a brilliant new personality in the theatre thus now becomes fully recognized. His virtuoso rhyming, sardonic humor, fresh turns of phrases in his lyrics was matched by the sensuality, smartness and exciting vigor of his melodies. All this could be found in songs like

'Find Me a Primitive Man,' 'You've Got That Thing' and 'You Do Something to Me.' The last two are still hardy perennials. The score also included two songs about Paris: "You Don't Know Paree" and "Paree, What You Did to Me?"

Fifty Million Frenchmen was one of the big box-office successes of the season. Two other musicals with Porter's songs in 1929 and 1930 were less fortunate financially. But they, too, contained song classics. Out of *Wake Up and Dream* in 1929 came "What Is This Thing Called Love?," while in *The New Yorkers* in 1930 "Love for Sale" was introduced. Qualities found in all later Porter song gems are here recognizable: the Slavic kind of melody often in a minor mode and just as often rising to passionate climaxes; the throbbing rhythmic pulse that dramatizes the background; and the lyrics which are filled with double entendres and sophisticated allusions both to places and things and to the delights of a bon vivant.

The now great demand for his services led Porter to make New York rather than Paris the base of his social and business operations. The Porters finally established residence at the Waldorf Towers of the Waldorf-Astoria Hotel on Park Avenue. This was their home for several months each winter as Porter labored on new scores for the theatre and participated in the preparation and production of new musicals. Usually, once a musical firmly established itself on Broadway, Porter would be traveling to far-off places or revisiting favorite haunts in Europe. The festivities that used to whirl around Porter in Paris, the Lido, and the French Riviera were now localized principally in New York. Though this was a sober period for most of America—it was the time of the Great Depression—the festivities at the Porters' had lost none of their extravagance or abandon. As far as the Porters were concerned, they were still living in the "gay twenties."

Porter's career as composer-lyricist went into high gear in

the 1930s, in spite of his preoccupation with the good life, and in spite of a tragedy that almost destroyed him. The 1930s saw the production of four outstandingly successful Cole Porter musicals: *Gay Divorce* in 1932, *Anything Goes* in 1934, *Leave It to Me* in 1938, and *Du Barry Was a Lady* in 1939.

There are two good reasons why the *Gay Divorce* is important. It is for this musical that Cole Porter wrote one of his greatest songs, "Night and Day." In addition, the *Gay Divorce* was made in 1934 into a highly successful motion-picture musical for Fred Astaire and Ginger Rogers—one of their earliest screen song-and-dance triumphs. (The screen version altered the title slightly, to *The Gay Divorcee.*) The plot was not of great consequence. It was a convenience for the presentation of song and dance, telling of the attempt by the heroine to get a divorce in the process of which she falls in love with the hero, posing as a co-respondent.

Fred Astaire, who appeared as the star of the stage musical as well as of the screen adaptation, introduced "Night and Day." It was the giant hit song of the production, so much so that the musical was often described at the time as the "'Night and Day' show." The unusual verse, in which the melodic line consists of a repeated single note, was said to have been inspired by the consistent beating of a tom-tom heard by Porter from a distance while traveling in Morocco. The chorus, unusual in that it extended for forty-eight instead of the usual thirty-two measures, had a melody which came to Porter from the chant of a Mohammedan priest.

Porter's next musical was *Anything Goes.* As first conceived by Guy Bolton and P. G. Wodehouse, *Anything Goes* was an amusing play about the impact of a shipwreck on a number of offbeat characters. Just as *Anything Goes* was about to enter rehearsal, a real major sea tragedy hit the country's front pages. One hundred and thirty-four lives were lost when the luxury liner *Morro Castle* went afire off the coast of New Jersey. To stage a musical that laughed at the plight of a ship's disaster was now unthinkable. A new script had to be prepared, for which a fresh pair of writers were recruited, Howard Lindsay and Russell Crouse. (Incidentally, this was the first time these two men worked together. In the years that followed they made stage history with two nonmusical plays, *Life with Father,* which had the longest run in Broadway history up to that time, and *State of the Union,* which received the Pulitzer Prize for drama in 1946. They also wrote a number of texts for highly successful musicals.)

Lindsay and Crouse retained a luxury ship as part of their setting for *Anything Goes,* and they populated it with a strange assortment of characters. This liner was carrying across the Atlantic to Europe a stowaway playboy, a female nightclub singer turned evangelist, and Public Enemy No. 13 disguised as a clergyman. The action opens in a smart New York bar; its entertainer, Reno, on the eve of leaving for Europe, uses a dynamic song, "I Get a Kick Out of You," to reveal how much she loves the playboy, Billy. He stows away on the same luxury liner on which Reno is sailing: having come to say good-bye to Reno he learns that his old flame, Hope, is also a passenger, and he is determined to go along with her. Aboard ship, Billy confides his romantic ardor to Hope in "All Through the Night" and engages in a saucy exchange of compliments with Reno in "You're the Top." As for Public Enemy No. 13—the only reason he is disguised is that he is fleeing from the law. As played by Victor Moore, Public Enemy No. 13 is a pathetic, meek little man afraid of his own shadow; yet he harbors a secret ambition to graduate to Public Enemy No. 1. After the ship lands at Southampton, all the principal characters find themselves at the estate of Sir Evelyn, an English nobleman whom Hope has come to marry.

By this time Hope, of course, knows full well she is in love with Billy. She can extricate herself from Sir Evelyn when the latter finds Reno much more to his liking. While all this is going on, a government investigation reveals that Public Enemy No. 13 is thoroughly harmless and that the law is no longer interested in him, a development that almost breaks the little man's heart. "Sometimes I don't understand this administration in Washington," he whines.

Ethel Merman was happily cast as Reno, the nightclub singer. By virtue of her sensational debut in the Gershwin musical *Girl Crazy,* in 1930, she was, by 1934, a fixed star in the Broadway firmament. And her star here shone with all its accustomed brilliance as she delivered numbers that Cole Porter fashioned for her voice, delivery, and personality. These numbers were not only "I Get a Kick Out of You" and "You're the Top" but also a ballad in the style of a religious hymn, "Blow, Gabriel, Blow," which she delivered with electrifying impact at an improvised revival meeting aboard ship.

Early in 1935, Porter took a cruise around the world with the dramatist Moss Hart to work on a new musical, *Jubilee.* This was a comedy about a royal family exiled from its mythical kingdom. This musical did not become one of Cole Porter's big successes. But it will not be forgotten, since it was the birthplace of another Cole Porter's song masterpieces, "Begin the Beguine." Strange to say, when *Jubilee* was first produced, nobody seemed to notice that "Begin the Beguine" was anything special; and after the show closed, the song was temporarily forgotten. Then, in 1936, the young bandleader Artie Shaw revived it in an RCA Victor recording that sold two million discs; it was through this version that the world of music was made aware that Porter had here produced another classic. There was another remarkable song in the score of *Jubilee,* "Just One of Those Things."

The soaring popularity of "Begin the Beguine" in 1936

and the more than four hundred performances enjoyed by *Anything Goes,* both provided ample evidence that Cole Porter had become one of the established "greats" in American popular music and in the American musical theatre. His friends were saying he was truly a pampered child of destiny, having been born wealthy, talented, and with an inexhaustible zest for living. They envied the way in which he had fulfilled himself creatively and how his immense talent was being recognized. They did not fail to point out that in addition to all these blessings he was a happily married man whose devoted friends were too numerous to count.

In fact, Porter did appear to be the most enviable of men when destiny, which for so long had showered its favors upon him, suddenly turned its back. One day in 1937, while riding horseback on Long Island, Porter was thrown to the ground when his horse slipped, reared, and fell on top of him. This accident smashed both of Porter's legs and brought about a serious nerve injury. One operation followed another. For twenty months Porter was bedridden in the hospital, tormented not only by physical agony but also by melancholia that at times made him think of suicide. After that, he was a prisoner to a wheelchair for five years, incapable of moving his legs; and during all that time pain was a constant companion.

He lifted himself from the depths of despair and physical torment to write the score for *Leave It to Me,* a comedy about the Soviet Union, for which Bella and Sam Spewack wrote the text based on their own stage play. Victor Moore appeared as a hapless American ambassador to the Soviet Union who is hopelessly homesick for Topeka, Kansas. In order to convince Washington to send him home, he plans all kinds of incidents to discredit his country with the Soviet regime, only to find that on each occasion he emerges a hero. When he finally decides to do a serious job, by devoting himself to the promotion of better relations between the two powers and to the advancement of peace in the world, he gets into hot water and has to be recalled.

Leave It to Me came to Broadway on November 9, 1938. This is the musical in which Mary Martin made her stage debut. She appeared in a small role, hardly calculated to attract and hold the limelight. In spite of the competition offered her by the other members of that cast—including such hardy veterans as Victor Moore, Sophie Tucker, William Gaxton, and Tamara—she not only attracted the limelight but stole it. She accomplished all this in an insignificant little episode contrived to find time for the change of scenery. Here she sang "My Heart Belongs to Daddy," which she accompanied with a mock strip tease that proved a provocative contrast to her baby tones and inflections. "She has the freshness and vitality of youth," wrote Sidney Whipple, "but she also has poise and the gift of devilish humor, and I think she is a find."

Despite the fact that he was suffering continuous pain—which frequently could not be dulled by sedatives—and despite periodic returns to the hospital, Cole Porter continued working industriously on new shows, and kept on pouring into them a wealth of melodic and verbal invention. Before the 1930s ended, *Du Barry Was a Lady* became a smash box-office success. Bert Lahr was cast as a washroom attendant in a nightclub who in his dreams sees himself as Louis XV of France with Ethel Merman becoming in those dreams Madame Du Barry. Here, Ethel Merman continually stopped the show with her vigorous renditions of "Katie Went to Haiti" and "Friendship," sharing the latter with Bert Lahr.

The late 1930s also found Porter in Hollywood. In 1936 he wrote his first original screen score, for *Born to Dance* starring

Eleanor Powell and Nelson Eddy. After that came *Rosalie* in 1937 and *The Broadway Melody of 1940.* For the screen as for the stage a Cole Porter score was a treasurehouse of hit songs. From these three screen productions came "I've Got You Under My Skin," "Rosalie," "In the Still of the Night," and "I Concentrate on You."

The years of World War II continued to bring a succession of Cole Porter triumphs to Broadway, beginning with *Panama Hattie* in 1940. It starred Ethel Merman in an old-fashioned spy plot set in Panama, made timely by the then-recent outbreak of war in Europe. Foreign agents in the musical are involved in a scheme to blow up the Panama Canal. Hattie, a nightclub singer, learns of this plot and thwarts it. A high spot of the production was the song "Let's Be Buddies" which Ethel Merman sang with an eight-year-old girl whom Hattie had befriended because she was the daughter of the man with whom she was in love. This song provided a few moments of undisguised sentimentality, and the audience loved it; as Brooks Atkinson prophesied in his review: "Gruff old codgers are going to choke up a little this winter when tot and temptress sing 'Let's Be Buddies' and bring down the house."

World War II was casting an ever larger and darker shadow over the United States in 1941. Then came Pearl Harbor and American involvement. The impact of the war on American life was reflected in the texts of the next two Cole Porter musicals, *Let's Face It,* in 1941, and *Something for the Boys,* in 1943. The first of these was a musical version of a successful stage comedy modernized for war-conscious audiences. The libretto followed the amatory experiences of three GI's stationed at Camp Roosevelt on Long Island as they get involved with three society matrons out to teach their wayward husbands a lesson. One of these GI's was played by Danny Kaye. (Only a few months before *Let's Face It* opened, he had stepped out of total obscurity as a comedian of first importance in the musical *Lady in the Dark,* with music by Kurt Weill.) As an inductee, trying to extricate himself both from military obligations and red tape and from the schemes of a determined woman, he was the unqualified hit of *Let's Face It.* A thoroughly ingratiating performance was also contributed by Nanette Fabray, for whom Cole Porter wrote "You Irritate Me So" and "Ace in the Hole."

Something for the Boys divided its interest between a defense plant and the nearby air base. Blossom Hart (a vehicle for Ethel Merman) is a onetime nightclub singer turned defense worker. She is in love with Sergeant Rocky Fulton of the air base. Obstacles and misunderstandings slow down their romance until Blossom proves herself a war heroine. The carborundum fillings in her dental bridgework are able to catch radio reception by which she saves the lives of several airmen.

Mexican Hayride, in 1944, was an escape from the war. With Mexico as its background, a female bullfighter as its heroine, and an American fugitive from justice as principal comedian, *Mexican Hayride* was the kind of musical that prospered before the war, completely divorced of the realities of current life and problems. Its somewhat difficult-to-believe plot had as its main concern the setting forth of the comic talents of Bobby Clark, the charm and sex appeal of June Havoc, and the haunting beauty of the ballad "I Love You."

When the war ended, Cole Porter discovered he had a personal war of his own. Together with physical pain and difficulty of locomotion—neither of which prevented him from resuming his active social life and his extensive travels to far-off places—came a growing feeling that his career was over; that he had given the best that was in him and that he had nothing more to say. Even some of his most devoted friends and colleagues were sure he was through. They pointed out that the resounding successes of the early 1940s had failed to produce songs hits of the quality, appeal, and durability of his classics of the 1930s. They also pointed to the sorry fact that in *Mexican Hayride,* Cole Porter's musical writing had gone into an all too obvious decline. And after *Mexican Hayride* Cole Porter began to experience the torment of failure. *Seven Lively Arts,* a revue produced late in 1944 with a cast headed by Bert Lahr and Beatrice Lillie, ran only 183 performances. The musical comedy *Around the World* lasted only 76 performances in 1946. The only motion picture for which Porter had completed a new score had proved a "dud." It was *The Pirate,* in 1948, starring Gene Kelly and Judy Garland. Not a single song from any of these productions gave promise of survival.

Porter's friends and colleagues also could not fail to remark that the only time he was now able to achieve any kind of success with his songs came with things he had written many years earlier. A song like "Don't Fence Me In"—which became one of the most successful songs of 1945 after being introduced by Roy Rogers in the movie *Hollywood Canteen*—had been written in the 1930s to satirize cowboy ballads popular over the radio. Then there was the Cole Porter screen biography, *Night and Day,* which Warner Brothers released in 1946 with Cary Grant as Porter. This picture was, to be sure, a success—but this was due mainly to the fact that it served as a means of offering a cavalcade of Porter's past hit songs. Not one of those songs had been written after 1940.

There could be no doubt that Porter had made formidable contributions to the music of stage and screen, said his friends and critics. But they had become convinced that his long tussle with pain had finally sapped his creative energies and had left him effete. They also suggested that a new kind of musical theatre had come to prominence on Broadway with the Rodgers and Hammerstein triumph *Oklahoma!* Porter's wit and sophistication, maintained his critics, were strong suits in a stage production in which the song, and not the play, was *the* thing. In a musical play, as opposed to musical comedy, the text was more important than the song. In such a scheme of things, it was felt, Cole Porter would be a misfit.

In short, the belief that Porter was "through" had begun to take hold, even in Porter's own mind. Then Porter went on to write what is undoubtedly the greatest music he was to create, in a production that became one of the greatest successes Broadway has known, a musical that is undoubtedly a permanent monument in theatrical history.

That musical was *Kiss Me, Kate* in 1948. At the time of conception, it gave little promise of restoring Porter to his former success and greatness. There were too many hurdles for it to leap over, any one of which could spell doom. The producers were novices, and they had no financial backing to speak of. *Kiss Me, Kate* was an adaptation of a Shakespeare play—and Shakespeare plays were not usually the source from which successful musical comedies sprang, even though Rodgers and Hart had once managed to do so with *Boys from Syracuse. Kiss Me, Kate* was being planned by its authors as a musical play and not as musical comedy, and in the writing of musical plays Cole Porter was an inexperienced hand. None of the performers selected for leading roles were box-office attractions; at that time, one of them (Alfred Drake) was believed to be on the decline in popularity, while another (Lisa Kirk) was a comparative newcomer and unknown.

In spite of all these handicaps, *Kiss Me, Kate* jelled into a production without a blemish. By the time rehearsals ended, every element fell neatly into place. The inexperienced producers had become veterans overnight. Performers, those who were on the decline and those who were unknown, established or reestablished themselves as stars. The direction was sure-handed. The scenery and costuming were a joy to the eye. The text was fresh and novel. And the music by Cole Porter was a miracle of variety and invention.

Though the prime source of the text came from Shakespeare's comedy *The Taming of the Shrew,* the librettists (Bella and Samuel Spewack) had no intention of merely adapting the Shakespeare text for song and dance. What they did do was to use the play-within-a-play technique: A present-day theatrical company is presenting the Shakespeare comedy in Baltimore, Maryland. *Kiss Me, Kate* reveals the various personal problems and involvements of the principals in this company; then it shifts to old Padua, Shakespeare's setting, by presenting a production of *The Taming of the Shrew,* dressed with songs. Fred Graham and his ex-wife, Lilli, are the two principals in the touring company. They are still much in love with each other, though it takes them a while to realize this. A subsidiary love interest engages two other members of this troupe—a chronic gambler, Bill, and his girl friend, Lois. They, too, have problems, brought about mainly through Bill's weakness for games of chance and his involvement with professional gamblers. In Shakespeare's Padua, Petruchio marries the shrew, Kate, and tames her by going her one better in the display of temper, irrational behavior, and quixotic moods. Petruchio finds a happy resolution to his marital problem, for Kate gets tamed. And in today's Baltimore, the four members of the company find happiness through a solution of their own problems.

Kiss Me, Kate was a musical play in which all the parts were beautifully assembled into an artistic whole. The present-day Baltimore and old Padua, the action and the song and dance, the sentiment and the humor—all this was skillfully fused in a production that carried conviction, in which the characterizations were always neatly drawn, and in which the line of the story progressed on a straight course toward a logical direction. "There is next to nothing wanting in *Kiss Me, Kate,* the proud and exultant musical which opened at the Century Theatre," reported Howard Barnes in the *Herald-Tribune.*

Since *Kiss Me, Kate* proved such an integrated production, with no single element more important than any other, the laurels could be distributed equally to each of the collaborators: to the librettists; to Hanya Holm, who conceived the dances; to Lemuel Ayers, who was responsible for the scenic and costume designs; to John C. Wilson, the director; to the four stars—Alfred Drake, Lisa Kirk, Harold Lang, and Patricia Morison. Nevertheless, *Kiss Me, Kate* could hardly have turned out to be the masterpiece it was without that remarkable score by Cole Porter. This was the peak toward which he had been scaling since the 1920s. This was the top of Mt. Everest, higher than which he could no longer ascend. Never before had he been so versatile in the projection of a wide gamut of emotion and mood; never before had he been so consistently at the acme of his powers as composer and lyricist, with hardly one of the seventeen numbers that was not pure diamond. From the sensual ("So in Love" and "Were Thine That Special Face") to the light and flippant ("Always True to You in My Fashion" and "We Open in Venice"); from broad humor and satire ("Brush Up Your Shakespeare," "I Hate Men," and "Too Darn Hot") to parody ("Wunderbar") —Porter was the consummate master of words and music who led Walter Kerr to say that this score was "one of the loveliest and most lyrical yet composed for the contemporary stage."

Kiss Me, Kate became the kind of box-office triumph it deserved to be. Its run exceeded one thousand performances.

The national company toured three years. Its original cast recording sold a million discs. The show was translated into eighteen languages and was successfully performed in Vienna (where it ran ten years!), Berlin, Turkey, Japan, Czechoslovakia, and South America. In 1952 it became a stunning motion picture starring Kathryn Grayson and Howard Keel.

Porter was never again to soar as high as he had in *Kiss Me, Kate*. But he did write two delightful, characteristically Porterish scores for successful musical comedies. Both had a Parisian setting, to which Porter had always been so partial, and both boasted nostalgic songs about Paris.

Can-Can, in 1953, went back to the nineteenth century when the can-can dance was the rage but was prohibited by law because it was regarded as morally outrageous. In the musical the action is focused on a Montmartre night spot which is raided because it featured this illicit dance. La Mome Pistache, the owner, is cleared in the courts—principally because the judge, sent out to investigate her place, succumbs to her charms. The dance once again becomes legal. Some of Porter's songs have a piquant Parisian flavor carrying nostalgic memories of the city of light: "C'est magnifique," "Allez-vous en," and most significantly and popularly, "I Love Paris." Other songs had the identifiable Porter ingredients of wit and urbanity, such as "It's All Right With Me."

Can-Can remained on Broadway for more than eight hundred performances. It was later brilliantly produced, sung, danced, and acted in a motion picture starring Frank Sinatra. This film, incidentally, contributed a footnote to the history of twentieth-century international relations. During his much publicized visit to the United States, Premier Khruschchev of the Soviet Union came to Hollywood where he was invited to the studios to witness the can-can number then in the process of being filmed. His expressions of outraged shock at this spectacle were duly reported in newspapers around the world, contributing still additional chill to the prevailing cold war.

Porter's last Broadway musical was *Silk Stockings,* in 1955. This was based on *Ninotchka,* a movie satire on Soviet bureaucracy that had starred Greta Garbo. George S. Kaufman, Leueen McGrath, and Abe Burrows made the adaptation. In Paris, Ninotchka is a female Soviet agent come to convince a Soviet composer—long at work on a movie filmed in France—that he must come home now that his job is finished. Softened by the luxuries and delights of Paris and by her romance with an American newspaperman, Ninotchka finds it hard to give up the world of capitalism and return to the socialist state. She does return, but her American lover follows her and induces her to escape with him back to France.

The text throughout has a keen-edged scalpel touching the flesh and nerves of Soviet ideology, way of life, and governmental red tape. Cole Porter's score was in kind, with several songs parodying Russian folk music, and several others commenting satirically on Soviet diversions. But Porter also tapped his familiar melodic vein, with a fine love ballad, "All of You," and with still one more hymn of praise to Paris, "Paris Loves Lovers."

Silk Stockings was Porter's twenty-fourth Broadway musical. It was also his last. After 1955, he wrote two new scores for motion pictures and one for television. From his music to *High Society* (which starred Bing Crosby, Grace Kelly, and Frank Sinatra in 1956) stepped forward Porter's last important love ballad, and one of his best, "True Love." His last motion picture score was heard in 1957 in *Les Girls,* starring Gene Kelly and Mitzi Gaynor. Porter wrote an original score for *Aladdin,* a TV "special" based on the familiar tale from *The Arabian Nights;* it was presented on the Du Pont Show of the Month over CBS on February 21, 1958.

By the time *Aladdin* was produced, Cole Porter was a sad, lonely man who had lost the will to live, and the will to create. The death of his wife in May of 1954 had been a shattering blow that sapped him of all his onetime enthusiasm for travel, for good times, for the society of friends, for theatre, for creation. To make matters still worse, his old leg injury was beginning to harass him again. In 1958 he was once again brought into a hospital for surgery. It now became evident that he was suffering from a chronic bone tumor, and that the only way to save his life was to amputate the leg. The operation took place on April 3, 1958.

After that, Porter was helplessly sucked up into a quagmire of despondency. He now rejected life by becoming a virtual recluse, refusing to read, work, attend the theatre, see visitors, or entertain friends. On the occasions when now one intimate friend, now another, kept him company at his dinner table, he would ignore them, frozen into silence as he nibbled at food for which he had no appetite. Every effort to get him to learn to use an artificial limb proved futile. He preferred to be carried about by his two valets.

Porter had long made it a practice to visit his home in California each June. Always a man of habit, he made the trip again in 1964. There he had to be taken to a hospital for the removal of a bowel obstruction. The operation took place on October 13. Two days later Porter died. The irony of the immense tragedy of Porter's last years was this: The man who most of his life had had more friends and admirers than he could count died practically alone. The only one at his bedside was his nurse, and she was a comparative stranger.

IX

RICHARD RODGERS

(1902-)

RICHARD RODGERS has had two careers in the musical theatre. Either one would have placed him with the most significant composers our theatre has produced. Both have made him unique.

His first career lasted twenty-two years when he worked with Lorenz Hart as lyricist. This was the time when Rodgers and Hart created a new age for musical comedy through their original approaches, techniques, and subject matter. Rodgers' second career involved his collaboration with Oscar Hammerstein II. It began with *Oklahoma!* which marked a new day for the American musical—the age of the musical play. During the next sixteen years, and largely through the achievements of Rodgers and Hammerstein, the musical play became an art form commanding the following and admiration of the civilized world.

Rodgers was born on July 28, 1902, at Hammels Station, near Arverne, Long Island, where the Rodgers family was spending the summer. William Rodgers, the head of the family, was a physician. His wife, Mamie, was an excellent amateur pianist. They had only one other child. He was Mortimer, who preceded Dick by four and a half years and in adult life became a distinguished physician.

Dick began fumbling at the piano keyboard when he was four, and was given his first piano lessons by an aunt when he was six. His sixth year was also a time of awakening for the future composer for the theatre. It was then that he saw a stage production for the first time—an operetta, *Pied Piper*. This first experience with a stage production transformed the boy at once into a passionate theatregoer. He now spent Saturday matinees attending live shows, drinking in the production so that he could recall later in the week every detail, most particularly the songs.

The ambition to become a theatre composer became crystallized in his mind when, in his fourteenth year, he saw Jerome Kern's *Very Good, Eddie*. What he liked about this show was its thoroughly American content; the other operettas he had seen up to now had foreign backgrounds and characters. In addition, Kern's songs, to which he was being introduced for the first time, represented for him a brave new world which he himself longed to penetrate. He went to see *Very Good, Eddie* half a dozen times. After that, whenever he could, he went to Kern's musicals. Some he saw not once but several times. All this while he continued studying the piano, having progressed from his aunt's instruction to a music school in Harlem.

His academic education was taking place in the city public schools, where he was hardly better than an average student. He was a normal boy. He was interested in sports (mostly tennis, swimming, and boxing), and he had periodic crushes on girls. Summers were spent in a boys' camp in the mountains. It was there that he wrote his first song, words as well as music. He called it "Campfire Days." Soon after this, back home, he was the proud author of a second song, "The Auto

Show Girl," which his father multigraphed for distribution to friends and relatives.

Rodgers now kept writing songs all the time, while dreaming of the time when, like his hero Jerome Kern, he could place them in the musical theatre. For a while he had to satisfy himself with amateur productions put on by a boys' club of which his brother, Mortimer, was a member. The first was called *One Minute Please,* produced in the Grand Ballroom of the Hotel Plaza in New York on December 29, 1917. Another amateur production, *Up Stage and Down,* in 1919 yielded Rodgers' first songs to be published: "Twinkling Eyes," "Love Is Not in Vain," and "Love Me By Parcel Post."

Sometimes he wrote his own lyrics, and sometimes his lyrics were written by his brother, by his father, or by friends. Finding a permanent collaborator proved an event in Rodgers' early life that had a decisive impact on his creative growth. That partner was Lorenz Hart, to whom Rodgers was introduced by a mutual friend in 1918. Hart was seven years older than Rodgers. The lyricist was a little man, about five feet tall, with babylike feet and hands, and a head too large for his small body. But he had a giant intelligence and culture. He had studied journalism at Columbia University where he had acted in and written material for its Varsity Shows. Since leaving Columbia he had produced summer shows at a boys' camp and had done translations from foreign languages for Shubert productions on Broadway. He knew a good deal about opera, symphonic music, the theatre, literature. His hobby was writing verses, for which he had a marked talent. Rodgers was delighted with these verses when Hart read some of them to him at their first meeting. And, in reciprocity, Hart liked the tunes Rodgers played for him. Then and there, and without hesitation, they decided to set up a words-and-music partnership.

One of their earliest efforts was "Any Old Place With You."

This was a love song—but with a difference. Typical of the later Hart, the verses sidestepped sentimentality for urbanity, assuming a romantic attitude with a good deal of flippancy. "I'll go to hell for ya, or Phil-a-del-phi-a, any old place with you," is one of its many breezy lines in which sentiment is compounded with cynicism. Hart's lines skipped nimbly, hand in hand with Rodgers' agile musical phrases spiced with unusual harmonies. "Any Old Place With You" became the first Rodgers and Hart song to be published—Remick released it in 1919; it was also the first Rodgers and Hart song to get heard on Broadway—in *A Lonely Romeo,* which came to the Casino Theatre on August 26, 1919.

In the fall of 1919 Rodgers graduated from high school and matriculated at Columbia College. There he became the first freshman ever to write songs for the Varsity Show. That production, *Fly With Me,* was seen at the Hotel Astor on March 24, 1920. Before 1920 ended, Rodgers and Hart were also represented on Broadway, in the first musical to which they contributed more than one song. In fact, half of the score of *The Poor Little Ritz Girl* was their work, while the other half came from Sigmund Romberg, the veteran of Shubert productions. One of the Rodgers and Hart numbers, "Mary, Queen of Scots," attracted the interest of the celebrated New York critic (and later a distinguished columnist) Heywood Broun, who praised the fanciful phraseology and the skill of versification in Hart's lyrics. Other Rodgers and Hart songs were described by various critics as "tuneful" and "light-handed."

In spite of such favorable comments, Rodgers and Hart did not find it easy to interest either publishers or producers in their work. About the only places where their songs were welcome were in amateur shows, which earned them nothing in cold cash and just as little in public recognition. Disappointed and frustrated, Rodgers finally decided to leave Columbia, forget about songwriting for the time being, and improve his musical equipment through additional study. He enrolled at the Institute of Musical Art in New York in 1921. During the next two years he studied piano, theory, and music history with Henry E. Krehbiel, George Wedge, and Percy Goetschius. This was the time when a novitiate and a dilettante became a competent musician. Rodgers has never stopped being grateful for this experience. He has said: "Whenever I think about what happened to me at the Institute of Musical Art, I get a little religious about it."

Once his musical training ended, he went back to songs, back to working with Lorenz Hart, back to placing numbers in amateur shows and also trying to find a spot for them in Tin Pan Alley and Broadway. They found plenty of work among amateur groups. But all they could accomplish in the professional theatre was with a comedy with songs, *The Melody Man,* which they wrote in collaboration with Herbert Fields. This was a satire on Tin Pan Alley in which the songs were planned as a travesty on the kind of hackneyed tunes and lyrics then being manufactured for public consumption. *The Melody Man* opened on May 13, 1924, and left fifty-five performances after that. Nobody thought much of it.

Rodgers now became convinced that as far as his career was concerned he had come to the end of a dead-end street. He was twenty-two. He was incapable of earning his living through songs. More than that, he was losing faith in his talent. All this led him to give up the idea of becoming a professional musician and to think of entering the world of business. One of his friends found him a job as salesman of children's underwear at a salary of fifty dollars a week.

He never got the chance to begin work. Just before he had to report for his first morning as salesman, he learned from

Hart that the Theatre Guild wanted them to write songs for a revue. The Theatre Guild was one of the most important producing companies on Broadway. At that time it was building a handsome new theatre on 52nd Street. The idea occurred to a group of young performers and co-workers affiliated with the Guild to contribute expensive tapestries to the new house. To raise the money for this gift, they decided to put on a show—a revue, which they themselves would write, produce, design, and act in.

The kind of revue these young people had in mind was far different from the splendiferous productions then being put on annually by such master showmen as Ziegfeld, George White, or Earl Carroll. Their revues cost a good deal of money to mount. All the Guild youngsters possessed were a contagious enthusiasm, a fresh point of view, and an adult intelligence. All they could afford was an economical, intimate kind of revue, dependent exclusively on smart and original textual and musical material and the bright, sparkling, effervescent performances of young unknowns.

This intimate kind of revue, however, was not the invention of these Guild youngsters. A successful experiment in this direction had already taken place in downtown New York, at the Neighborhood Playhouse on the East Side. There other young people were presenting a revue called *The Grand Street Follies,* filled with the kind of wit, cynicism, iconoclasm, and satire to which the 1920s was so partial. The first edition of *The Grand Street Follies* had been mounted in 1922. By 1925 it had established a pattern and *modus operandi* that revolutionized the existing concept of what a revue should be, while setting a new standard and procedure the Guild young people could imitate.

These Guild people baptized their show *The Garrick Gaieties*—the Garrick Theatre being the place where their revue was presented. It had an abundance of sketches, dances, novel ideals for production numbers, and talented performers. What it needed most of all was—songs. The Guild members asked Rodgers and Hart to write them. Once again no payment would be forthcoming for their effort. But this time, at least, Rodgers and Hart would have a showcase that would restore their songs to Broadway and would attract the attention of critics and cultured audiences. Beyond all this, an affiliation with the Theatre Guild (whose directors were powers in the theatre) might very well lead to some important professional assignment. Rodgers, therefore, allowed Hart to convince him to forget the salesman's job and to go to work writing some new melodies for the *Gaieties*.

The Guild planned just two performances—a matinee and evening presentation on Sunday, May 17, 1925. But the critics were so enthusiastic, and the demand for more performances so insistent by the public, that four additional matinees were scheduled for June. Even this was not enough. A decision was finally arrived at to place the revue on a regular run beginning with June 8. That run lasted twenty-five weeks.

The critics remarked, with apparent delight, that *The Garrick Gaieties* was continuously novel, irreverent, and a bountiful source of joy. Broadway stage successes and Broadway stars were burlesqued; grand opera was mimicked; the White House was lampooned. Unusual routines included a choreographic episode worked out in black and white. And the best of the Rodgers and Hart songs—notably "Manhattan" and "Sentimental Me"—possessed the same kind of a bright, young, sparkling face and the same exuberance of spirit found in the sketches and dances.

For both Rodgers and Hart, the success of *The Garrick Gaieties* meant that, at long last, they could make a living from writing songs. Each was paid fifty dollars a week during the show's run, while Rodgers was paid an additional weekly salary of eighty-three dollars for conducting the orchestra. Both "Manhattan" and "Sentimental Me" were published by Harms, royalties of which added further to their income. This sudden affluence indicated that Rodgers and Hart had finally arrived.

Ignored only a few months earlier, their work was in sudden demand. By the end of 1925, Rodgers and Hart were each receiving several hundred dollars a week in royalties from a musical comedy, *Dearest Enemy,* which came to Broadway only four months after *The Garrick Gaieties.* In 1926, five Rodgers and Hart musical comedies could be seen on Broadway. The weekly income of each collaborator mounted to a thousand dollars.

The Rodgers and Hart epoch on Broadway, begun so auspiciously in 1925 with *The Garrick Gaieties* and *Dearest Enemy,* lasted seventeen years. During that time, twenty-three productions had songs by Rodgers and Hart, the best of which are still heard today through every possible medium and in many different places. With Herbert Fields often providing them with the text, Rodgers and Hart helped bring to the musical stage at least a dozen musical comedies which marked a new age. The three men were creators who were never satisfied with the status quo in the theatre; they never followed the lead of others; they were never even interested in continuing a pattern they themselves had helped make successful. Each successive Rodgers and Hart musical sought out unusual, provocative material to interest an adult audience. New methods, new techniques were always being tried out. And throughout, Rodgers and Hart succeeded continually to bring an ever fresher, an ever newer, and an ever more subtle expression and wit to the words and the melodies of their songs.

Already in *Dearest Enemy,* their first successful musical

comedy, an independence of thought and method could be discovered. Here for the first time a Broadway musical comedy went to the American history book for its plot: an incident during the Revolutionary War when Mrs. Robert Murray, at the request of General Washington, detained British officers at her home while the Continental Army could make a safe, strategic retreat.

Into such an unusual plot, Rodgers and Hart introduced a musical score of an amplitude and scope altogether new for the stage of 1925. We encounter not only songs capable of becoming hits, such as "Here in My Arms," but also fetching choral numbers, delightful vocal duets and trios, and even an atmospheric old-world gavotte for orchestra.

More radical still in theme and its development was *Peggy-Ann* in 1926. This was the first musical comedy to discuss the subject of dream psychology. The story was built from the dream fantasies of its heroine, a girl bored with her humdrum existence and her unromantic boy friend in Glens Falls, New York. Translating dreams into the language of the musical stage, Herbert Fields introduced into his text the often incongruous, absurd, even mad stuff out of which dreams are made. Policemen wear pink moustaches; fishes speak with an English accent; horses are interviewed; Peggy-Ann's wedding ceremony uses a telephone book for a Bible while her wedding gown consists of underclothes. To carry conviction to such a theme and its adventurous treatment, some of the long-accepted ritual of musical comedy had to be discarded. Musical comedies habitually opened with a big musical number. In *Peggy-Ann* no song was heard, nor was the chorus called upon to appear, in the first fifteen minutes. The dancing was not of the tap variety then so familiar in musical comedy but almost ballet in concept as it carried on the surrealistic nature of the text. Musical comedies invariably ended with a production number featuring the entire cast. *Peggy-Ann* closed with a slow comedy dance on a darkened stage. Rodgers' music was made up not only of songs but also of orchestral episodes as a suitable background for a dream world.

In *A Connecticut Yankee,* in 1926, American literature was the source, once again virgin territory for American musicals. Mark Twain's celebrated story, *A Connecticut Yankee in King Arthur's Court*—about a modern-day American returned to old Camelot—proved choice material for a trio of young men to whom satire was meat, and razor-edged wit, drink. In the musical comedy, Martin gets hit over the head with a champagne bottle at a party. Losing consciousness, he sinks into dreams in which he is back in the sixth century. As Sir Boss at Camelot, he introduces some of the developments of American life in the twentieth century, such as the telephone, radio, big business, advertising, efficiency experts, and so on. Gradually, Camelot becomes transformed into a typical American city whose inhabitants begin to talk in American slang, and whose king gives the appearance and suggests the behavior of the then President of the United States, Calvin Coolidge.

Some of the Rodgers and Hart songs carried on this anachronism by employing Arthurian phraseology, even while creating a delicious incongruity through combining this with present-day slang. "Thou Swell," "On a Desert Island with Thee," and "I Feel at Home with You," found Hart more nimble than ever in his rhyming, even as it put him in his preferred posture of coating love words with a generous sprinkling of acid. In the last of these three songs, the lover explains to his lass he is at home with her because she knows "no better words than three-letter words."

But for all the spice and pepper, this Rodgers and Hart score also possessed moments of deep feeling—for example, the main love ballad, "My Heart Stood Still," which its authors had actually written a year earlier for a London musical but whose value they recognized by buying it back from the English producer for interpolation into *A Connecticut Yankee.*

After *America's Sweetheart* in 1931—a take-off on Hollywood, its stars, manners and mores—there came a three-year hiatus for Rodgers and Hart during which they abandoned Broadway for Hollywood. This was not the first time Rodgers and Hart worked in Hollywood. They had gone there during the summer of 1930, Rodgers accompanied by his wife, Dorothy, whom he had married on March 5 of that year. The first screen assignment for Rodgers and Hart was three songs for *The Hot Heiress,* which proved a dismal failure. This first none too happy experience in Hollywood had given them the idea to write *America's Sweetheart.* Then, in the spring of 1931, Rodgers and Hart were called back to Hollywood to work for Paramount. This time the Rodgers family numbered three: a daughter, Mary, was born in New York on January 11, 1931. (Mary grew up to emulate her father by writing songs for the stage. Her biggest success has been the musical comedy *Once Upon a Mattress,* in 1959.) This time their screen efforts proved fruitful. Their first Paramount picture was *Love Me Tonight,* in which Maurice Chevalier was starred with Jeanette MacDonald. This delightful comedy, sprightly in its humor and engaging in its charm, was enhanced by songs like "Isn't It Romantic?," "Mimi," and "Lover." Then came *The Phantom President,* in which George M. Cohan made his debut in talking pictures; after that one or two more films that were failures. One of the best songs Rodgers and Hart wrote during this Hollywood interval, however, was never used on the screen, though intended for it. It was "Blue Moon," deleted now from one production, now from another, and then being issued in New York as an independent number to become the biggest hit song Rodgers and Hart had known up to this time.

Their three-year absence from the stage had provided both Rodgers and Hart with a new perspective on what they already had accomplished on the stage and what they yet hoped to achieve. More and more they were thinking in terms of "integration." By "integration" they meant coalescing all the various parts of a musical production into an indivisible unity. A musical comedy, they now came to realize more strongly than before, must be a whole and not just a sum of interesting parts. Song, dance, humor, staging, all must serve the story line, and when any of them failed to do so it must be dispensed with. As Hart told an interviewer soon after his return to New York: "Our aim is a new form of musical show for Broadway which is neither musical comedy nor operetta but in which the songs will be part of the progress of the piece, not extraneous interludes without rhyme or reason."

Rodgers also had clear ideas about the purpose and techniques of theatre music. The goals toward which he had been groping in the past were now clarified in his mind. A score should sometimes have a bit of the amplitude of operatic music, with the song often allowed to have dimensions far larger than the usual sixteen-measure verse and the thirty-two measure chorus. Choral and orchestral writing should be allowed greater representation as well as greater spaciousness of design.

The musical comedy with which Rodgers and Hart made their reentry into the Broadway scene, however, gave no indication of the new directions toward which they were now aiming. This was *Jumbo,* an old-fashioned kind of musical—part extravaganza, part circus. Billy Rose produced it in 1935 at the Hippodrome. The plot was inconsequential; the characters lacked conviction. The main interest lay in animal acts, tight rope stunts, and the broad humor. However circumscribed was the territory in which they were asked to move, Rodgers and Hart managed to produce one of their most infectious scores in which could be found "The Most Beautiful Girl in the World," "My Romance," and "Little Girl Blue." Better songs than these could not be heard on the Broadway stage in 1935.

But beginning with *On Your Toes,* in 1936, and ending with *By Jupiter,* in 1942, Rodgers and Hart consciously set out to bring their vital, progressive ideas about the musical theatre to fruition. During this period they continually opened new vistas, continually explored new territory. In the process, musical comedy became transfigured.

On Your Toes was even more adventurous than most of the Rodgers and Hart musicals of the 1920s in seeking out a subject never before used by the musical stage. The subject was the world of ballet. Writing their own text for the first time (though they did receive valuable assistance from George Abbott), Rodgers and Hart symbolized the conflicts between classical and modern jazz ballets in the person of their hero. He is a young dancer, the son of vaudevillians, who joins a ballet company to be near one of its ballerinas, with whom he is in love. As a performer in classical ballet he is a total failure. But when he convinces the company to put on a modern jazz ballet he not only establishes himself as a dancing star but also rehabilitates the fortunes of a bankrupt company.

Keeping in mind that ballet was the heart and core of their musical comedy, Rodgers and Hart contracted George Balanchine to prepare the choreography. He was the onetime director of the world-famous Ballet Russe de Monte Carlo and had become one of the most distinguished choreographers of his time. This was the first time Balanchine was called upon to work for the Broadway theatre; in fact, this was the first time that the Broadway theatre ever employed a distinguished member of the ballet world. Balanchine devised two ballets for *On Your Toes.* One was a satire of a classic dance; the other was a modern jazz ballet that brings the show to its climax. With the latter, "Slaughter on Tenth Avenue," serious modern ballet invaded musical comedy for the first time. For this ballet, Rodgers produced his most ambitious symphonic score, a score so richly atmospheric and melodic, so intriguing in its use of jazz materials, that even when it is heard without the dancing it remains a joy. This music has acquired a permanent place at orchestral concerts of semi-classical or "pop" music.

With *Babes in Arms,* in 1937, Rodgers and Hart brought into the professional musical theatre the fresh and welcome infusion of youth. The cast was made up mainly of youngsters; the two principals (Mitzi Green and Wynn Murray) were each only sixteen years old at the time. The cast included many other teen-agers, several of whom later became stars (Alfred Drake, Dan Dailey, Ray Heatherton, and Robert Rounseville). These young people represented the children of touring vaudevillians. Left behind in Long Island by their parents, they put on an amateur show to raise funds that will keep the sheriff from their doors. The whole production was charged with enthusiasm, excitement, verve, and energy. Each of the musical numbers was intended to develop the story line. The songs accomplished this aim, without losing any emotional impact or melodic appeal when divorced from the text. In fact, the score represented a veritable harvest of songs that became standards: "Where or When," "My Funny Valentine," "The Lady Is a Tramp," "Johnny One Note," "I Wish I Were in Love Again."

Later in 1937 came a trenchant satire on national politics in Washington, D.C., very much in the style and manner of the Gershwin musical *Of Thee I Sing!* seen a half a dozen years earlier. In *I'd Rather Be Right* we meet not a fictional American President (as had been the case with the Gershwin musical), but an actual one—Franklin Delano Roosevelt, America's President in 1937, portrayed by George M. Cohan in one of his rare appearances in a play not of his own writing, and in one of his most remarkable roles. Specifics rather than generalities govern the text. Names and issues very much in the news in 1938 are talked about and laughed at—names and issues which, perhaps, have long since been forgotten. The Rodgers and Hart songs discuss these items with brisk verses and leaping tunes. In this instance, however, songs separated from the play lose a good deal of their interest and flavor, the single exception being "Have You Met Miss Jones?"

Fantasy intruded into *I'd Rather Be Right* by having the hero and heroine, victims of the economic Depression, meet face-to-face with the President of the United States on a park bench in Central Park, New York. Fantasy invaded the next Rodgers and Hart musical comedy even more boldly. In *I Married an Angel,* in 1938 (book once again the work of Rodgers and Hart, an adaptation of a Hungarian play), a man of the world, disenchanted with women, marries an angel who comes flying through his window. He discovers that being the husband of somebody who is the paragon of virtue is not quite as desirable as he had hoped. Vera Zorina, in her Broadway stage debut, played the part of angel turned wife. Since she was a graduate of ballet, a good deal of attention was paid to dance sequences, the choreography once again created by George Balanchine.

Three more Rodgers and Hart musicals helped carry the musical theatre away from its onetime clichés and toward total integration. *The Boys from Syracuse,* in 1938, represented the first successful attempt to use Shakespeare for the commercial musical stage—*The Comedy of Errors.* The text remained consistently faithful to its source. In the Rodgers and Hart musical, the setting stayed in ancient Greece. The main characters are two pairs of twins—the Antipholus boys and the Dromio boys—one Antipholus and one Dromio coming from Ephesus, and the other pair from Syracuse. One pair of twins becomes confused with the other pair, a situation involving mistaken identity that provides most of the hilarity. "If you have been wondering all these years just what was wrong with *The Comedy of Errors,*" said Richard Watts, Jr., "it is now possible to tell you. It has been waiting for a score by Rodgers and Hart, and direction by George Abbott."

Pal Joey, in 1940, was undoubtedly the most courageous of all the Rodgers and Hart attempts to depart from accepted ways in the musical theatre. If there was any single tradition to which musical comedy had remained steadfast it was to have the audience sympathetic to its main characters; to have those characters turn out at the final curtain to be the essence of kindness and virtue, however much they may have been misunderstood in earlier scenes. In *Pal Joey,* the main character is a scheming, double-dealing opportunist whose only ingratiating trait is his personal charm, which he knows how to use to good advantage. His patroness is a hard-boiled socialite, willing to buy love for a price. The setting is a disreputable district of Chicago, populated by blackmailers and other highly unsavory characters. The main love story ends on a note of frustration. All in all, *Pal Joey* was a distasteful dish in place of the sweets musical comedy devotees had long come to expect. And in adapting his own stories for the stage—stories originally published in the *New Yorker*—John O'Hara did not yield to the temptation of sugarcoating a bitter pill. In the musical, as in the stories, Joey remains a brash nightclub entertainer who manages to get his own nightclub by embarking on an affair with a middle-aged socialite he does not love and deserting his girl friend. The musical comedy ends with Joey broken and disenchanted. He has lost his nightclub; he cannot get a job as an entertainer; and he is abandoned by both his patroness and his onetime girl.

The Rodgers and Hart music was thoroughly in character with the text—numbers like "In Our Little Den of Iniquity," "What Is a Man?" and especially the major song in the show, "Bewitched, Bothered and Bewildered," with which the female socialite expresses her confusion at her growing interest for Joey. Even Joey's love song to the girl he really loves—"I Could Write a Book"—has an undercurrent of insincerity, for here he is not giving vent to honest emotions half as much as ruminating over the kind of emotion his girl expects from him.

In a theatre habitually consecrated to escapism, *Pal Joey* was strong stuff. The year of 1940 was still a bit too soon for audiences and critics to appreciate its genuine virility and originality. *Pal Joey* was a failure in 1940. But when *Pal Joey* was revived on Broadway a dozen years later, audiences of musical comedy had grown up and were ready to appreciate adult entertainment with substance and new viewpoints. The critics, formerly hostile, were now unstinted in their praises. One now called *Pal Joey* a "masterwork"; another said it "renews confidence in the professionalism of the theatre"; a third remarked that "it is perhaps easier to see now that it is and always was a fine piece of work." *Pal Joey* now profited from a run of more than five hundred performances (the longest up to that time of any musical revival in Broadway history). It received the New York Drama Critics Award (the first musical comedy to do so) and eleven Donaldson Awards.

Its original-cast recording was a best seller. Its two main songs—"Bewitched, Bothered and Bewildered" and "I Could Write a Book"—soared into the hit class.

By Jupiter in 1942 was the last of the Rodgers and Hart musicals. Greek mythology provided the text, which made sport of the ancient locale of Pontus where women were the hardy warriors while the men were the homemakers. *By Jupiter* had the longest run of any Rodgers and Hart musical on Broadway during its original presentation, 427 performances. All that time it played to capacity houses. When it closed down it was not for lack of business at the box office; it was a casualty of World War II. Its star, Ray Bolger, had been committed to tour the Pacific war area to entertain American troops, and the consensus of producers and writers was that Bolger was indispensable to their show.

Only one more Rodgers and Hart production came to Broadway after that during Hart's lifetime—a revival of *A Connecticut Yankee* in 1943. This was an updated version with a number of new songs including "To Keep My Love Alive."

And then the age of Rodgers and Hart was over. It had been a words-and-music partnership with few parallels: twenty-seven stage musicals (fifteen of them major successes); eight motion-picture scores; film adaptations of nine stage shows; over five hundred songs with a high batting average of solid hits. Lorenz Hart had transformed lyric writing from the tired and hackneyed routine it had been in the 1920s into the kind of poetic art it had become by 1942 through the accomplishments of men like Ira Gershwin, Cole Porter, and "Yip" Harburg among many others. Richard Rodgers' songs helped to maintain a standard for Broadway show music few others had been able to achieve. He even managed to elevate that standard a few notches higher through the individual stamp of his melodic writing, and the way in which the ear was continually surprised through his original procedures and techniques. Words and music formed such a perfect match for each other that they almost appear to have been written simultaneously, by one and the same person. Actually, Rodgers invariably wrote the melody first, and Hart fitted his lyrics to it.

Lorenz Hart died of pneumonia in a New York hospital on November 22, 1943. But long before he died, Rodgers knew that their partnership was over and that he would have to seek out a new collaborator. Late in the 1930s, Hart had become an unhappy man who plunged again and again into the depths of despair and melancholia. He was neurotically sensitive about his pygmy size, regarding himself as a freak; he had not been able to find a woman to love him enough to marry him; he was dissatisfied with his work. His unhappiness intensified a lifelong disposition to be rather lackadaisical about his work habits, about keeping appointments or meeting deadlines. In the late 1930s it had become more difficult than ever for him to keep his nose to the grindstone. Having lost his onetime zest for work, success, and the theatre he tried to find stimulation in alcohol. When, after *By Jupiter,* the Theatre Guild proposed a new project for Rodgers and Hart, Hart bowed out. He said the project did not interest him; that he was too tired to work; that he wanted to go off on a prolonged holiday in Mexico. He urged Rodgers to seek out a new writing partner.

Rodgers did. He found him in Oscar Hammerstein II, and having found him he went to work on the musical in which the Theatre Guild was interested, *Oklahoma!*

For Rodgers, *Oklahoma!* represented the dawn of a new day. Unbelievable though it appeared back in 1943, this day was to prove even more resplendent, and of greater significance to the development of the American musical theatre, than had been the one Rodgers knew with Hart.

Hammerstein was seven years older than Rodgers. In 1943, he was already a hardy veteran of the musical theatre. As a lyricist and as a librettist he had been involved in stage successes of the first magnitude which had given him a place of importance. He first achieved recognition in 1924 with a musical comedy, *Wildflower,* for which Vincent Youmans and Herbert Stothart contributed the score. During the next fifteen years Hammerstein worked with Sigmund Romberg, Rudolf Friml, George Gershwin, and Jerome Kern. *Rose-Marie, The Desert Song,* and *The New Moon* were some of the operettas in which he had had a hand. With Jerome Kern as his composer, he helped revolutionize the musical theatre with *Show Boat.* And just before he teamed up with Rodgers, he had achieved the highest award the motion-picture industry could bestow on a songwriter—an Oscar for the song "The Last Time I Saw Paris," for which Kern provided the melody.

The paths of Rodgers and Hammerstein had crossed many a time before they joined up into a single broad highway in 1943. Rodgers met Hammerstein for the first time at Columbia University in 1915. Hammerstein was appearing in a Columbia Varsity Show, and young Rodgers (aged thirteen) had been brought backstage to meet him. Four years later, the two young men collaborated in the writing of two songs for an amateur production, "Weaknesses" and "Can It."

It would be another two decades before Rodgers and Hammerstein would work together on songs again. But during that period, while each was making his own mark in the theatre, they maintained a personal relationship that blossomed into close friendship; and they nursed a healthy respect for each other's talent. Then, when it became apparent to Rodgers he could no longer count on Hart, the first man he sought out as Hart's replacement was Hammerstein. "What happened between Oscar and me was almost chemical," Rodgers later explained. "Put the right components together and an explosion takes place. Oscar and I hit it off from the day we began discussing the show."

The show, *Oklahoma!*, was a musical adaptation of an American folk play by Lynn Riggs, *Green Grow the Lilacs*, which the Theatre Guild had presented as a stage play. This was material such as the popular musical theatre had rarely if ever touched; and for this very reason, it was material demanding a completely new approach, new methods, a new set of stage values. The main action involves the romance of Curly and Laurey in Midwestern Indian country at the turn of the present century. Since Curly is too shy to reveal how much he really loves Laurey, she punishes him by going off to a picnic with Jud Fry, an ugly character. At the picnic, the girls' lunch boxes are auctioned off to the boys, the buyer then being given the right to share the food with the girl. By outbidding Jud for Laurey's box, Curly convinces her finally that he is genuinely interested in her. Their love affair can now proceed into high gear—toward marriage. The wedding ceremony is rudely interrupted by Jud's arrival. He is drunk and he menaces Curly with a knife. In the ensuing scuffle, Jud falls upon his own blade and is killed. Curly is exonerated by an improvised court, permitting him to leave with his bride on their honeymoon in territory soon to become known as Oklahoma.

The problem of total integration of music and text—the problem that had so deeply concerned Rodgers and Hart for many years—was here finally solved. In this process, a new musical stage form came to full maturity—the musical play, of which *Show Boat* had been the parent. In *Oklahoma!* the play was the thing. The play, and the play alone, dictated what materials should be used, and how. Humor had to spring naturally, logically from situation and character. Lyrics had to become an essential part of the text—so essential, in fact, that Rodgers and Hammerstein immediately came to the decision that the lyrics had to be written *before* the melody (a practice they would henceforth pursue). Dance had to be an extension of the plot development, and in addition it had to be in complete harmony with setting and characters; consequently, American folk ballet, rather than formal dance numbers, had to be conceived by one of America's leading dancers and choreographers, Agnes de Mille.

In making his adaptation, Oscar Hammerstein II remained true to the original intentions of the Lynn Riggs play. *Green Grow the Lilacs* required the musical play to open simply, on a subdued note, creating a relaxed atmosphere. Rodgers and Hammerstein met this challenge with "Oh, What a Beautiful Mornin'," sung by the hero offstage while a single character (a woman churning butter) is visible. *Green Grow the Lilacs* made no room for chorus girls or production numbers, and so both were dispensed with. *Green Grow the Lilacs* gave importance to the villainous character of Jud, and carried the play to its climax with Jud's death. Neither Jud nor his death was eliminated from the musical play, though neither would have been acceptable to the musical comedy of the past.

An American folk play begged for a musical treatment more in line with opera than musical comedy. Rodgers complied: now with a lengthy and expressive narrative, "Pore Jud," of dimensions larger than the musical comedy song and touched with sardonic humor; now with an ambitious dance sequence, "Laurey Makes Up Her Mind," which was symphonic in dimension and character; now with frequent musical fragments and quotations, sometimes played under the dialogue, sometimes introducing a mood, sometimes serving as transition from one scene to the next. The thirteen basic numbers evolved from the plot and character so inevitably that play and music became enmeshed inextricably. The most significant of these individual numbers were Curly's opening hymn to the morning and his closing paean to the state of Oklahoma, "People Will Say We're in Love," "The Surrey with the Fringe on Top," "Kansas City," and "The Farmer and the Cowman." Some of these numbers had the sound and personality of Western folk songs and dance tunes.

The whole concept of *Oklahoma!,* as well as the way the musical play was worked out, was revolutionary. The minute they started working, Rodgers and Hammerstein knew that their course would have to be experimental, "amounting almost to the breach of an implied contract with a musical comedy audience," as Hammerstein himself put it. "I cannot say truthfully that we were worried by the risk. Once we had made the decision everything seemed to work right and we had the inner confidence people feel when they have adopted the right and honest approach to a problem."

The cards were stacked against *Oklahoma!* becoming a winning hand at the box office. It lacked those elements that had attracted audiences to musical comedies for so many years: chorus girls and sex appeal, production numbers, broad humor, stars in the cast. Other elements joined in to work against *Oklahoma!* It had been derived from a play that had been a failure. In addition, the extensive use of American folk ballet placed it more in the art class than in entertainment, and art was poison to the box office. "When people come to Broadway," was the consensus, "they want to be amused and entertained, not uplifted." Herculean effort on the part of the Theatre Guild was required to raise the $83,000 needed for production costs. Most of this money, when it was finally collected, was contributed more out of a spirit of charity or allegiance to the Theatre Guild than faith in the production itself.

When *Oklahoma!* tried out in New Haven, word was flashed back to Broadway that this was a show with "no girls, no gags, and no chance." In Boston, the musical made a better impression, but those who insisted that it was not commercial far outnumbered the admirers. When *Oklahoma!* finally opened in New York on March 31, 1943, the house was one-quarter empty. Many of those who came expected to be bored.

The production had not progressed very far before one after another in that audience was made conscious that something very special—indeed, something historic—was taking place before its very eyes. With each successive episode the musical play grew increasingly irresistible, until the audience succumbed to it completely. After the final curtain, the ovation was thunderous. The following morning the critics vied with one another for superlatives. Burton Rascoe called it "fresh, lovely, colorful, one of the finest musical scores any musical ever had." John Anderson found it "as enchanting to the eye as Richard Rodgers' music is to the ear." Lewis Nichols described it as a "folk opera."

There were no empty seats at the St. James Theatre after that—not for many years to come. The message that had been sent back from the New Haven tryouts was now altered to read: "No girls, no gags, no tickets." *Oklahoma!* remained on Broadway for five years and nine months—its run of 2,248 performances without precedence for a musical. A national company toured 250 cities in a ten-year period. Even all this was not enough to meet the demand throughout America for the sight and sound of *Oklahoma!* The New York company undertook a national tour of its own, once the Broadway run had been terminated, covering seventy cities. *Oklahoma!* was also produced in Europe, Scandinavia, Australia, South Africa —and for the American armed forces throughout the Pacific. In London, as in New York, stage history was made: All box-office records were broken for the Drury Lane Theatre as *Oklahoma!* became London's second longest running musical production.

Oklahoma! made history on other counts as well. It received a special award from the Pulitzer Prize committee. Its first appearance in the state from which it took its title was declared a holiday by the Governor. It became the first musical to issue its entire score in a recording, selling over a million albums (this was during the period before the long-playing record). The various stage productions grossed over a hundred million dollars. The motion picture adaptation, released in 1955, grossed almost ten million dollars in the United States alone. Each investor of $1,500 was returned over $50,-000. The Theatre Guild profited to the tune of more than five million dollars, and Rodgers and Hammerstein each earned over a million dollars.

Before undertaking a successor to *Oklahoma!*, Rodgers and Hammerstein left for Hollywood in 1944 to write their only original screen score: for *State Fair*, in which Will Rogers and Janet Gaynor were starred. One of its songs, "It Might As Well Be Spring," was a masterpiece—recognized as such by the Motion Picture Academy of Arts and Sciences when it conferred on it the Academy Award. In 1962, *State Fair* was remade into a fresh screen production, this time with Pat Boone, Bobby Darin, and Ann-Margret. "It Might As Well Be Spring" remained the musical high point of the production, though several new songs had been added.

But, in spite of their success in Hollywood, Rodgers and Hammerstein belonged on Broadway, and it was to Broadway that they henceforth directed their extraordinary creativity. *Carousel* came in 1945, *South Pacific* in 1949, *The King and I* in 1951. Each is a masterwork. Each has survived its initial long run to become a continually revived classic.

What is perhaps most remarkable about these three productions is the way in which each differs from the others in style, setting, artistic purpose, and even methods of procedure. The greatness of Rodgers and Hammerstein lay in their continual growth and change; they were never willing to stand still by repeating themselves, by trying to buy a new success with the techniques and materials of an old one. Experiment was the meat upon which these, our stage Caesars, fed and grew strong. And experiment would continue to dominate Rodgers' work even after his partnership with Hammerstein ended with the latter's death.

Carousel was a second attempt to write music for a Theatre Guild stage production. In this case it was Ferenc Molnar's *Liliom*. But translating *Liliom* into a musical play posed problems of its own. *Liliom* was a fantasy with a Hungarian background. Using Budapest as the locale for a new musical play was not feasible in the early 1940s: Hungary had become an ally of Nazi Germany during World War II and could not be expected to inspire nostalgia or sentimentality in an American audience. This touchy question was eventually answered by shifting the locale to New England, a healthy change of scene as it turned out, since it enabled the adaptors to draw upon such picturesque local New England characters as sailors, mill workers, fishermen. A second problem was no less serious. The hero died midway in the play, something which no musical had ever permitted and which no musical audience would be expected to accept. But this death was basic to the plot and could not be sidestepped—and so it was accepted for the musical play.

The first part of *Carousel* placed its accent on realism and romance. After the climax, which came with the hero's death, the story passed on to pure fantasy. Billy Bigelow, our hero (the prototype of Liliom in the stage play), is a brash, shiftless, happy-go-lucky fellow, who earns his living by helping operate a carousel in a New England amusement park in 1873. When two mill girls are insulted by the carousel proprietress, he comes to their defense, for which he is summarily dismissed from his job. He takes this development lightly; he even offers to take one of those mill girls, Julie Jordan, for a drink of beer. Romance develops between them, even though they are opposites in every possible way. After they get married, Julie tells Billy she is to become a mother. This fills Billy with a sudden welling of pride, but also with a smothering awareness of his own shortcomings as a provider. He is now determined to find the money with which to assure the upbringing of his child. He gets involved in a holdup, is caught, and rather than submit to arrest, commits suicide.

The rest is fantasy. Billy is doomed to spend fifteen years in Purgatory because he does not regret having committed his crime. After that, he is permitted to spend a single day back on earth to redeem his soul. He seizes a star to bring back as a gift to his child, now a grown girl. But the girl is suspicious of the stranger and refuses it. His intense disappointment leads Billy to slap her sharply. But Billy loves his daughter intensely. Through that love—and the tenderness and understanding it brings him—he is able to inspire his daughter with hope and courage. He attends her graduation from school, happy in the knowledge that he was responsible for her salvation, and that through this deed he has won redemption for himself.

Carousel did not boast quite the spectacular performing history previously enjoyed by *Oklahoma!*—though its run of 890 performances represented a monumental success—but in some ways it proved a more distinguished artistic achievement than its predecessor, a happier realization of the aesthetic aims and purposes of musical playwriting. It is also a more endearing work of art. It has a compassion, a humanity, a tenderness only rarely encountered in *Oklahoma!* For *Carousel,* Hammerstein began tapping a vein of poetic beauty that touched his lyrics and dialogue with an incandescent glow. Rodgers emerged in *Carousel* as a musical dramatist rather than merely the creator of wonderful songs and effective sequences. A new dimension that was almost operatic entered his writing of the now celebrated soliloquy in which Billy speaks of his hopes and dreams for his unborn child. Rodgers' orchestral writing also betrayed a new breadth, particularly in the set of waltzes played under the opening scene as a whirling carousel comes into view. His score as a whole is a complex network of pieces large and small—vocal, choral, orchestral—with the orchestra ever present to provide provocative comments on what is happening on the stage. At the same time he voices new depths of intensity and feeling in numbers like "If I Loved You," "June Is Bustin' Out All Over," and "You'll Never Walk Alone." The last of these has a spirituality which Cole Porter once described as "a kind of holiness." Throughout, *Carousel* blends song and speech, speech and song. Large sequences are made up of song, speech, recitative. Music and text are of one piece.

"When somebody writes a better play than *Carousel,* Richard Rodgers and Oscar Hammerstein will have to write it," said Robert Garland in 1945. Indeed, it did take a Rodgers and Hammerstein to surpass Rodgers and Hammerstein. This happened in 1949 with *South Pacific.*

Where *Oklahoma!* and *Carousel* had sprung from the American past, *South Pacific* was as contemporary as the war that inspired it, that endowed it with its setting, plot, and characters. The musical play emerged from *Tales of the South Pacific,* a set of stories about the American fighting forces during World War II. James Michener wrote it, and for it he received the Pulitzer Prize in fiction. The transition from book to stage musical was made by Oscar Hammerstein II in collaboration with Joshua Logan.

They took their material from two of those Michener tales —"Fo' Dolla" and "Our Heroine." They made as principal character Emile de Becque, a middle-aged French widower, a wealthy planter who had made his home on a South Pacific island long before it had become involved in World War II. All of the action, however, takes place during the war, and much of it concerns the love that develops between De Becque and an American nurse stationed on the island, Ensign Nellie Forbush. The island is also the base for American soldiers, Seabees, and Marines. Bloody Mary, a Tonkinese, sees in Lieutenant Joseph Cable a suitable candidate as husband for her daughter, Liat. Bloody Mary introduces the pair to each other on the nearby island of Bali Ha'i where they fall in love. The romance between De Becque and Nellie is complicated when she discovers that he is the father of two Eurasian children. As for Cable and Liat, he soon comes to the conclusion that their racial difference makes marriage impossible. Cable, dispatched on a dangerous war mission, convinces De Becque to accompany him, since De Becque is so familiar with the terrain. They get information on a Japanese-held island that enables the American forces to destroy a Japanese flotilla and thus make possible a successful invasion. Cable is killed during the mission. But De Becque returns safely to find that Nellie has had a change of heart: She will not allow her prejudices to stand in the way of her happiness with the man she loves.

Once again—as had been the case with *Oklahoma!* and

Carousel—problems posed by the text demanded courageous thinking and decisions. Artistic issues had to be met squarely and honestly; concessions to expediency could not be made. To have a middle-aged gray-haired man as the romantic hero defied the traditions of a musical theatre that had always glorified youth; and the subsidiary love interest between an American Marine and a Tonkinese girl was even more iconoclastic. The first of these problems was well worked out by getting Ezio Pinza, the handsome star of the Metropolitan Opera, to assume the role of De Becque. He made the role so convincing and so alluring that before the show had progressed far into its extended Broadway run, he had become a matinee idol for young and old alike. The second problem endangered the box office. Would an American public—especially a Southern public, when the show went on tour—accept an interracial love affair? Rodgers and Hammerstein compounded problem upon problem by writing a song that was a plea for racial tolerance, "Carefully Taught," completely ignoring the possible implications for the play's success. As it turned out, neither the love affair nor the song found opposition. As Rodgers later remarked wisely: "You can do anything in the theatre, just so long as you do it right."

More than he had done in his two earlier productions, Rodgers went out of his way to illuminate character through music. As he himself explained: "I tried to weave De Becque's character into his songs—romantic, rather powerful, but not too involved—and so I wrote for him 'Some Enchanted Evening' and 'This Nearly Was Mine.' Nellie Forbush is a Navy nurse out of Arkansas, a kid whose musical background probably had been limited to the movies, radio and maybe a touring musical comedy. She talks in the vernacular, so her songs had to be in the vernacular. It gave me a chance for a change of pace, and the music I wrote for her is light, contemporary, rhythmic: 'A Cockeyed Optimist,' 'I'm Gonna

Wash That Man Right Outa My Hair,' 'I'm in Love with a Wonderful Guy.' Cable's songs—'Younger than Springtime' and 'Carefully Taught'—are like the man, deeply sincere, while Bloody Mary's songs, 'Bali Ha'i' and 'Happy Talk' try to convey some of the languor and mystery of her race."

The actress chosen to play Nellie Forbush—opposite Ezio Pinza's De Becque—was Mary Martin. She fell in love with the role and the score from the moment she received the song "I'm in Love with a Wonderful Guy." This is a number that achieves a powerful emotional impact in the closing line of the chorus, through the five-time repetition of the phrase "I'm in love"—an effect Rodgers had suggested to Hammerstein. Mary Martin tried the song early one morning at Joshua Logan's apartment. "I almost passed out," she later confessed. "I was so excited. After the repeats I fell off the piano bench and I remember that the management had to call up to complain of the noise."

Long before *South Pacific* arrived at the Majestic Theatre on April 7, 1949, word had begun to spread like contagion throughout the Broadway sector that this was an exceptional show, possibly the greatest Rodgers and Hammerstein had thus far written. On opening night expectation ran high. The enthusiasm reached the heat of fever by the final curtain. Arthur Hammerstein left the theatre insisting that this was the perfect musical, the only such he had encountered in half a century of personal experiences within the theatre. Michael Todd said it was the greatest show he had ever seen. By the time the critics had had their say, the queues started forming outside the Majestic to deplete the box office of all available tickets. For a long time after that, a pair of seats for *South Pacific* remained a rare commodity—so rare, in fact, that many a tale was told about the extravagant lengths to which people went to capture them.

South Pacific threatened the historic run of *Oklahoma!* but failed short by only 323 performances. On most other counts, it surpassed its distinguished predecessor. It received the regular drama award of the Pulitzer Prize Committee, instead of just a special one as had been the case with *Oklahoma!* (This was only the second time in Pulitzer Prize history that the award went to a musical.) *South Pacific* also captured the Drama Critics Award, nine Donaldson and seven Antoinette Perry awards. Three and a half million customers paid nine million dollars during the Broadway run. A national company toured several years to establish box-office records across the country, grossing over three and a half million dollars during its first year. A run of two and a half years in London was followed by a two-year run throughout England. The production also proved a triumph in Australia, Denmark, and Spain. The motion-picture adaptation in 1958 grossed over sixteen million dollars in America and twice that in the rest of the world—one of the all-time box-office successes for a motion picture. In addition to all this: The initial original-cast recording sold over two million discs; over two million copies of sheet music were bought; and licenses to use the name of "South Pacific" on various products yielded a small fortune.

It seemed almost incredible to believe that whatever Rodgers and Hammerstein would write next could be anything but an anticlimax after a trio of masterworks like *Oklahoma!*, *Carousel*, and *South Pacific*. The two collaborators accomplished the incredible with *The King and I*. They had the foresight, wisdom, and fortitude to embark on a project completely fresh for both them and the the musical theatre; a project completely divorced from American experiences and materials; a project with distant and exotic Siam as a setting, with characters who were mostly Orientals (except for the heroine and three others, who were Anglo-Saxon), and with a plot in which almost no love interest touches the two principals, and which ends with the death of the leading male.

There was still one other way in which *The King and I* represented a radical departure for the musical theatre. This was the first stage musical adapting a motion picture (reversing the accepted procedure of adapting stage musicals into motion pictures). The film from which *The King and I* was derived was *Anna and the King of Siam,* a nonmusical production starring Irene Dunne and Rex Harrison (in turn taken from a novel by Margaret Landon). Gertrude Lawrence had been impressed by that movie, saw herself as Anna in a stage musical production, and urged Rodgers and Hammerstein to write it for her.

Rodgers and Hammerstein forthwith became fascinated with the idea of doing an Oriental musical play in which artistic dignity and sensitive feeling for Oriental splendor would replace what Hammerstein described as "this business of girls dressed in Oriental costumes and dancing out onto the stage and singing 'ching-aling-aling' with their fingers in the air." For Rodgers, the special problem of writing Oriental-type music—rather than Oriental music about which he knew little—was a particular challenge. "What I tried to do," he explained, "was to say what the Far East suggested to me musically, to write a score that would be analagous in sound to the look of a series of Siamese paintings by Grant Wood. I myself remained a Broadway character, not somebody in Oriental getup." The Oriental atmosphere sometimes faintly touched and sometimes completely pervaded the fifteen basic numbers, two finales, and the forty-six musical clues that made up the score. But the music itself remained basically of the Western world.

Rodgers was more successful than ever before in combining action with musical continuity. The technique of getting a song to spring effortlessly from a sequence of dialogue or situation is achieved with total assurance. Completely natural is the way in which dialogue interrupts song and then reverts to the spoken word; in which instrumental music provides a background for dialogue to heighten and intensify emotion; in which snatches of orchestral sequences tie scenes together.

The score also contained songs with the unmistakable Rodgers identity and style: "I Whistle a Happy Tune" and "Shall We Dance?" "A Puzzlement" is in the expansive mold and in the effective narrative style Rodgers had previously used for his famous *Carousel* "Soliloquy." New altitudes of poetic eloquence and lyrical beauty are reached in "Hello, Young Lovers," "We Kiss in a Shadow," and "I Have Dreamed," each of which has the expressiveness of an art song.

Notable, too, in the musical play was a remarkable ballet, "The Small House of Uncle Thomas," choreography by Jerome Robbins. To the primitive background of percussion sounds from woodblock and ancient cymbals, there transpires on the stage a re-creation, in terms of the Siamese dance, of the story of *Uncle Tom's Cabin.* It is told with a literalness, a childlike naïveté and humor, that is thoroughly captivating in every detail. John Lardner called it in the *New Yorker* "the most beguiling ballet I have ever seen."

As for the story of *The King and I:* In the 1860s a prim schoolteacher, Anna, arrives in Siam from London to teach Western ways to Oriental people. At first she is repelled by the despotic ways of the king, but she soon finds a good deal to admire in him. She also becomes completely devoted to the princes and princesses, as their teacher. Her ingenuity helps save the king and Siam from diplomatic disaster. But because the king has broken his word to her she insists she can stay in Siam no longer. This decision is changed when the king dies, and Anna realizes how much the royal children need her.

The king was played by Yul Brynner, who had come to this all-important role with only minor stage experience and less recognition. A single audition was enough to convince both Rodgers and Hammerstein that he was truly their king. His swagger, his self-assured, blustering yet strangely likable characterization would have thrown every other performance in that play into a shade, had not Gertrude Lawrence been cast as Anna. Here she gave one of her most luminous, most subtle, and most winning performances. Here, too, she gave her last performance. With *The King and I* still running on Broadway, Miss Lawrence died of cancer on September 6, 1952.

The King and I was the third Rodgers and Hammerstein musical play achieving a run that passed the thousand mark. The fourth and last of their productions to do so was *The Sound of Music,* opening on November 16, 1959. Sweetness and sentimentality, and an overdose of charm, might seem out of place in a story that reached its dramatic peak with the Nazi invasion of Austria and the flight of its main character from pursuing Gestapo. Nevertheless, since the musical play ends on a note of exaltation, the warm glow generated earlier in so many of its scenes does not lose its radiance. This was true not only of the stage production but also of the stunningly beautiful motion picture version released in 1965 by 20th-Century Fox, starring Julie Andrews and Christopher Plummer. That film won the Academy Award. It established new box-office records in all parts of the civilized world to become the most successful motion picture ever made. And the eight-million-disc sale of its soundtrack recording is the largest ever achieved.

The idea for *The Sound of Music* had originated with

Mary Martin, who became convinced that a good musical could be made out of the real-life history of the Trapp Family Choir. This was an Austrian singing family who had fled from Nazi-dominated Austria to tour the world in choral concerts. Consulting the autobiography of Maria Augusta Trapp, Howard Lindsay and Russell Crouse went to work fashioning a book in which we first meet Maria as a postulant at the Nonnberg Abbey in Austria. She is unhappy, since she seems incapable of conforming to abbey discipline. This is the reason why the Mother Abbess sends her off to the nearby home of Captain Georg von Trapp, a retired naval officer and widower, to serve as governess to his seven children. The Captain falls in love with her, after Maria had succeeded in winning over completely the hearts of the children. He breaks his engagement to Elsa and marries Maria in an impressive religious ceremony. The invasion of Austria by the Nazis jeopardizes their happiness, for the Captain is an outspoken anti-Fascist. After the family performs at a local Austrian festival, they escape from the country by going on foot over the mountains into Switzerland, the Gestapo on their heels.

Mary Martin was Maria. She and the seven delectable children, together with the songs, combined to create what Frank Aston called "the loveliest musical imaginable." Mary Martin and the children were heard in "Do Re Mi"—built on the ascending tones of the diatonic scale as Mary teaches the children to sing notes—and "The Lonely Goatherd." Mary Martin herself introduced "My Favorite Things" and the children, without Miss Martin, "So Long, Farewell." "Sixteen Going on Seventeen" was assigned to two adolescent lovers. Nor have we yet exhausted the melodic riches. "Climb Every Mountain" is in an inspirational vein, with strong spiritual overtones. "Edelweiss" has the character of authentic Austrian folk music, just as the opening "Preludium" (replacing the traditional orchestral overture) suggests authentic church music. The stylistic gamut of the music is a wide one. The musical production itself is also eclectic, being part musical play and part operetta.

In providing memories of an older stage form, operetta, *The Sound of Music* was not the first Rodgers and Hammerstein musical to direct a backward glance at the theatre's past. Before they wrote *The Sound of Music,* they had tried reverting to old-fashioned, traditional musical comedy in *Flower-Drum Song*. This was in 1958. A song like "I Enjoy Being a Girl" (fetchingly presented by Pat Suzuki in her Broadway stage debut) and the buck-and-wing dance that followed the rendition of "Don't Marry Me" are the kind of material musical comedy had always favored strongly. Also more in character with musical comedy than musical play was a nightclub scene which featured a strip tease. The plot pitted an older generation of American Chinese in San Francisco's Chinatown against the younger generation, who are more American than Chinese. The old world of Chinese culture is represented by "A Hundred Million Miracles" and a Chinese wedding procession down Chinatown's main street. The new world is found in a character like Linda Low, the proprietress of the nightclub where the strip tease takes place.

The Sound of Music was the final chord of the Rodgers and Hammerstein partnership that had changed the destiny of the American musical theatre. On August 23, 1960, at his home in Doylestown, Pennsylvania, Hammerstein died, a victim of cancer.

For Rodgers, the death of Oscar Hammerstein represented a double tragedy. One of his dearest friends was gone, leaving an emptiness that could never again be filled. But Rodgers had lost not only a friend but a collaborator and co-worker, whose inspiration and wisdom had made it possible for him to soar to heights. Henceforth, Rodgers would have to find somebody else to work with. Having collaborated with only two men all his life, this problem of adjusting himself creatively to another personality, to a fresh point of view, to a new set of habits, and to other ideals and ideas became formidable.

At first Rodgers tried going it alone by writing his own lyrics for *No Strings,* in 1962. The basic idea for this musical was his own, but Samuel Taylor, an experienced hand at playwriting, worked that idea out in a text. Once again, as in the past, novelty and experiment are the keynotes with Rodgers. The basic story involves a love affair between different races—a Negro Parisian fashion model and a white Pulitzer Prize novelist. This romance transpires in Paris and Deauville, and ends with frustration to both when the novelist feels he must go home and return to his writing and realizes he cannot take his sweetheart with him. What made the treatment of this relationship so unusual was the natural way in which this involvement of two people, of different-colored skins, is treated. There is no suggestion that there is anything unusual for a white man and a Negro girl to be in love; there is no intrusion of any interracial problems. The two main characters are developed as they should be—as two attractive human beings interested in one another.

Unconventional approaches are found in both the staging and the music. Rodgers wanted to give the musical stage a new dimension by "pushing out the walls of the theatre," as he explained. A minimum of scenery, suggesting only the essentials of any given background, is required; this scenery is sometimes moved about by the actors and actresses themselves as part of the action. The stilted tradition of keeping the orchestra players in the pit was broken for the first time. This orchestra (composed exclusively of wind instruments, as befitting the title of the musical) was grouped in the wings of the stage. Every once in a while, now one orchestral player, now two or three, would stroll leisurely across the stage and take a stance behind a performer or performers to provide a discreet musical commentary to what was being said or done. "In short," reported Walter Kerr, "the composer's hirelings are used to support rather than to intercept the principals. . . . Mr. Rodgers' impudent resettlement works."

Rodgers' lyrics were professional, neatly trimmed, carefully molded, and always serviceable. They revealed forcefully that if he wished he was fully capable of dispensing with a collaborator. But Rodgers was not satisfied. He sensed the need of working with somebody with whom he would exchange suggestions and ideas while working out his songs; somebody who could excite his imagination; somebody with whom to share his own aspirations and visions. What he needed, in short, was another working partner—another Hart or another Hammerstein.

For a short while it seemed that Rodgers had found that man in Alan Jay Lerner. Lerner was already one of the most distinguished lyricists and librettists on the theatrical scene, by virtue of his monumental success with *Brigadoon, My Fair Lady,* and *Camelot.* At first glance, he seemed to be the kind of forceful, inventive creator who could step into the shoes of a Hammerstein and work harmoniously with Rodgers. With Lerner, Rodgers tried to work out a project about a girl with extrasensory perception. For a time it appeared that the two writers were in perfect accord. But this honeymoon was brief. Soon they failed to see eye to eye on details big and small. Rodgers withdrew from the partnership, allowing Lerner to keep his libretto. It came to Broadway as *On a Clear Day You Can See Forever,* music by Burton Lane.

Then—with *Do I Hear a Waltz?* in 1965—Rodgers worked

with Stephen Sondheim, a young writer who had distinguished himself in *West Side Story* as Leonard Bernstein's lyricist. *Do I Hear a Waltz?* turned out to be a mild-mannered little story about an American girl in Venice who falls in love with a romantic Italian. The whole thing was presented *sotte voce*—but unfortunately this kind of understatement invited only ennui. *Do I Hear a Waltz?* was a failure. Another attempt to find a writing partner had collapsed for Rodgers.

But the need to write songs for musicals, the compulsion to project new themes and evolve new techniques, is not to be denied. Retirement for Rodgers is not to be contemplated. Rodgers and Hart . . . Rodgers and Hammerstein . . . Rodgers and Rodgers . . . The common denominator is a man with a passion to create, and a genius for bringing large dreams to fulfillment. "I'd like to keep on doing work for the theatre," Rodgers has said, "and write one or two more shows that will leave an impression." If the past is any guide to the future, those one or two shows *will* get written, and in all probability they *will* leave a further indelible impression on the American musical theatre.

X

KURT WEILL

(1900-1950)

KURT WEILL was the only significant composer for the musical theatre whose first experiences and successes were in Europe. He was, as a matter of fact, the most successful composer for the popular musical theatre in Germany in the years just before the rise of Nazism. A thoroughly trained musician, who had initiated his career with works in a modern style and technique, Weill soon felt uncomfortable in his ivory tower. He wanted to reach an audience much larger than the scattered few who came to concerts of modern music. The need to communicate with the masses, rather than with the intellectual elite, led him to throw a cold objective eye of appraisal on where he had thus far gone in music and where he really wanted to go. He knew what he wanted. He aimed to write music for the theatre utilizing popular idioms and treating modern subjects—music that a large public can understand and respond to at first hearing. He was thinking in terms of opera, but *popular* opera interpreting modern life and mores. "I want to reach the real people," he told an interviewer, "a more representative public than any opera house attracts. I write for today. I can't care about writing for posterity." And so he evolved a new operatic form for everyday people, and he called it "song-play."

The rise of Hitler and Nazism uprooted him and sent him across the ocean to find a new home, a new sphere of activity, and in the end a new stage medium. He became an American citizen. He oriented himself thoroughly to the American way of life. And he began writing music for the Broadway theatre. He contributed scores for musical comedies, and after that scores for musical plays. The latter were virtually operatic in their seriousness of artistic purpose and significance of musical treatment. And so, the man who had won his first success in Germany by transforming opera into musical comedy, ended up his career in America by making musical comedy into opera.

He was the son of a synagogue cantor in Dessau, Germany, where he was born on March 2, 1900. His musical talent was inherited from his father, a trained singer, and his mother, who played the piano well. Kurt, however, did not receive formal instruction in music until he was fourteen when he took piano lessons with Albert Bing. Bing detected that Weill had a flair for composition. On his teacher's urging, Weill started to study theory. Several years later, in 1918, Weill went to Berlin where he enrolled in the High School of Music for one semester, a pupil in composition of Engelbert Humperdinck (the composer of the opera *Hansel and Gretel*). Weill then served as an opera coach in Dessau and as a conductor in a theatre in Lüdenscheid.

He was back in Berlin in 1921, once again deeply immersed in the study of composition, this time with one of the most highly esteemed musical scholars, pianists, and theoreticians of his generation, Ferruccio Busoni. He studied with

Busoni for three years, supporting himself all that while by playing the piano in beer halls.

As Busoni's pupil, Weill became interested in the aims and methods of modern music. Like so many other young composers in Germany he wrote a number of concert works in an abstract, complex, discordant style. Several of his compositions were later performed at important European festivals. Meanwhile, in 1922, on a commission, he wrote a little ballet for children, *The Magic Night*. Bearing his audience in mind, he produced music that was simplified in approach and aesthetic aims, music that emphasized pleasing tunes. The young audience was delighted, and Weill in turn was delighted with its reaction. This was the first time that Weill began thinking in terms of writing music more readily assimilable by a large audience than the concert works he was then producing for the esoteric few.

By 1925 he had reached the decision to write operas. The first was *The Protagonist,* in 1926, with a text by Georg Kaiser, a distinguished German dramatist with futurist tendencies. Produced in Dresden, it was a minor success.

In trying to reach out to a wider audience, Weill now began experimenting with new methods. In 1927, his second opera, *The Royal Palace,* used pantomime and movies as well as stage action. In 1928, in *The Czar Has Himself Photographed,* Weill experimented with jazz. Jazz in those years was in vogue in Germany, and the way Weill used it in his opera had an enormous appeal. *The Czar Has Himself Photographed* was performed in eighty German theatres.

Weill now became increasingly interested in operas with modern stories and characters, dealing with situations and problems a modern audience could respond to. At the same time, he began to use popular tunes and styles in his writing, American jazz especially. To emphasize that he had broken with operatic traditions and was creating a new medium of his own, he baptized the form in which he was working as "song-play."

His first full-length song-play brought him world fame, for it was *The Three-Penny Opera.* Since this musical production is almost as well known to Americans as many a Broadway musical comedy success, its history deserves to be detailed.

The libretto was the work of Bertolt Brecht, a writer with strong leftist political leanings. Brecht had attended a German revival of John Gay's historic ballad opera, *The Beggar's Opera. The Beggar's Opera* had been written in the early eighteenth century and had created a furor in London when first produced. Gay's text was a travesty on Italian opera while mocking and laying bare the corruption of English politicians and the sham of English high society. To this text, a composer named John Christopher Pepusch had contributed a musical score made up largely of popular English and Scottish ballads and tunes of his day. *The Beggar's Opera* had been responsible for creating a vogue for ballad opera that lasted almost a century, and at the same time it did much to discredit the more serious form of opera then being written by George Frideric Handel.

Brecht decided to modernize Gay's ballad opera and make it applicable to the Germany of Brecht's times. He opened his play with a prologue in which a Soho street musician tells the history of Macheath, a highwayman. The story unfolds in the next three acts. Peachum, chief of the Beggars' Guild, is upset to discover that his daughter, Polly, has married Macheath, known as Mack the Knife. He threatens to go to the police to incriminate Macheath. The highwayman goes into hiding, but is apprehended. He manages to escape from prison, but once again he is captured, and this time he is condemned to die at the gallows. At the zero hour, as the rope is about to be tied around his neck, Macheath gets a royal pardon. The Queen does more than that: She presents Macheath with a castle and a yearly pension.

Since Brecht had already worked well with Weill on a one-act opera, the composer was asked to provide the score for this libretto. Weill complied with lively, melodious, catching music that combined elements of opera with jazz, Bach-like chorales with beer-hall tunes. Play and music became a delightful brew mixing together cabaret, opera, operetta, theatre, music hall, the beer hall. When *The Three-Penny Opera,* as the Brecht-Weill song-play was called, went into rehearsal, most of the performers were convinced that the production was both too unusual and too eclectic to achieve acceptance. The final dress rehearsal went so badly that the owner of the theatre might have cancelled the production if he had had another play to present in its place.

The Three-Penny Opera opened in Berlin on August 31, 1928. Lotte Lenya, who played one of the leading roles (and who since 1926 had been Kurt Weill's wife), recalled many years later how that first-night audience reacted. "Up to the stable scene the audience seemed cold and apathetic, as though convinced in advance that it had come to a certain 'flop.' Then . . . an unbelievable uproar went up, and from that point on it was wonderfully, intoxicatingly clear that the public was with us. However, late the next morning as we were waiting for the first reviews, there persisted a crassy unreality about what had happened; nobody quite dared believe in our success. Nor did the reviews confirm it for us—they were decidedly mixed. Hollander wrote that he had slept through the entire performance."

Nevertheless, *The Three-Penny Opera* soon created a fever in Berlin. It was the topic of conversation everywhere. Its tunes were heard in the streets; a special bar, called *The*

Three-Penny Opera, was opened to play only the music from the score. The first year found over one hundred German theatres presenting it. Within five years, the work had been given over ten thousand times, in eighteen languages, throughout central Europe. It had also been made into a highly acclaimed German-language motion picture.

For a time it appeared that *The Three-Penny Opera* was too Germanic to appeal to Americans. When first given in New York, in 1933, it limped through thirteen performances before expiring. But two decades after that, Marc Blitzstein rewrote and modernized the text without changing Weill's music. (Blitzstein was the brilliant American composer whose social-conscious opera *The Cradle Will Rock* had been inspired by and imitative of Kurt Weill's song-plays.) Blitzstein's version of *The Three-Penny Opera* was produced off-Broadway on March 10, 1954, where it stayed more than six years to become New York's longest running musical up to that time. Two national companies toured the rest of the country. The most popular number from the Weill score, "Mack the Knife," now sold over ten million discs in forty-eight versions, including the one that first made Bobby Darin a recording star.

In 1929, Kurt Weill and Bertolt Brecht wrote *Happy End,* a song-play about gangsterism in Chicago. A recording by Andy Williams of one of its numbers, "The Bilbao Song," became a hit in America in 1961. On March 9, 1930, Weill and Brecht created a sensation in Germany with *The Rise and Fall of the City of Mahagonny* (an expansion into three acts of a one-act opera they had written some years earlier). It was produced simultaneously at the Frankfort and Leipzig Operas. Here, too, the writers lay a sharp-edged scalpel to the body of modern society and capitalism to reveal the corruption and degradation they felt grow under the skin like a cancer. Mahagonny was a fictional town in America's Alabama, a town established in the wilderness by three ex-convicts. In their society, people could do whatever they wished without a second thought about morality or ethics. The important things in Mahagonny were eating, love, boxing, and drinking—in that order. The only sin was to be poor. Mahagonny is menaced by an economic crash and a hurricane, but it withstands both successfully, just as it is able to cope with the decaying influence of the corruption and vices of its citizens. "The atmosphere of Berlin of the 1920s," wrote H. H. Stuckenschmidt, a distinguished German music critic, "has found no more anguished expression than in this opera . . . a document of its times."

Embellished with a procession of ragtime, blues, music-hall tunes, and Tin Pan Alley melodies, *The Rise and Fall of the City of Mahagonny* proved as iconoclastic and as irreverent in music as it was in text. "Alabamy Song" became one of Germany's leading hit songs of the early 1930s. This was a number with gibberish English lyrics that sounded as if they came from Tin Pan Alley without making any sense.

The Nazi Swastika was now beginning to rise over the horizon of Germany. At the opening night performance of *The Rise and Fall of the City of Mahagonny,* brown shirts provoked a riot by throwing stink bombs, yelling disapproval, and instigating fist-fights in the audience. In Leipzig, the management decided to keep the theatre lights on throughout the performance to prevent matters from getting out of hand. In Frankfort, one man in the audience was shot and killed.

The Nazis, then, did not like the Weill song-play, because of its pronounced left-wing propaganda and because Kurt Weill was a Jew. Once the Nazis seized power, the composer became *persona non grata,* and his song-plays were censored. Upon opening a Museum of Degenerate Art, the Nazis exhibited *The Three-Penny Opera* as an example of decadence; tunes from the opera were played constantly in one of the rooms. This exhibit had to be summarily removed when the Nazis saw how many people crowded into the room to listen to the music. A number of years later, during World War II, the German underground movement used the song "Mack the Knife" as a signal for its members.

Just before the control of Germany fell into Nazi hands, Kurt Weill's song-play *The Silver Lake* opened simultaneously in eleven German cities. This was a thinly disguised indictment of Hitler and Nazism. A month later, when Hitler and the Nazis were in power, Weill's life was in danger. With his wife, Lotte, he managed to escape from Germany. For the next two years, the Weills lived on the outskirts of Paris where he wrote the music for a number of stage productions mounted both in Paris and in London.

In the fall of 1935, Weill came to New York to write the music for *The Eternal Road.* This was an elaborate pageant tracing the history of the Jewish people. This mammoth production was not seen until 1937. Before then, however, on November 19, 1936, Weill made his debut as a composer for the Broadway theatre with *Johnny Johnson,* a bitter satire on war which Robert Benchley called "the most effective of all satires in its class . . . the first anti-war play to use laughing gas in its attack on the stupidity of mankind." For all the brilliance of the text (the work of Paul Green) and the haunting impact of the music, *Johnny Johnson* was a box-office failure. Audiences in late 1936 were perhaps not yet ready to accept a musical fantasy developed with such daring and originality.

But Weill did not wait long for success, even if at first it proved only a minor one. It came on October 19, 1938, with *Knickerbocker Holiday,* text and lyrics by Maxwell Anderson, one of America's most distinguished dramatists. The place of this text was New Amsterdam, and the time 1647. Peter Stuyvesant is Governor General. He is married to a girl many years younger than he and who, in turn, is loved by Brom Broeck, a young political rebel. The writers went back to distant American history to point a moral very much needed to be told in 1938, what with Europe in the thralls of Fascism and Nazism and Communism, the world on the brink of war, and liberties in America seriously endangered by the international situation. The tyrannical Peter Stuyvesant became the predecessor of the twentieth-century Fascist, and the ruthless way he controls and rules New Amsterdam is a warning to twentieth-century Americans of what can happen when freedom is curtailed. The political message is emphasized in the song "How Can You Tell an American?," in which true Americans are identified by their love of liberty.

Peter Stuyvesant was played by a hardy veteran of the stage, here making his first appearance in musical comedy—Walter Huston. The thoroughly pragmatic manner in which Kurt Weill operated—one of the reasons for his sustained success in several different media of the musical theatre—is demonstrated by the way in which he wrote the hit song of this musical while bearing in mind Huston's vocal limitations. "September Song" was a number in which Peter Stuyvesant ruminates on the problems facing a middle-aged man married to a young girl. In planning his songs for Huston, Weill wired the actor, then in Hollywood, inquiring about the range of his voice. Huston wired back: "No range, no voice"—which was true. Huston's singing left much to be desired, since he possessed unattractive, rasping, nasal tones. Weill was introduced to Huston's nonsinging style on a coast-to-coast broadcast in which Huston was starred. Faced with the necessity of consigning the most important song of *Knickerbocker*

Holiday to Huston, Weill kept Huston's highly personal, non-vocal delivery in mind in shaping the melodic line. The result was not only a song with a unique personality but also a song that profited from Huston's individual vocal delivery.

If *Knickerbocker Holiday* represented a minor success for Weill (its engagement extending for only 168 performances), his next musical proved a major one. It was *Lady in the Dark,* in 1941. Having himself recently undergone psychoanalytic treatment, Moss Hart felt that there was good musical comedy material in psychoanalysis. He fashioned a book in which the heroine, Liza Elliott, a highly successful magazine editor, undergoes psychotherapy, to avert a nervous breakdown. Much of the text is devoted to dream sequences that help the psychoanalyst to seek out the cause of her emotional disturbance. The story also takes place partly in the heroine's real world as editor and in her romantic involvement with Charles Johnson, on the one hand, and Randy Curtis, on the other. A tune, "My Ship," which keeps haunting Liza's memory continually, and which she had learned in childhood, helps to unlock the door to Liza's problem. As a girl she had come to regard herself as an ugly duckling, having lost a succession of boy friends. She then found refuge in plainness, in a rejection of her womanhood. Once this truth dawns on her, she can love Charles Johnson without inhibitions and arrive at a fuller and happier life both as an editor and as a wife.

Moss Hart's exceptional text, Ira Gershwin's adroit and subtle lyrics, and a fresh and ingratiating score by Weill that included songs like "My Ship," "This Is New," and "Saga of Jenny" were not the only components to make *Lady in the Dark* the remarkable success it was. Two performers were also significant contributions. Gertrude Lawrence, as Liza, was in her element, whether as the introverted and aloof editor or as the brazen and irresponsible lady who couldn't make up her mind in "Saga of Jenny." "Suddenly, startlingly," wrote her husband Richard Aldrich, in recalling the first time he heard her sing the saga, "the exquisite, glamorous Gertrude Lawrence was transformed into a tough, bawdy dive singer. As a piece of impromptu impersonation it was superb with few parallels."

The other performer who helped make *Lady in the Dark* as good as it was was a comedian making his bow in a musical show. Danny Kaye was cast as Russell Paxton, a photographer employed by Liza's magazine. This was at best a minor part, but it was enough to allow Kaye to reveal for the first time his enormous potential as a comedian and his remarkable agility in delivering patter songs. Ira Gershwin provided him with one of the latter, a set of fleeting lyrics made up almost entirely of the names of Russian composers. That song, "Tchaikovsky"—which, in the show, immediately preceded Gertrude Lawrence's presentation of "Saga of Jenny"—was a show-stopper and remained a Danny Kaye tour de force.

One Touch of Venus, in 1943, was an even greater box-office success than *Lady in the Dark.* Here Kurt Weill's principal collaborator was Ogden Nash, one of America's most celebrated creators of light verse. Nash provided the lyrics and helped S. J. Perelman in writing the text. Mary Martin was here starred as the statue of Venus come to life. She falls in love with Rodney Hatch and thereby complicates his romance with Gloria. He succumbs to Venus's beauty and charm. But in a dream sequence he is made forcefully aware of what his life would be like were he to marry Venus and live with her in a suburban development. Renouncing Venus, who now reverts to her former inanimate state as a statue in a museum, Rodney begs for Gloria's forgiveness. Gloria, however, refuses to have anything more to do with Rodney.

He now pays a visit to the museum to look with longing eyes on the statue he had recently loved as a woman. A young girl, who resembles the statue of Venus in appearance, comes to him with a question. They exchange small talk and then walk out of the museum, hand in hand.

The problem of integrating music and text had concerned Weill from the beginnings of his career on Broadway. With *Street Scene,* in 1947, he embraced the medium of the musical play, for which he was so extraordinarily well equipped through his musical training, sound musical instincts, and innate creative gifts. *Street Scene,* described in the program as a "folk play with music," was an adaptation of a celebrated stage play by Elmer Rice that had won the Pulitzer Prize in drama in 1929. This was a realistic play of life-in-the-raw in a tenement house in one of New York City's slum areas. No escapism, here, no glamour, no star dust! This was a picture of frustrated people driven by elemental passions and seemingly hopeless dreams. Anna Maurant is a middle-aged woman starving for love which her husband does not give her. She tries to find romance with a milkman, whom her husband murders in a fit of jealousy. Their daughter, Rosa, and a young college student, Sam Kaplan, are also searching for love and understanding. Sam is willing to give up his education—and his ambitions to become a lawyer—in order to marry Rosa, but she refuses to let him make a sacrifice that would ruin his life the way ignorance and poverty destroyed her parents. She flees from the tenement and from Sam to try finding a new life elsewhere with her little brother.

Music with text are here woven into a single fabric. As Weill himself told an interviewer: "Not until *Street Scene* did I achieve a real blending of drama and music in which the singing continues naturally where the speaking stops, and the spoken word, as well as the dramatic action, is embedded in the overall musical structure." With the experienced hand of a man who had written operas, Weill was able to find the musical *mot juste* for every emotional nuance in the text. "His music," said Rosamond Gilder in *Theatre Arts,* "reflects the hot night, the chatter and gossiping housewives, the sound of children at play, the ebb and flow of anonymous existence." It also caught and fixed the high dramatic moments in several unforgettable individual numbers: "Somehow I Never Could Believe," for example, "Lonely House" or "We'll Go Away Together," for all of which Langston Hughes, the distinguished Negro poet, wrote the lyrics.

Realism and stark drama could also be found in Weill's last musical play, *Lost in the Stars,* in 1949. The problem of racial conflict in South Africa (as detailed in a powerful novel, *Cry the Beloved Country* by Alan Paton) is the substance of a musical drama that combines high tension with conflict, and compassion with deeply moving human values. Absalom, son of a small-town Negro parson, falls in love with Irina in the South African metropolis Johannesburg. Needing money to support her, he gets involved in a robbery during which he murders a white man. He confesses his guilt and is sentenced to be hanged. The old parson is broken by the tragedy befalling his family. When the father of the murdered man comes to visit him, he is moved by the old man's touching and dignified sorrow. Their common grief suddenly becomes a bond of sympathy and understanding between them.

Music and text are one and indivisible. With eloquent individual numbers and stirring choral pages, Weill reflects both the immense grief of the two old men (one black, the other white) at the loss of their respective sons and their awakening to tolerance and a feeling of brotherhood brought about by the sorrow they shared.

Some authorities have long maintained that when American operas get written they will come from the Broadway musical theatre. Weill was one of them. He told an interviewer: "You hear a lot of talk about 'American opera' that's going to come along some day. It's my opinion that we can and will develop musical-dramatic form in this country, but I don't think it will be called 'opera,' or that it will grow out of the opera which has become a thing separate from the commercial theatre. It will develop from, and remain a part of, the American theatre—'Broadway theatre' if you like."

Weill himself proved the wisdom of this belief. Both *Street Scene* and *Lost in the Stars* have been successfully produced by the New York City Opera as part of its regular repertory and as notable examples of American opera. Regrettably, Weill did not live to see this development, which would have given him much personal satisfaction. He died of a heart attack in New York on April 3, 1950. "He was probably the most original single workman in the whole musical theatre, internationally considered, during the last quarter of a century," wrote Virgil Thomson in an eloquent eulogy. "He was an architect, a master of musico-dramatic design, whose structure, built for function and solidity, constitutes a repertory of models that have not only served well their original purpose but also had wide influence on composers as examples of procedure." Brooks Atkinson was also fully appreciative of Weill's significance. A number of years after Weill's death he wrote: "Everyone agrees that Mr. Weill was one of the finest composers we have had in the last twenty-five years, and there is reason to think he was the best."

XI

FREDERICK LOEWE

(1904-)

TO FREDERICK LOEWE goes the distinction of having written the score for *My Fair Lady,* the most successful musical production in Broadway history. Its original run of 2,717 performances established a new record for musicals, and so did its London run of 2,281 for that city. A national company touring the United States for several years grossed over twenty million dollars. Twenty-one foreign productions were given in eleven languages, in countries from Iceland to Japan, from Israel to the Soviet Union. In all, the total gross of productions the world over exceeded eighty million dollars.

The motion-picture rights sold for an all-time high: five and a half million dollars and a percentage of the gross. Released in 1964 (starring Rex Harrison and Audrey Hepburn) it captured eight Academy Awards, including the one as best picture of the year. Its take at the box offices throughout the world placed it solidly among the all-time cinema leaders.

Fifty recordings were made of the score, not only in English but also in Hebrew, Spanish, and Italian. The original-cast recording made by Columbia sold more than five million discs, something without even a close parallel up to that time. The original soundtrack recording of the motion picture sold another million discs.

In contemplating these and other staggering figures, a representative of the publishing house of Chappell, which by issuing all the music gathered a windfall all its own, said this of *My Fair Lady:* "It's the biggest thing we've seen since we've been in business, and that's three hundred years."

A high-water mark in the history of the American theatre, *My Fair Lady* was, of course, also the high-water mark in the career of Frederick Loewe.

Loewe's individuality and strength as a composer spring from his ability to combine a dramatic expressiveness and an American identity with a haunting, poetic, and at times sententious lyricism that has a good deal of Viennese *Gemütlichkeit* to it. This *Gemütlichkeit* comes to him by way of heritage, birth, and early upbringing. Loewe was born in Vienna on June 10, 1904. His father was a distinguished operetta tenor who had appeared in the world premières of two of the most famous Viennese operettas ever written—Oscar Straus's *The Chocolate Soldier* and Franz Lehar's *The Merry Widow.* The waltzes and sentimental songs of these and other Viennese musicals were what Frederick heard most often at home; and his earliest experiences in the theatre came from hearing and seeing these operettas.

Frederick was precocious in music. He began showing an interest in the piano when he was five, and at seven he took his first lessons. Once he had some facility in picking out tunes at the keyboard, he started inventing them. He wrote a few popular songs while he was still a child, which his father sang in variety theatres throughout Europe. When Frederick was fifteen his song "Katrina" became so popular all over Europe that it had a sheet-music sale of two million copies.

Despite this early preoccupation and success with popular music he was thinking of a concert career as pianist. He went to Berlin for intensive study at the Stern Conservatory. In the ensuing years he received some of the best piano training available in Europe at the time—with Ferruccio Busoni (Kurt Weill's teacher later) and Eugene d'Albert. Loewe made such progress that when he was thirteen he appeared as soloist with the Berlin Symphony, the youngest piano virtuoso ever to get a hearing with that distinguished organization. By the time his piano studies had ended in 1922 he received one of the most highly regarded German awards for pianist, the Hollander medal. He now turned for a year of study of composition with Nikolaus von Reznicek.

He came to the United States in 1924, hoping to advance his career both as concert pianist and as composer. (This was not his first visit to America. That had taken place in 1906 when, as an infant of two, he had been brought to the United States by his father for a brief visit.) Loewe failed to make headway in music. A piano recital at Town Hall, New York, attracted little attention. An assignment to play the piano at the Rivoli Theatre, a motion picture house in New York, proved temporary, and so did a job to perform in a nightclub in New York's Greenwich Village. There followed for Loewe a picaresque career during which he worked in many different jobs, in many different places. He was a busboy in a cafeteria. He taught horseback riding in a New Hampshire resort. He engaged in professional prize fights in Brooklyn, New York (for five dollars an engagement!), winning his first eight bouts in the bantamweight class, and then getting such a terrific beating that he decided he was through with boxing for good. He went out West where he was a cowpuncher, a gold prospector, and a mail carrier on horseback.

Returning East, he went back to his piano as a means of

livelihood. In those days of Prohibition, boats plied regularly between Miami and Havana, carrying fun-loving Americans to a place where the sale of hard liquor was legal. Loewe was hired to entertain the travelers. Later, in the early thirties, he found a steady job in a German beer hall in the Yorkville section of New York. He was beginning to write songs again. He joined the Players Club, on Gramercy Park—haunt of theatrical folks—with the hope of finding somebody influential to promote his music. He did find such a person—Dennis King, an established star of operetta and musical comedy. In 1934, King sang a Loewe song, "Love Tiptoed Through My Heart," in a nonmusical Broadway play, *Petticoat Fever*. Another Loewe song, "A Waltz Was Born in Vienna," was danced by Gomez and Winona in a production, *Illustrators Show,* that had a five-day run at the 48th Street Theatre in 1936. Neither represented a particularly auspicious beginning for Loewe's career in the theatre. But it was a beginning, nevertheless.

Loewe now tied up with Earl Crooker, a script writer for radio and the movies. They wrote a musical comedy, *Salute to Spring,* produced by the St. Louis Opera during the summer of 1937. A successful Broadway producer, Dwight Deere Wiman, thought so much of its songs that he signed both Crooker and Loewe to write the numbers for a Broadway musical. *Great Lady,* in 1937, was an elaborate production with a star-studded cast, but its whole lifespan was just twenty-eight performances. Loewe's songs proved too Viennese and saccharine for American consumption, particularly at a time when the Viennese-type operetta had lost its audience on Broadway.

Songwriting, Loewe now had to realize, was no way to support himself and his wife (he had married an Austrian girl in 1931). He went back to playing the piano in restaurants. He also made one more futile try at concert work, with a recital in Carnegie Hall in New York, in 1942, that found most of the hall empty, and most of the critics silent.

One day in 1942, Loewe was at the Lambs Club discussing with a Detroit producer the possibility of using the songs from *Salute to Spring* for a farce by Barry Connor, *The Patsy*. The producer was interested—but only if Loewe could adapt the songs for the new show in two weeks' time and if he could find somebody to revamp and spruce up the old Crooker lyrics. Pondering this problem, Loewe espied at the club Alan Jay Lerner, a young writer of radio scripts. Loewe invited Lerner to join him in the assignment. As it happened, at this very time Lerner had also come to a dead end as far as his career was concerned. Loewe's proposition offered Lerner a new route, and he grabbed it. It was his first commission to write for the stage.

Lerner and Loewe left for Detroit where they spent two weeks shaping a musical which they now named *Life of the Party*. It was produced in that city in October of 1942, and then was forgotten. Its sole significance is that it marked the debut of the songwriting team of Lerner and Loewe.

Their next collaboration did reach Broadway. It was *What's Up?*, a musical comedy opening on November 11, 1943. Jimmy Savo, the gifted pantomimist and comedian, played the part of the Rawa of Tanglinia, an East Indian potentate, come to America for conferences in Washington. The plane on which he and his entourage are traveling is grounded near a school for girls. The East Indian visitors are quarantined for eight days because of a measles epidemic, but they make the most of this development by running after the girls. Jimmy Savo notwithstanding, *What's Up?* was a "dud" both in the text and in the music. "I could say it was a disaster," Lerner commented some years later, "but disaster is too cheerful a word."

They returned to Broadway with *The Day Before Spring* in 1945. This time they did much better, not so much at the box office as with the critics. The text described a tenth-anniversary class reunion, attended by Peter Townsend and his wife Katherine. Katherine meets an old school beau, Alex; when they were seniors they had planned to elope but were frustrated when their car broke down. Meeting again, even though after the passing of a decade, they find they are still interested in each other. In fact, they plan to run off together. Once again the breakdown of their car thwarts them. Katherine now reconciles herself to spending the rest of her life with her husband.

This inconsequential plot was developed with a lightness of touch and a most ingratiating humor. The songs contributed a charm all their own, the best being "God's Green World," "I Love You, This Morning," and "My Love Is a Married Man." Wolcott Gibbs described them as "fresh and bright" springing "spontaneously from the action rather than from spasmodic impulses on the part of the singers."

While working on *The Day Before Spring,* Loewe happened to mention to Lerner something about the ability of faith to move mountains. "This started me thinking," says Lerner. "For a while I had a play about faith moving mountains. From here we went to all sorts of miracles occurring through faith, and eventually faith moved a town."

This was the origin of *Brigadoon,* a musical play with which Lerner and Loewe finally reached heights in 1947. *Brigadoon* was "a whimsical musical fantasy" with a Scottish setting, Brigadoon being a magic village which had disappeared in 1747 but which comes back to life once every hundred years. Whoever stumbles upon Brigadoon during its brief return to existence becomes a part of its life and activity until the town once again evaporates into the Highland mists.

Two American tourists, Tommy and Jeff, find Brigadoon on that one day in a century when it becomes alive again. They are enchanted with it. Tommy falls in love with one of the lasses, Fiona, even though he has a sweetheart back in America. He now wants to stay in Brigadoon forever. By thumbing through an old album and identifying some of the characters he had come across with people living a hundred years earlier, both he and Jeff are made aware of the fact that this is no ordinary town, that in fact it exists in fantasy rather than reality. Reality dictates they go home, Tommy to marry his American sweetheart. Back in New York, Tommy cannot forget either Brigadoon or Fiona. He returns to Scotland with Jeff to try to find them again. They are nowhere to be seen. Suddenly Brigadoon's schoolmaster appears out of the mists. He tells Tommy that love can accomplish anything, even miracles. He takes Tommy by the hand and leads him away, as Tommy waves a final farewell to Jeff, who is left behind.

The utter enchantment evoked by Lerner's story and poetic dialogue, and Loewe's thoroughly compatible music, remains irresistible, however many times the play is revived (which is repeatedly) or even if it is transferred to some other medium, such as motion pictures or television. "The plot works beautifully," wrote Brooks Atkinson. "Mr. Lerner organized his story. He does not get down to the details of the fairy story until the audiences had already been won by the pleasant characters, the exuberant music, and the grim though fiery dances. After that, the incantation is complete and easy." As for the music—many of Loewe's songs beat with the pulse of true Scottish folk tunes: "Come to Me, Bend to Me," "The Heather on the Hill," and "Waitin' for My Dearie." The main love song, "Almost Like Being in Love" (it became one of the major hit songs of 1956), has more Broadway in it than Scotland—a significant indication that Loewe had been able to free himself from his onetime all too strong Viennese mannerisms. But what was most important about these and other songs, whether Scottish or Broadwayish, was the way in which they continually caught the spirit and enhanced the fanciful mood of the play. This spirit and mood were also captured in three remarkable ballet sequences. Play, music, and dance were combined into what Brooks Atkinson did not hesitate to describe as a "vibrant work of art." The Drama Critics Circle, recognizing the artistic importance of this musical play, singled it out as the best of the year, the first time it had conferred this honor on a musical production.

Where *Brigadoon* had been Scottish, *Paint Your Wagon,* in 1951, was thoroughly American—early American. This musical play was a greater artistic than financial success. Its major significance lies in that it demonstrated a further strengthening of those creative forces soon to come into full play in the writing of *My Fair Lady.*

The background of *Paint Your Wagon* is the Western Gold Rush of the mid 1800s. The thread of the story ties together the history of a mining camp from its beginnings, through its boom days, and up to the time it has disintegrated into a ghost town. The American folk element is given strong emphasis in all the departments: in Lerner's homespun dialogue, in episodes involving saloon brawls, and in the raucous humor and uninhibited horseplay of miners; in Oliver Smith's evocative designs and costumes; in Agnes de Mille's thoroughly American folk ballets; and in songs that almost have the quality of authentic American folk ballads—such as "They Call the Wind Maria," "I Talk to the Trees," and "Wand'rin' Star."

Almost five years went by before Lerner and Loewe were

again represented on Broadway. This return took place on March 15, 1956—a truly historic event, for this was when *My Fair Lady* had its New York première.

Whereas in each of the earlier Lerner and Loewe musicals the text had been original with Lerner, in *My Fair Lady* it was an adaptation—the source being George Bernard Shaw's comedy *Pygmalion*. Pygmalion is that legendary Greek character who fashions the statue of Galatea with which he falls in love. In the Shaw play, Galatea is Liza Doolittle, a Cockney flower girl, and Pygmalion is Henry Higgins, professor of phonetics. Under his guidance and instruction the uncouth and illiterate Liza is transformed into a young lady of refinement and culture who is welcomed with open arms by London's high society.

Pygmalion was the first Shaw play to be filmed, produced by Gabriel Pascal. Pascal was then fired with the ambition to make *Pygmalion* into a stage musical, but Shaw failed to show any interest. Not until Shaw died was Pascal able to acquire short-term rights for a musical adaptation. His negotiations with various Broadway producers and musical comedy writers led nowhere. When Pascal died in 1954 the whole project seemed to have perished with him.

On the strength of their work in *Brigadoon* and *Paint Your Wagon,* Lerner and Loewe were among the writers Pascal had approached. They were fascinated by the project from the very beginning, and retained their enthusiasm even after Pascal died. They started negotiations of their own to gain the rights for the Shaw play, which were finally consummated with the Shaw estate in July 1955. Herman Levin was singled out as producer, and Rex Harrison was immediately engaged to play the part of Higgins. Largely because of the enthusiasm and faith of Goddard Lieberson, president of Columbia Records, the Columbia Broadcasting System took over the financing exclusively, to the tune of $400,000.

The search to find an actress for Liza Doolittle ended with the engagement of a comparative newcomer—Julie Andrews, who had then recently made her American debut in an off-Broadway musical, *The Boy Friend.* After that, the other distinguished collaborators fell into place: Moss Hart as director; Hanya Holm as choreographer; Cecil Beaton as costume designer; Oliver Smith as set designer.

The Shaw play posed a number of disturbing problems for the adaptors. In Shaw's *Pygmalion* the love interest was so amorphous that hero and heroine never even exchanged a kiss. Shaw himself had even insisted that there was no romantic tie between them. How to develop a musical play without a love story was a question that disturbed Lerner no end. But there was a greater problem still. The main point of interest in the play is Liza's transformation, and the high climactic point arrives when the Cockney girl finally masters phonetics to a point where she can pronounce "rain" and "Spain" correctly, and not in the Cockney fashion of "rine" and "Spine." How can an adaptor make an exercise in diction a moment to seize the fascinated interest, and arouse the excitement, of an audience?

After wrestling with these and various other thorny problems, Lerner and Loewe came to the conclusion that the best method of operation would be to permit the play to stand as it was, to make no attempt either to change it or to improve it. "All we had to do," Lerner has explained, "was to add to our adaptation those things that Shaw had happening offstage."

As in the Shaw play, so in the musical adaptation. Liza Doolittle is a Cockney flower girl selling bouquets outside Covent Garden, London, in 1912. Henry Higgins, a phonetician, becomes interested in her accent and behavior, both of which betray her humble background and her lack of education and refinement. Higgins is convinced he can teach her to be a lady and so transform her speech, manners, behavior, and appearance that she can be mistaken for a duchess. A wager with his friend, Colonel Pickering, leads Higgins to embark on the experiment. Liza comes to live with Higgins and he takes great pains to convince Liza's father, a Cockney partial to the bottle, that his interest in Liza is solely to make her into a great lady.

The process of reeducation proves arduous and painful. But Higgins's efforts are not in vain. Liza turns into an elegant and beautiful woman, the last word in social poise, grace, and diction. She makes her first appearance in high society at the races at Ascot, where she attracts the interest of young Freddy. But her real test comes at the Embassy Ball, to which she comes exquisitely gowned, and where she is taken for Hungarian royalty.

Her triumph is complete, but Liza herself is not satisfied. She turns angrily on Higgins, wanting to know what will become of her now that she has been made into a lady. It would have been better by far to have allowed her to remain a Cockney flower girl. When Higgins suggests she go out and find a nice young man to marry, she packs her belongings, and angrily storms out of Higgins' house. She returns to the flower mart where nobody recognizes her, not even her father, whose thoughts are focused on his imminent marriage. Liza then pays a visit to Higgins's mother. Higgins finds her there and becomes aroused when Liza tells him that Freddy has asked her to marry him. To Liza, Higgins's reaction is most unreasonable. She insists she is free to marry anybody she wishes and that she has no interest in Higgins's advice or guidance.

Back at his home, Higgins is restive and lonely. He misses the presence of Liza, for he has become accustomed to her face. Although deep in thought he becomes aware that Liza has slipped into the house. As he orders Liza to bring him his slippers, the final curtain descends slowly.

The combined gifts of librettist-lyricist, composer, stage director, costume and stage designers, and choreographer all blended harmoniously into a production that Brooks Atkinson regarded as "one of the best musicals of the century . . . close to the genius of creation." For the races at Ascot and for the Embassy Ball, Hanya Holm created stunning ballet sequences, abetted and supplemented by the opulence with which the stage and the characters were dressed up and the thoroughly seductive lilt and pulse of Loewe's elegant music. The production was all of one piece in which the imagination of several highly gifted creators coalesced into a single artistic concept. This happy union of many minds and many imaginations proved particularly felicitous in carrying the play toward its climax when Liza reveals for the first time that Higgins's experiment is successful. An extended song sequence with Spanish overtones, "The Rain in Spain" achieves both dramatic and comic interest, particularly when the joy of Higgins, Pickering, and Liza finds expression in an uninhibited fandango dance. Song, dialogue, dance, pantomime, and comedy are here combined to create a moment to seize the audience and hold it spellbound. "You listen astonished because you believe in her so completely that you didn't really suppose she could make it," Walter Kerr wrote. "Suddenly her delight becomes yours. And when Mr. Harrison, together with an equally astonished Robert Coote, bounces irresistibly to the center of the stage and begins to kick out a tango rhythm to the sound she has just made, there is no controlling the joy in the theatre."

There was joy in that theatre in many another sequence. There is the moment when Liza makes her first appearance as a lady of quality and her rapture at having been accepted as such at the Embassy Ball, expressed in her song "I Could Have Danced All Night." In other numbers a rich slice of Cockney humor is cut from the delicious cake in old man Doolittle's two main numbers, "Get Me to the Church on Time" and "With a Little Bit of Luck"; insights are given into Liza's personality in "Wouldn't It Be Loverly?," "Show Me," and "Without You"; and Higgins's sophistication is found in "Why Can't the English?," "I'm an Ordinary Man," and "A Hymn to Him." Other songs reach toward the romantic and the sentimental: "On the Street Where You Live," which achieved hit status, and "I've Grown Accustomed to Her Face."

Bountiful, glamorous, spellbinding, at turns gay and sentimental, *My Fair Lady* had every possible ingredient in a recipe for an unforgettable musical play. This was exalted musical theatre, and its fabulous success was the expression of gratitude by public and critics alike.

The next two musical productions upon which Lerner and Loewe collaborated—one for the screen, the other for the stage—were attempts (conscious or otherwise) to use once again some of the ingredients that made *My Fair Lady* so good.

The motion-picture musical *Gigi,* in 1957, carried more than one recollection of *My Fair Lady.* Besides Lerner and Loewe, a third member affiliated with the stage triumph, had been recruited—Cecil Beaton—to design sets and costumes. The plot, based on a story by Colette, also carried an echo or two from Shaw's *Pygmalion.* Gigi is a gawky, teen-age tomboy in Paris who resists all the efforts of her grandmother and grandaunt to learn the refinements of a great lady. She is cynical about love and disgusted with elegant Frenchmen.

But a young man comes into her life—an attractive, dashing bachelor—and he helps to bring about Gigi's transformation. Leslie Caron played the girl; Louis Jourdan, the bachelor. The title song in which the young bachelor recognizes that Gigi is a young lady of beauty and quality is not much different from "I've Grown Accustomed to Her Face"—and this similarity is possibly not altogether coincidental. "The Night They Invented Champagne," "I Remember It Well," "Thank Heaven for Little Girls," "I'm Glad I'm Not Young Anymore," are other memorable song treasures to remind us again and again of *My Fair Lady*. The title song and the motion picture itself were recipients of Academy Awards, while seven other Oscars were bestowed upon other departments. This was the first time in the history of the Academy that a single motion picture got nine awards.

When they finally returned to Broadway with *Camelot,* in 1960, Lerner and Loewe carried the heavy responsibility of creating a musical that would not be obliterated by the enormous, far-reaching shadow of *My Fair Lady*. Their subject was King Arthur and his Round Table in eighth-century Camelot, by way of a novel by T. H. White, *The Once and Future King*. The musical-stage adaptation finds Guinevere come to marry King Arthur. Shy and nervous, he is hiding in the woods where he is discovered by Guinevere, who does not know who he is. Charmed with one another, they finally reveal their respective identities, delighted upon discovering that they are to become husband and wife. After they are married, the king forms his Round Table. Lancelot comes from France with the hope of being a Round Table knight. He is a cocky, self-assured fellow who instantly arouses Guinevere's displeasure. She instigates him to engage three knights in a jousting match to prove his valor. When he emerges triumphant, Guinevere's contempt turns to admiration. Realizing he is falling in love with the queen, Lancelot leaves Camelot. He comes back two years later when, at long last, he is made a knight of the Round Table in an impressive ceremony. The love between Guinevere and Lancelot now blossoms, a situation about which King Arthur is fully aware. During the king's absence, Lancelot visits Guinevere in her chambers where they are discovered by Mordred and his men. Found guilty of treachery, Lancelot is imprisoned, but he escapes. Guinevere is then doomed to die at the stake, but she, too, manages to flee to France. Because of these developments, Arthur and his knights go to war against France, but on encountering Lancelot and Guinevere on the field of battle he forgives them.

Most of the component parts that had gone to make up *My Fair Lady* were once again used: Lerner and Loewe; Moss Hart as stage director; Hanya Holm as choreographer; Oliver Smith as scenic designer; Julie Andrews as the heroine and Robert Coote in a subsidiary role; Franz Allers as musical director; and Robert Russell Bennett as orchestrator. All the same *Camelot* was no *My Fair Lady*. Yet it was not without visual and aural appeal. It was magnificently mounted with emphasis on glamour. It was magnificently cast, with Julie Andrews supplemented by Richard Burton playing King Arthur and Robert Goulet as Sir Lancelot, the last in his American stage debut. And some of its songs were appealing, such as "How to Handle a Woman," "What Do Simple Folk Do?," "If Ever I Would Leave You," and the title number. But expectations had been too high: *Camelot* arrived on Broadway with the largest advance sale in its history, about three million dollars. And expressions of disappointment were keen. Many critics felt that it was too much of an old-fashioned operetta and too little a musical play. Howard Taubman felt that Lerner and Loewe badly missed "their late collaborator—Bernard Shaw." Richard Watts, Jr., felt that "a curious air of heaviness" hung over it. Robert Coleman called *Camelot* "an expensive disappointment."

Camelot was a child of sorrow. While it was being planned and projected in 1958, Frederick Loewe suffered a serious heart attack, and while working on the score a year later, he had to husband his energies and strength. Nor was Loewe the only one who was handicapped physically. While the production was getting into shape, two other major collaborators had to go to the hospital—Moss Hart, with a heart attack, and Alan Jay Lerner with bleeding ulcers. These calamities were not all that afflicted *Camelot*. It was no secret that Lerner and Loewe were no longer working harmoniously. Tension, strain, poor health made each man increasingly irritable, increasingly critical of the other's efforts, increasingly intolerant of the other's idiosyncrasies. Even as they worked on *Camelot*, each knew that he was working with the other for the last time.

Long after *Camelot* had begun its substantial run on Broadway and had been sold to the movies for a fabulous price, Loewe told an interviewer that he had become too rich to go through any longer the kind of anguish that the writing and the production of a musical entails. He said he could afford to indulge himself now, to spend his time in leisure. He had no intention of writing anymore.

For Lerner, the theatre was a way of life. He could no more stop working than he could stop breathing. He had to seek out other composers to work with: Burton Lane for *On a Clear Day You Can See Forever* and, after that, André Previn for *Coco*.

But for Frederick Loewe the termination of his partnership with Alan Jay Lerner meant creative silence.

XII

FRANK LOESSER

(1910-)

AFTER WORLD WAR II, the American musical theatre followed two separate paths. One led to the musical play, the other to musical comedy. The development of the musical play as a vibrant new art did not make the musical comedy obsolete. Even while adhering to the same basic methods and stereotypes that had characterized it through the years, musical comedy continued to flourish in the middle 1940s and in the 1950s and 1960s. It attracted to itself new writing and performing talent, new stage techniques, while bringing an enriched invention to well-set patterns. Some of the new composers, lyricists, and librettists come to prominence after the second World War preferred writing musical plays; others were partial to old-fashioned musical comedies. Frank Loesser was a composer-lyricist who was impartial. He wrote musical comedies and he wrote musical plays. Both areas were fructified by his fertile imagination and remarkable creativity.

He was born in New York City on June 29, 1910, the youngest of three children. His father was a piano teacher, and his older brother, Arthur, became a distinguished concert pianist and critic. The Loesser household encouraged intellectual and cultural interests. Frank alone seemed to resist this influence. In the handling both of words and of music, with which he ultimately achieved such significance, he received virtually no training, counting almost entirely upon sound instincts and those bits of knowledge and information he could absorb through the less painful process of osmosis.

He early revealed an interest in music. At six he was improvising on the piano and composing his first song, "The May Party." At seven, while listening from his window to the distant rumble of a passing elevator train, he invented little verses to the rhythm of the passing train. His father made a try at giving him piano instruction. He would have none of it. He preferred picking out tunes on the keyboard in his own haphazard way—and since the tunes he was picking out were invariably of the popular kind, his father preferred to leave him to his own devices. Frank's musical nature further expressed itself through the harmonica, with which he captured third prize in a city contest. Beyond music, he also revealed a gift for words and for putting pictures down on paper. In both of these endeavors he avoided any sort of formal guidance.

He was no scholar. In high school he had to be disqualified from the swimming team because his marks were substandard. Somehow he managed to graduate and enter the College of the City of New York. He stayed there only one year before he was summarily dropped. Sixteen years old, he deserted the academic halls for good to make his way in the world.

His first job was as office boy in a wholesale jewelry firm. After that he worked as a reporter for a small New Rochelle paper where he became city editor. In this job he went to cover a dinner of the Lions' Club. There he provided couplets identifying each of the guests. One read: "Secretary Albert

Vincent, Read these minutes, right this instant!" From such unpretentious beginnings sprang one of America's most distinguished lyricists.

He gravitated from one job to another, all the while remaining faithful to his main hobby of writing verses for song. One was called "Armful of You," which he sold to a vaudevillian for fifteen dollars. He also wrote special material for vaudeville acts and later on for radio programs. Leo Feist, the music publisher, became interested in him and paid him forty dollars a week to write lyrics to be used in talking pictures. This assignment lasted a year, during which Loesser wrote words for about a dozen numbers, none of which were published.

His first publication came in 1931, soon after his one-year contract with Leo Feist ended. Leo Feist, however, published it, and it was called "In Love With the Memory of You." Being Loesser's first published song was not its sole distinction. The composer was a young man named William Schuman, who had been Loesser's classmate and then had become a close friend. In later years, Schuman became one of America's most distinguished serious composers as well as President of the Juilliard School of Music, and after that of the Lincoln Center for the Performing Arts.

"In Love With the Memory of You" was a failure. So were several other Loesser songs that followed. A minor victory was registered in 1934 with "I Wish I Were Twins," which had music by Joseph Meyer and Eddie De Lange. In 1936, with Irving Actman as his composer, he wrote most of the lyrics for *The Illustrators Show,* a revue that had only a five-day run on Broadway. Since his earnings from this venture were miniscule, Loesser went to work for a night spot on 52nd Street, The Back Drop, where he sang and played the piano. One evening, a young blonde radio singer, Lynn Garland, dropped in. She liked what she heard and returned. Before long Frank Loesser found himself writing love songs and singing them to her at The Back Drop.

If *The Illustrators Show* accomplished nothing else, it brought Loesser his first movie assignment. An executive from Universal Pictures liked the songs in this revue and gave both Actman and Loesser a movie contract. Loesser arrived in Hollywood in 1936, where on October 19 he married Lynn. The year spent on the Universal lot was not particularly productive. Some of his songs were used, but none made enough of an impression to get published. The Universal contract was allowed to expire. Loesser then went to work for Paramount, where he stayed six years. Those were the years when a struggling novice, in a continual tussle to make ends meet, developed into a dapper songwriter who lived in the grand manner befitting a Hollywood success.

His first big hit came in 1937 in an early Paramount picture, *The Hurricane,* starring Dorothy Lamour; it was "The Moon of Manakoora," with music by Alfred Newman. The next five years found Loesser contributing lyrics to more than fifty songs by various composers. They were heard in thirty motion pictures. Since half a dozen or more were among the leading song successes of their respective years, Loesser soon achieved recognition as one of Hollywood's most talented and most highly paid lyricists. The best remembered of these cinema songs were "Small Fry" (Hoagy Carmichael); "Two Sleepy People" (Hoagy Carmichael); "Says My Heart" (Burton Lane); "See What the Boys in the Back Room Will Have" (Fredrick Hollander); "I Don't Want to Walk Without You, Baby" (Jule Styne); "Jingle, Jangle, Jingle" (Joseph J. Lilley). His royalties from the sheet music and record sale of "Jingle, Jangle, Jingle" alone were in excess of $50,000.

Sheer chance made Frank Loesser a composer. Pearl Harbor, and America's entry in World War II, had made an overwhelming impact on him, as it did on all Americans. As emotional release he wrote the lyrics of "Praise the Lord and Pass the Ammunition"—getting his title from the words reputed to have been shouted by Chaplain William Maguire of the United States Navy during the Japanese attack on Pearl Harbor. Here, as earlier, he concocted a dummy tune of his own with which to try out the lilt and rhythm of the words. He used that dummy tune to demonstrate his lyrics to friends. They insisted the tune was as good as the words, that it possessed a simple folklike character called for by his lyrics. Loesser allowed himself to be convinced to publish the song exactly as he wrote it, melody as well as words. With the help of Kay Kyser's Columbia recording that sold over one million discs, it became the first giant hit song of World War II. It was heard so often over the radio that the Office of War Information asked radio stations to refrain from broadcasting the song more often than once every four hours, lest it be played and sung to an early death.

Loesser was inducted into the Army in 1942. He was first attached to a military band unit stationed at the Santa Ana air base. His job was to write songs for the various service forces, for the Wacs, the War Loan Drive, the Bombardiers, and so forth. The most significant of these numbers was "What Do You Do in the Infantry?" which became the most popular song to identify that branch of the armed services. Still in uniform in 1945, Loesser produced the words and music of one of the war's most eloquent ballads, possibly the most eloquent ever written about an army private, "Rodger Young." The infantry had asked Loesser to write a song glorifying a member of its service, and he complied by describing the heroism of a private who, in the Solomons, lost his own life but saved those of his comrades by singlehandedly attacking a Japanese machine-gun nest. For this act of valor, he was posthumously awarded the Medal of Honor.

With the war ended, Loesser returned to Hollywood to write for the movies, this time producing his own melodies most of the time as well as lyrics. He scored successfully with "Tallahassee" in *Variety Girl* and "I Wish I Didn't Love You So" in *Perils of Pauline.* He also achieved hit status with a number published independently in 1947 and introduced by Danny Kaye in a Decca recording, "Bloop-Bleep." The year of 1949 found him clutching to his bosom an Oscar for the song, "Baby, It's Cold Outside." Actually he had written the song not for the screen but for his own delectation, confining its performance to private parties. But when he was working on songs for *Neptune's Daughter,* starring Esther Williams, he decided to place the song in that score.

By 1949, Loesser also had to his credit a solid box-office success on Broadway. This was his first attempt at writing a stage musical. *Where's Charley?* was a musical comedy adaptation of Brandon Thomas's farce, *Charley's Aunt,* an English play first produced in 1892, after which it became a prime favorite in America with amateur groups and stock companies. The idea of making a musical out of it was born with two young producers about to make their Broadway bow—Cy Feuer and Ernest Martin. Feuer was head of the music department at Republic Pictures in Hollywood. A close friend of Loesser's, he was able to convince the songwriter to make the shift from Hollywood to Broadway.

George Abbott was called in not only to make the necessary adaptation but also to direct the production. Oxford in England remained the setting. There Charley Wykeman is a chaperon at a party being celebrated by two couples. For this occasion he dresses up as a woman, posing as one of the young men's maiden aunts from Brazil. An Oxford lawyer, believing him to be a woman of wealth, becomes interested enough to pursue "her" relentlessly. Charley eludes him as best he can until he can discard his disguise and follow his own romantic bent for Amy.

Charley's Aunt was an old and not easily reheatable chestnut. Milking laughter from an audience with the antics of a man assuming a woman's clothes, gestures, voice, and affectations is not the freshest possible piece of stage business. *Where's Charley?* made no pretense at innovation or subtlety. But it was briskly paced by George Abbott's direction, and it boasted an extraordinary performance by Ray Bolger as Charley, who had a highly personal way with song, dance, and pantomime. Old routines acquired vigor and freshness when he was on the stage. He stopped the show regularly when he sang "Once in Love with Amy," in which he encouraged the audience to participate.

The main ballad was "My Darling, My Darling." It reached and stayed on the top spot of the Hit Parade for several weeks running. When it slipped to second place, the Number One position was usurped by another Frank Loesser song, "On a Slow Boat to China," which came from no movie or stage show but which Kay Kyser helped to popularize in a recording. For a few weeks, "My Darling, My Darling" and "On a Slow Boat to China" exchanged between them the first and second positions on the Hit Parade, the only time that such a thing happened to a single composer.

Where's Charley? ran on Broadway for almost 800 performances beginning on October 11, 1948. The next Broadway musical with Loesser's songs, *Guys and Dolls* in 1950, was an even greater triumph. It drew more than twelve million dollars to the box office on Broadway during its run of 1,200 performances. Then it was sold to Samuel Goldwyn for a movie adaptation, receiving an advance of one million dollars, a high for motion picture sales at that time.

Where's Charley? had been a stereotype as musical comedy; *Guys and Dolls* was consistently adventurous, imaginative, and exciting theatre. In fact it is one of the best musical comedies ever written. Characterization was its strongest suit, the characters stepping out of the pages of Broadway stories by Damon Runyon. These people were as unconventional, uninhibited, and colorful as the names they carried: Nicely-Nicely Johnson, Nathan Detroit, Angie the Ox, Harry the Horse. This was as curious an assortment of noncomformists as the Broadway musical theatre has assembled on one stage at one time: a pragmatic people whose answer to life was to shrug off its responsibilities, who were always on the lookout for the easy buck and the passing romance. They were the Broadway high livers, gamblers, free spenders, and the scantily dressed entertainers at night spots.

With a consistently lively text that never flagged in interest (fashioned by Jo Swerling and Abe Burrows), and given a dynamic thrust by George S. Kaufman's fast-moving direction, *Guys and Dolls* never relaxed the momentum that was started with the rise of the opening curtain on a Broadway street coming alive with movement. The hubbub subsides to reveal three gamblers picking their choices for the day's races in a song called "Fugue for Tinhorns." Nearby is the Save-a-Soul Mission, which is under the direction of Abernathy and his attractive young helper, Sarah Brown. Sky Masterson, a happy-go-lucky fellow, is attracted to Sarah, but confronts stout resistance when he tries to win her with his easy ways and charm. Spurred on by a bet, he breaks down Sarah's will to resist and gets her to go with him to Havana; one of the reasons she accepts Sky's invitation is because he has promised to save her Mission, whose existence is being threatened.

Sarah, however, is now interested in Sky himself; and her brief interlude in romantic Havana fans that interest into love. After their return, Sky not only convinces Sarah of his sincerity but is also instrumental in saving the Mission, as he had promised to do.

Subsidiary to this central love interest is the affair between gambler Nathan Detroit and the nightclub entertainer Adelaide. They have been keeping company for fourteen years. Each time they seem to be on the verge of marriage, Nathan gets deflected by a crap game or a horse race. Because he is engineering a crap game, which finally finds a home in a sewer, he avoids Adelaide's pressure for matrimony until the final curtain.

To use the musical form of the canon for a song by three horse players making their selections is one of many tidbits that made *Guys and Dolls* both unusual and delectable. Another musical number was hardly less distinctive, though this time the novelty lay more in the lyrics than in the music. This was "Adelaide's Lament," in which she explains that her chronic colds are psychosomatic, the consequence of having had her wedding day postponed so often. To Moss Hart, this number represented one of the most original musical comedy sequences he had ever heard. Smart and sophisticated lyrics are also of prime interest in the title song, in "Take Back Your Mink," and in "A Bushel and a Peck." And strong romantic impulses are released in songs like "I'll Know," "If I Were a Bell," and "I've Never Been in Love Before."

The way in which songs often enhance action or throw new light on character suggests a musical play rather than a musical comedy. The production also leans toward the musical play in Michael Kidd's choreography, particularly in the memorable ballet depicting a crap game in the sewer, a climax in the play. Here, as in the staging of all the musical numbers,

Michael Kidd proved highly effective in projecting the nervous pulse and heartbeat of Broadway life and people.

Loesser made the transfer from musical comedy to musical play in *The Most Happy Fella* in 1956. Here he served as his own librettist (besides writing lyrics and music) by adapting *They Knew What They Wanted,* the play with which Sidney Howard had won the Pulitzer Prize in drama in 1924. In Howard's play and in Loesser's adaptation, Tony is a middle-aged California winegrower who, on a visit to San Francisco, falls in love at sight with a waitress, Rosabella. Back home in Napa, he starts to correspond with her, during which he proposes marriage. When Rosabella asks for his photograph he sends her that of his young and handsome foreman, Joe. Impressed, Rosabella comes to Napa. But no sooner does she arrive than she discovers she is to marry, not the attractive Joe, but the middle-aged Italian, Tony. She makes plans to return at once to San Francisco. Destiny intervenes. Tony, having gone to meet Rosabella at the bus stop, has met with a serious automobile accident. Brought back on a stretcher, he expresses such joy at seeing Rosabella that she finds it impossible to break his heart by insisting on leaving him. In fact, not only does she stay, but she even marries him. But she is young, and Joe, who is ever nearby, is handsome. Rosabella and Joe fall in love. In spite of this, Rosabella feels a growing sympathy and tenderness for Tony, who is gentleness itself. At a mammoth party that Tony throws for Rosabella, she decides to leave him for good, since she is pregnant, and the child is Joe's. When Tony tries to stop her, she blurts out the truth. At first, Tony succumbs to a violent rage in which he bitterly denounces Rosabella and threatens to kill Joe. But no sooner has Rosabella departed for the bus depot than he has a change of heart. He knows that he cannot live without his wife. Following her, he begs her to return home with him. He insists he is overjoyed that she is going to have a child, and he promises to regard it as his own *"bambino."*

The tensions, the strong dramatic effects, the highly charged emotion, together with an overall compassion and humanity, are all developed in the music as well as in the text. Three quarters of the play has some form of music. Dialogue is used to develop the story, but when emotion sets in, music enters to supplement words. The score has several outstanding individual numbers such as "Standing On the Corner" (a hillbilly-type tune), "Big D" (imitative of the song styles of the 1920s), and "Joey, Joey." But the score has much more too: arias, dance music, duets, instrumental passages, choral passages, folk hymns, recitatives, accompanied speech. Music as well as play points up the terrible loneliness and the harrowing need for love and companionship which so many people suffer—in songs like "My Heart Is So Full of You" and "Don't Cry." Other numbers—"Abbondanza" and "Benvenuta," for example—contribute an Italian flavor. So important is the music to the overall scheme of the entire production, and so good and so varied is this music, that some critics referred to *The Most Happy Fella* as an opera. Loesser did not agree. He preferred to consider it a musical play and nothing more. But whether it be opera or musical play, *The Most Happy Fella* was stirring, unforgettable theatre. "His musical drama," said Brooks Atkinson, "goes so much deeper into the soul of its leading characters than most Broadway shows, and it has such an abundant and virtuoso score in it, that it has to be taken on the level of theatre."

Robert Weede, a graduate from grand opera, was cast in the part of Tony. Rosabella was played by Jo Sullivan, whose stage experience had been gained in operettas and musical comedies. During the run of the show, a romantic interest developed between Miss Sullivan and Loesser. They were married in 1959, Loesser having divorced his first wife some years earlier.

With a New York run of more than six hundred performances, and the Drama Critics Award as the best musical of the year in hand, *The Most Happy Fella* could be regarded as an unqualified success. This could not be said of Loesser's next adventure within the musical play format. It was *Greenwillow,* in 1960, which Loesser and Lesser Samuels adapted from a novel by B. J. Chute. Greenwillow is an imaginary place on an imaginary river in an unspecified country and time. It is the home of Amos Briggs, a man who suffers from "wanderlust." He is continually on the move, but once every few years he returns to his family, who accept him on his own terms. His son, Gideon, is in love with a village maiden. But he fears he has inherited his father's weakness for wandering, and this is the reason he is afraid of getting married. But by the end of the play true love proves victorious.

The whole play has a quiet and pastoral character which Joe Layton sustained in his choreography and Frank Loesser in his music. If *Greenwillow* proved nothing else it demonstrated that Frank Loesser was not the man to stay put in a creative rut. It was as different from *Guys and Dolls* as that production was from *The Most Happy Fella.* Brooks Atkinson put it this way in a Sunday feature article: "In *Guys and Dolls* he captured the corrosive excitement and the adolescent sentimentality of Broadway. *The Most Happy Fella* . . . seemed to represent a drive to get free of the limitations of the Broadway show medium. In *Greenwillow* . . . he has written buoyant music of a romantic nature that illustrates the affable unreality of the fable." But Mr. Atkinson was in the minority in reacting favorably to *Greenwillow*. Most other critics, and the audiences with them, felt with Richard Watts, Jr., that "scenes and characters that possessed touching or humorous charm in the novel, became excessively whimsical, and uncomfortably coy, when not simply dull, on the stage. . . . Despite its pleasant moments, *Greenwillow* is gravely disappointing."

Greenwillow did not stay long on Broadway. But Loesser had by no means lost the touch of success. In fact, in *How to Succeed in Business Without Really Trying,* in 1961, he surpassed all earlier triumphs. With it he earned his first Pulitzer Prize in drama, together with the Antoinette Perry and Drama Critics Circle awards—a clean sweep of the most important stage honors a musical can get. It also had the longest run of any of Loesser's musicals, 1,417 performances.

In *How to Succeed in Business,* Loesser was reunited with Abe Burrows for the first time since *Guys and Dolls,* Burrows having had a hand in the writing of the libretto. This may very well be the reason why the later production is so much more like *Guys and Dolls* than it is like *The Most Happy Fella.* In other words, *How to Succeed in Business* is musical comedy entertainment *in excelsis;* it does not concern itself with artistic or dramatic values. Fashioned by expert showmen who brought imagination and skill to their tasks, *How to Succeed in Business* proved to be a shining example of musical comedy at its sophisticated best. Richard Watts, Jr., called it a "smashing success." Howard Taubman wrote that "it belongs to the blue chips among modern musicals."

This musical started out with a strong book, a devastating satire on big business and on the ruthless go-getter who allows nothing to stand in the way of his getting to the top. The go-getter is personified by Finch, brilliantly portrayed by young Robert Morse; big business is represented by J. B. Biggley, a role in which Rudy Vallee (crooning idol of the early 1930s) was belatedly making his musical comedy debut (although in the 1930s he had been starred in revues). As for the text, it came from a novel by Shepherd Mead, which Abe Burrows, Jack Weinstock, and Willie Gilbert made into one of the best musical comedy texts of the 1960s. Burrows was the one who interested Loesser in this project. "I convinced Frank," he explained, "if he could put a crap game to music in *Guys and Dolls,* he could put a big corporation to music. He did it too. Why, he even put a board meeting to music."

Being musical comedy rather than musical play, *How to Succeed in Business* did not have the elaborate and extended musical fabric of *The Most Happy Fella.* Individual songs are of prime importance. Pursuing the long-accepted methods of musical comedy, Loesser chose "song areas" (the term is his) within the text. Then, as he has said, he went on to "lay out the spots where to place the ballads, the comedy songs, the patter songs, dance numbers, like that." Emphasis was placed on satire and humor: on the rah-rah college spirit in "Grand Old Ivy"; on self-aggrandizement in "I Believe in You"; on big business habits, practices, and institutions in "Coffee Break" and "The Company Way"; on the career girl in "A Secretary Is Not a Toy"; on romantic or sentimental attitudes in "Happy to Keep His Dinner Warm" and "Love from a Heart of Gold"; on the golden rule in "The Brotherhood of Man."

Our hero, Finch, starts out as a window cleaner. Inspired by a do-it-yourself book on success, he is determined to follow its basic rules in order to get to the top. The book specified that the first rule was to get a job in a large firm. Finch finds such a job in the mail room of World Wide Wickets. When he turns down promotion "for the sake of the team," he attracts the interest of the firm's president, J. B. Biggley. Being a resourceful and opportunistic young man, Finch always finds ways and means of endearing himself to the president, such as saying he is a graduate of Biggley's alma mater, or that like Biggley he finds relaxation in knitting. Eventually, even the chairman of the Board of Directors is on Finch's side, having discovered that Finch had once been a window cleaner, the humble job with which the chairman had started his own career. When the chairman resigns his post to marry and devote himself to the firm's sex-pot, Hedy, Finch becomes his successor. During this long and steady ascent to the top rung in World Wide Wickets, Finch gets female adoration from one of the company's secretaries, Rosemary.

Despite his activity on Broadway, Loesser did not completely desert Hollywood. Above and beyond the transfer of his most successful musicals to the screen, his later association with Hollywood included a thoroughly charming score for *Hans Christian Andersen.* This was a Samuel Goldwyn production released in 1953 in which Danny Kaye was starred as the Danish storyteller. Not the least of the attractions of this lovable film were the songs "Anywhere I Wander," "Thumbelina," "Wonderful Copenhagen," "The Inch Worm," and "No Two People."

XIII

JERRY BOCK

(1928-)

In 1960, Jerry Bock received the Pulitzer Prize in drama for the musical comedy *Fiorello!* Four years after that, he gathered accolade upon accolade for having written the music for one of the great artistic triumphs the American musical theatre has known—*Fiddler on the Roof.*

Two such achievements—*Fiorello!* on the one hand, and *Fiddler on the Roof,* on the other—place Bock with the most important composers for the stage to step forward since Frank Loesser. The distinction of each of these two scores speaks eloquently on behalf of Bock's creativity and talent. The fact that they are so many miles apart in style and purpose, in background and atmosphere also offers testimony to Bock's versatility, to his chameleon-like capacity to change colors with whatever production he becomes involved.

He was born in New Haven, Connecticut, on November 23, 1928, the son of a salesman of Hungarian background. When he was an infant, the Bock family moved to New York. As a two-year-old he would sit near the loudspeaker of his radio, keeping perfect rhythm on a toy drum to popular songs being broadcast. At nine he began taking piano lessons. He detested practicing, was thoroughly impatient with the necessity of learning a piece down to its last note before embarking on a fresh one. Nevertheless, as he has communicated to this writer, "I can remember rather well the curiosity I had for exploring along those musical lines, away from the exactness and care of acquiring a formidable piano repertoire, and towards the more frivolous and exciting adventure of personal musical expression. The variations led to improvisations, all of this overlapping into what I considered to be composing original themes." Somewhere between learning Schumann's *The Happy Farmer* and Bach's two-part *Inventions,* he got the urge to write his own music, an urge that remained permanent. His teacher was patient with these escapades into extracurricular musical activities and did what she could to canalize this creativity into a study of theory and composition —but without much success. "The moment music became more work than fun," Bock confesses, "I found it less desirable."

Bock's boyhood years were lived in Queens, New York, where he attended elementary and high school. By the time he entered Flushing High School he had given up formal music study for good. At the same time he intensified his efforts at composition and improvisation. Both parents encouraged him in his musical diversions without exerting any pressure for him to abandon this time-consuming hobby or to apply himself to it with the kind of system and training music required. Music, however, was not Bock's sole interest. He was almost as deeply involved with literature and creative writing. He edited the school paper, and contributed prose and poetry to various nonpaying journals. In his last year at school, he combined his musical and literary interests into a single activity by writing texts and songs for a musical comedy, *My Dream,* presented locally in Queens to raise money for recreational equipment for a Navy hospital ship. "It was my first taste of theatrical excitement," he says, "and may have influenced me to begin thinking about that special field of music."

Somewhere at about this time the idea came to him that the best way to earn a living was to enter the advertising profession. With this plan in mind he went to register at the University of Wisconsin. During registration week, however, he succumbed to a sudden impulse to try and gain admission to the music school at the university. An audition before four members of the music faculty was required. The other candidates arrived with volumes of music under their arms, ready to demonstrate their readiness to pursue advanced study. Since it had been some five years since Bock had had his last piano lesson, and since he was totally unprepared to perform anything at all, his first impulse was to flee. Some inexplicable force, however, kept him in the line waiting to get heard. When he entered the audition room he explained how inadequate his training had been, and that he had come with more hope and enthusiasm than preparation. "If they mistook these confessions for exaggerated modesty they swiftly learned to take me at my word. I was asked to sight read some simple hymns and incurred not only theirs but the wrath of God as well." Bock then performed his own arrangement of bugle calls in the style of the masters—Bach, Beethoven, Rachmaninoff, and so forth—ending up the piece with improvised jazz. The judges listened with amusement. "Finally one spoke and said I showed signs of inventiveness, but I needed basic training. Would I be willing to start at the beginning? I said I'd be willing to start prenatally if there was a chance. They consented."

In music school, Bock did not change either his character

or habits. He still preferred extracurricular musical activities to formal study. He also stood ready and willing to leave a class assignment undone so that he might engage in the college's theatrical activities, contribute to its magazines, or take courses in English, philosophy, and the political sciences. In his third year at the music school he wrote the score for a musical, *Big as Life,* produced by the college dramatic society; this was a fanciful treatment of the Paul Bunyan legend. "The memory of that experience ignited a hotter creative urge to follow through on some specific aspect of my musical bent. I was beginning to get the theatre into focus as an ultimate aspiration, and writing songs for a living as an immediate one."

One of those impressed by his creative efforts was Patti Faggen, a university student interested in acting and a performer in college productions. This interest in Bock's music was the catalytic agent to unite them. While still in college they fell in love. Then on May 28, 1950, they were married in New York. This was one year after Bock had left Wisconsin with the hopes of invading the Broadway theatre. A fellow student from Wisconsin had similar ambitions—a young writer, Larry Holofcener. Bock and Holofcener decided to join forces. They auditioned for Max Liebman, at that time beginning a career as producer of musical shows for television. Liebman signed the pair to write songs for his shows. During the next three seasons numbers by Bock and Holofcener were heard on the "Admiral Broadway Revue," which subsequently became the highly successful "Your Show of Shows," starring Sid Caesar and Imogene Coca. Summers were spent by Bock and Holofcener writing songs for revues produced at Camp Tamiment, an adult vacation resort in the Pocono Mountains of Pennsylvania.

Those three years were, as Bock does not hesitate to recall, a wonderful period of continual creativity, of writing songs and hearing them performed. This was feast. Then came famine. Television began to lose interest in, or felt it could no longer foot the bill for, original songs and had begun to tap the standard repertory. To keep working and paying their bills, both Bock and Holofcener changed over from song-writers to writers of continuity and sketches for a number of television shows, including the Kate Smith Hour. They also fashioned material for nightclub entertainers. All this work was profitable financially and made it possible for Bock and Holofcener to continue writing songs on their own, and once in a while placing one in some television show or nightclub act. And writing a song was a reward all its own. "Even under the most difficult circumstances," says Bock, "even at the very nadir of hoping for something to happen, there was always the ability to create. In the very midst of disappointment, of discouragement, of depression, I could always steal away to compose. My basic need was the ability to create, my basic love was the act of writing, audience or not. The reward comes at a moment when you've finished a song, and you sing it to your collaborator, or your wife, or your dog, or yourself, and you taste the deep personal joy of having written, of having created. And if nothing else follows, that will keep you alive, it will feed your spirit, and be enough nourishment to tie you over somehow."

By 1955, Bock and Holofcener were beginning to earn some money from their songs through an arrangement with a publisher by which they were paid a modest weekly salary for their exclusive services, the salary being an advance against royalties. This year also found them writing four songs for a motion-picture travelogue about New York, *Wonders of Manhattan,* in which songs replaced the more usual spoken commentary. This short documentary won honorable mention at the Cannes Film Festival in 1956. And, on September 7, 1955, Bock and Holofcener finally made their debut in the Broadway theatre by placing three numbers in *Catch a Star,* a revue. The critics found the songs appealing, but the revue itself much less so. The show lasted only three months. It was later produced in California under the title of *Joy Ride,* when it enjoyed a somewhat longer run.

Catch a Star brought the songwriters an assignment for a new Broadway show—*Mr. Wonderful,* starring Sammy Davis, Jr., in 1956. This was a musical manufactured to serve as a frame for the many facets of Davis's performing talent. The story line was maintained for an act and a half, after which the show lapsed into an extended nightclub routine for Sammy Davis. Singing, dancing, miming, ad libbing, he was the heart of the show, and the main reason for the show's success. Highly professional, too, was the score. Two of the songs became standards (the first by Jerry Bock to have survived)—the title number and "Too Close for Comfort."

For Jerry Bock, *Mr. Wonderful* represented a new and significant turn in his career. It established him once and for all as a successful composer for the stage whose services would henceforth be in demand. It lifted him into a high earning bracket. It also marked the end of his collaboration with Holofcener. Bock explains: "A growing separation in creative ideologies, working techniques and ultimate ambitions between Larry and myself which had been accumulating finally split us apart, irrevocably."

For his next Broadway musical, *The Body Beautiful,* in 1958, Jerry Bock worked with a new lyricist, Sheldon Harnick. "It was love at first write," Bock says of his new partner.

The Body Beautiful was rejected by audiences. This may well be the reason why, as a neglected brainchild, it has held a special place in Bock's heart. "It was much closer to me than *Mr. Wonderful,*" says Bock. "The labor pains were more prolonged, the child born was more helpless, and so the concern at all times was more intense. Also, Sheldon and I had great *sympatico,* mutual respect, and the first blush of collaboration was marvelously exciting. I was involved more intimately with every aspect of the show and felt a sense of deeper participation than had been true of *Mr. Wonderful.* It unravelled more slowly, more sensationally, with greater trials and tribulations in terms of raising money, no protection from 'stars' in any department, and just generally an underdog in all respects. It opened a year and a month, I think to the day, after *Mr. Wonderful* closed. It received better reviews and eked out a two-month run, and proved to be a major heartbreak, capped by the cancellation of an original cast album. In my most objective mood I still feel the show and the score deserved a longer life."

But *The Body Beautiful* was not a total loss. The songs had so impressed Robert E. Griffith and Hal Prince, two young producers, that they engaged Bock and Harnick to write songs for a musical they were projecting based on the life of Fiorello H. La Guardia, New York's fiery pint-sized Mayor.

When *Fiorello!* came to the Broadhurst Theatre on November 23, 1959, it arrived without ringing promises or soaring hopes inspired by the out-of-town tryouts. Its entrance was a thoroughly modest one, and expectations on opening night in New York did not run particularly high. Many of those who attended doubted very seriously if a commercial musical could possibly be fashioned from the career of an iconoclastic, rambunctious little Mayor who, for all of his personal dynamism as a politician, was hardly the kind of figure you could shape into a musical comedy romantic hero. There were other factors about *Fiorello!* that were discouraging at the box office. Five performers were making their Broadway debuts, including Tom Bosley cast as La Guardia; not a single big name could be found in the cast. Jerome Weidman, author of the text, was a prominent novelist, but he had never before written a musical comedy libretto. The question stood uppermost in many minds: Would tying up a theatrical novice like Weidman with the veteran George Abbott, as collaborator, help to bring him the necessary know-how to write a slick, professional book? Uncertainty about the musical, then, hung over the production like an ominous cloud warning of a storm to come—and it persisted right through rehearsals and out-of-town tryouts and up to opening night in New York. "There wasn't a moment that resembled anything like smug satisfaction," Bock recalls. "It wasn't until the early hours of a Tuesday morning when a member of the company, standing high on a table in Sardi's, read us Atkinson, and soon after that Kerr, and then Chapman, that we all began to loosen and share the glow, and breathe deeply and explode in screams of joy, catching a glimmer, a sense of achievement, excitement and victory. Fiorello was elected again, and oh, what a beautiful morning after. I absolutely forgot that we opened on my birthday, and I'll never have a happier one."

Fiorello! is the portrait not only of a man but also of a colorful political era in New York. The story begins in 1914 when La Guardia is still practicing law in Greenwich Village. He is a young man of remarkable energy and integrity, with an enormous concern for the underdog and the underprivileged, whose battles he champions without thought for personal gain. Since Fiorello is politically ambitious and wants to run for Congress, he tries to gain the support of Ben Marino, the Republican leader of La Guardia's Congressional district. The only reason he gets that support is because no Republican has ever won an election in that Democratic district, and nobody else is eager to run. As a champion of the working class and as an opponent of sweatshops and ruthless employers, La Guardia manages to gain the support of the masses—especially after he has invaded the Italian and Jewish districts, talking to these audiences in Italian and Yiddish. The masses vote and elect him. As a Congressman, La Guardia alienates a good many of his constituents by supporting the Draft Act, this being the period of America's involvement in World War I. But La Guardia insists that the draft is the only democratic way to build an army. When the Draft Act becomes law, he enlists in the army. His active involvement in the war is flashed in a quick series of montages, some of them staged, others in motion pictures. Ten years later, we find La Guardia married to Thea, a onetime employee of a shirtwaist factory. He is now planning to run for the office of Mayor in New York City in an effort to crusade against crime, corruption, and big-time political operators. His enemies band together to murder him, but their plan is thwarted. La Guardia survives, but he suffers a personal major tragedy in the death of his wife, Thea, who had long been ill. He also knows the disappointment and frustration of having been beaten in the mayoralty election. Nevertheless, he continues to fight for honesty and good government. Through his efforts, Tammany Hall and New York's dapper Mayor, James J. Walker, are discredited by the Seabury investigation. Running once again for the Mayor's office, this time on a reform fusion ticket, La Guardia is finally victorious. He also finds personal happiness by marrying Marie, who had long served as his faithful secretary.

The picture of New York's political life between 1914 and 1932 was drawn in strong lines, and sometimes voiced with pronounced satirical accents. Two of Bock's best numbers are in a satirical vein. One is "Politics and Poker," sung by the Republican leader and his cronies during a poker game; they find a striking parallel between these two pursuits. The same politicians also indulge in a delightful travesty on investigations of graft and corruption in city politics in "Little Tin Box." But Bock and Harnick reveal an equally felicitous touch in sentiment—in the nostalgic waltz " 'Til Tomorrow" and in the ballads "Look Who's in Love" and "When Did I Fall in Love?"

Fiorello! became the third musical comedy in stage history to capture the Pulitzer Prize for drama. It also received the New York Drama Critics Circle Award, while sharing the Antoinette Perry Award with *The Sound of Music.* "Hard boiled . . . raucous, honest, blisteringly funny," was the way Frank Aston described *Fiorello!*. Together with *Guys and Dolls* it is one of the best musicals inspired by the sidewalks of New York.

Bock and Harnick returned to the New York scene in their next musical comedy, *Tenderloin* in 1960. *Tenderloin* is a period piece placed in the 1890s and it describes the efforts of a Presbyterian minister to clean up a disreputable New York neighborhood. The mixture is the same as before—satire, nostalgia, sentiment—but the final stew is far less delectable. *Tenderloin* is no *Fiorello!* It lacks the pace, excitement, and consistent point of view of its predecessor. Its stay on Broadway was brief, and so was that of *She Loves Me,* in 1963, a musical comedy based on the delightful motion picture *The Little Shop Around the Corner,* which the public found too bland for its taste.

It was the general consensus of the Broadway cognoscenti that *Fiddler on the Roof* would also be vigorously rejected. Subject, characters, *Weltanschaaung,* ritual were all too alien to American experiences to be readily understood. At least, this is what almost everybody thought when *Fiddler on the Roof* came to Broadway in the fall of 1964. "No smash, no blockbuster," is the way *Variety* regarded it during the out-of-town tryouts. "May have a chance for moderate success." Even its creators were apprehensive. "It wasn't the sort of show where, from first blush, you knew you had a hit," says Jerry Bock. Sheldon Harnick feared "it might be too special."

Once the ordeal of opening night was over, the critics left no doubts about how good the show was or how successful it would become. Howard Taubman said it was "filled with laughter and tenderness. It catches the essence of a moment in history with sentiment and radiance. Compounded of the familiar materials of the musical theatre . . . it combines and transcends them to arrive at an integrated achievement of uncommon quality." Seeing it on Broadway, *Variety* now had no hesitancy to call it "the first blockbuster of the new season," adding: "It is a cinch to satisfy almost anyone who enjoys the musical theatre." And a blockbuster it surely was! It instantly became the "hottest" ticket on Broadway and stayed that way for several years. By the time it passed its one-thousandth performance it had returned over three million dollars to investors. It had also been sold to the movies for two million dollars and had earned over a million dollars for its original-cast recording. In addition to all this, it had spread its wings to soar far beyond Broadway, having been produced in Chicago, London, Copenhagen, The Hague, Sydney, Finland, Tel Aviv and, in 1967, in Japanese in Tokyo, providing uncontrovertible proof of its universality.

The thing that made *Fiddler on the Roof* so exotic was that it revived a world long dead, a world unknown to most Americans: that of the Orthodox Jew in Czarist Russia. This was a world all its own, with its unique dress, customs, mannerisms, ritual, and overall outlook on life. This was a world which the popular musical theatre had never before touched. The basic story stemmed from the tales of Sholom Aleichem, one of the foremost Yiddish writers. Joseph Stein molded this material into a text, while direction and choreography were assigned to Jerome Robbins. All involved in the production saw to it that *Fiddler on the Roof* remained true not only to Sholom Aleichem in all areas and departments but also to the background and traditions he described.

The basic story is a simple one. Teyve is a dairyman in the little Russian town of Anatevka in 1905. He pursues a simple, humble, poverty-stricken existence following his trade. He worships his God, and cares for Golde, his sharp-tongued wife, and their five unmarried daughters. His problem is to find a good match for his children, and his choices are based on practical considerations. But the girls have a mind of their own. One of them even runs off with a gentile. Teyve, who is not above arguing with God or posing Him with his own peculiar brand of rationalization and logic, convinces himself that his daughters have made wise decisions. But the play does not end on a happy note. The village is victimized by anti-Semitic persecution, and Teyve and his family must leave their home for good.

In Jerome Robbins's remarkable staging and choreography, in Zero Mostel's touching and human portrayal of Teyve, and in the evocative songs of Bock and Harnick, the old world comes vividly to life. The dances and the wedding ceremony as conceived by Robbins are deeply rooted in Russian-Jewish backgrounds and customs. In the songs, an inflection here, an augmented interval there, a plangent minor mode phrase in a third place, succeed in capturing a Semitic feeling and personality while remaining a basic part of Broadway. "Sunrise, Sunset" became the most popular song to come out of this score, but other numbers are equally memorable for hearty or wistful or nostalgic or robustly humorous attitudes

—for example, "Matchmaker, Matchmaker," "To Life," "If I Were a Rich Man," and "Far from the Home I Love."

For all its deep immersion into the past, into a foreign land, and into a religious and social ambiance that was *terra incognita* for most theatregoers, *Fiddler on the Roof* was able to establish a direct and immediate contact with its audiences, and for a number of reasons. To Jews, even those of American birth, it carried a reminder of tales and legends and memories recounted by parents and grandparents. To non-Jews, it brought a vital message that had contemporary meaning. Bigotry and persecution, after all, were very much in the news in the 1960s. The suffering of humble Jews in old Russia could readily be understood and sympathized with in terms of racial intolerance in America and religious bigotry in other countries. The revolt of Teyve's daughters against parental authority was also of modern-day significance. *Fiddler on the Roof,* then, was not just an interesting excursion into esoterica, but a profound human drama with ringing present-day overtones. This is undoubtedly the reason why non-Jews as well as Jews, why Japanese as well as New Yorkers, could respond to it with such warmth of feeling and such heartfelt enthusiasm.

In its own way, *The Apple Tree*—with which Bock and Harnick reappeared in New York in 1966—is quite as novel as *Fiddler on the Roof.* This is three musicals in one, based on short stories by Mark Twain, Frank R. Stockton, and Jules Feiffer, which Bock and Harnick themselves adapted. Woman is the center of interest in each of the three one-act musicals. We encounter her first as Eve in the Garden of Eden; then as Princess Barbara in a semibarbaric kingdom "a long time ago"; finally as a present-day motion picture sex symbol, Passionella, a kind of composite of Marilyn Monroe and Jayne Mansfield. The attitude maintained throughout the three plays is that of mockery, and mockery together with sardonic humor abounds in the songs. One of them is a parody on songs about romantic far-off places ("Forbidden Love"); another is a take-off on numbers exploiting sex interest ("I've Got What You Want"). Of more sober appeal and content is the ballad "What Makes Me Love Him." For Barbara Harris (later starring in the Burton Lane–Alan Jay Lerner musical, *On a Clear Day You Can See Forever*), *The Apple Tree* was a tour de force with which her career took another important step forward. For Jerry Bock, *The Apple Tree* presented a new facet to his creativity, further proof, if such were needed, that in the musical theatre of the present day he occupies a place of first importance.

XIV

LEONARD BERNSTEIN

(1918 -)

THERE IS NO AREA in music cultivated by Leonard Bernstein which he has not enriched and fructified. His creative "green thumb" has made it possible for him just to touch the soil of any artistic endeavor and have it sprout forth with rich blossoms. The world of the musical theatre has proved no exception. Bernstein has written the music for two highly successful musical comedies, and for a musical play which is now a durable classic in the theatre.

His career in the musical theatre, of course, has been only a single phase of his multi-faceted achievements which, by now, have assumed legendary proportions. As is well known and much publicized, Bernstein is one of the world's greatest conductors. For a decade he has been the musical director of the New York Philharmonic Orchestra, and as a guest conductor he has been heard throughout the civilized world not only in symphonic music but also in operas. He is also one of America's most important serious composers. His three symphonies, two ballet scores, and large choral works are now among the proudest achievements of American contemporary music.

In addition, Bernstein is the successful author of two books on music. He is also an outstandingly popular personality in television, both as a conductor and as music teacher to young and old. He is a fine concert pianist, often appearing in the dual role of virtuoso and conductor in performances of great concertos.

In short, whatever he does, he does superlatively well. This, by itself, is amazing enough. The wonder grows when we are suddenly reminded that in each of these endeavors he was able to scale the heights of success with a maiden effort.

This has proved true in the musical theatre as well. The first time he ever wrote music for the popular stage was in 1944 when he was only twenty-six. That musical was *On the Town,* whose Broadway run of 463 performances represented a solid box-office success. The musical was made in 1949 into a movie starring Frank Sinatra and Ann Miller. It was subsequently revived in two off-Broadway productions presented simultaneously—perhaps the first time in New York stage history that a musical was twice revived during a single period of time.

With this giant achievement out of the way, Bernstein went on to even more formidable successes in the theatre. *Wonderful Town,* in 1953, ran for 533 performances, received the Antoinette Perry and Donaldson Awards as the best musical of the year, toured the United States and Europe, and was given a lavish television production over the CBS network in 1958. After *Wonderful Town* came *West Side Story. . . .*

The life story of a man who accomplished all this, and so many things more, has been told in many different places and with considerable detail. The present writer has done so in *Famous Modern Conductors.**

Here and now, perhaps, it need be essential merely to

* New York: Dodd, Mead & Co., 1967.

record only a few of the salient biographical facts while concentrating on his work in the musical theatre.

Bernstein was born in Lawrence, Massachusetts, on August 25, 1918. His profound love for music, as well as his formidable talent for it, were revealed during his early boyhood, when a piano came into his household. "It was love at first sight," Bernstein now says about his first sight of that instrument, when he was eleven. From the moment he put fingers to keyboard he knew "with finality that I would become a musician." He began taking lessons with local teachers, the most important of whom was Helen Coates, while going to the Boston Latin School for his academic education. "He was frighteningly gifted," Helen Coates remembers. He was making music all the time, and when he was not making it, he was reading musical scores borrowed from the library, going to concerts, and talking about it.

From the Boston Latin School Bernstein went on to Harvard in 1935. There he attended classes in music while pursuing a regular academic curriculum leading to a Bachelor of Arts degree. At the same time he studied the piano privately with Heinrich Gebhard. At Harvard, he involved himself in the making of music whenever he could. He played the piano for the Harvard Film Society and for the Harvard Music Club. He wrote incidental music for a production of *The Birds* by Aristophanes. He conducted performances of Marc Blitzstein's provocative social-conscious opera, *The Cradle Will Rock*.

Upon being graduated from Harvard in 1939, Bernstein concentrated on music study. He attended the Curtis Institute of Music in Philadelphia—a pupil of Fritz Reiner in conducting, Randall Thompson in orchestration, and Isabelle Vengerova in piano. During the summers of 1940 and 1941 he studied conducting with Serge Koussevitzky at the Berkshire

Music Center at Tanglewood. In 1942, Koussevitzky recognized Bernstein's talent by making him his assistant in the conducting class.

Others, too, were made aware of his musical powers. Artur Rodzinski, then the new music director of the New York Philharmonic Orchestra, appointed him his assistant, even though up to that time Bernstein had never conducted a major orchestra. Then, on Sunday afternoon, November 14, 1943, there took place an event that suddenly and unexpectedly threw the limelight of national interest on Bernstein. Bruno Walter, scheduled to be a guest conductor of the New York Philharmonic that day, had fallen ill and could not appear. At virtually the zero hour Bernstein was called to take his place. He had had no opportunity to rehearse with the orchestra, and he had only one night in which to acquaint himself with the music. Nevertheless, he carried off that afternoon with flying banners—so much so that his debut made front-page news throughout the country. Unknown except to a handful of friends and admirers only one day earlier, Bernstein found himself famous and sought after.

From then on, through numerous guest appearances with great orchestras everywhere, Bernstein rapidly developed into not only one of the most gifted conductors in America but also one of the greatest box-office attractions in the world of music. But, apparently, conducting was not enough for a versatile young man whose talents reached out into so many different directions. On January 28, 1944 he led in Pittsburgh the world première of his own symphony, *Jeremiah.* Though this was his first work for orchestra, it was acclaimed at once as a major artistic achievement. It received the award of the New York Music Critics Circle (as the best new symphonic composition of the season), was performed by many leading American orchestras, and was recorded for RCA Victor.

Hardly had the impact of this symphony been fully felt when Bernstein once again made a mark as composer, this time with a ballet score. *Fancy Free,* with choreography by Jerome Robbins, was such a phenomenal success when introduced on April 18, 1944 that it had to be given more than 150 times that season.

Before the year of 1944 had ended, Bernstein invaded still another area of musical creativity, that of the Broadway theatre. *On the Town* opened on December 28, and almost at once Bernstein assumed a dominant place in the American musical theatre.

Actually, *On the Town* was an extension of an idea previously projected in that ballet, *Fancy Free.* The ballet scenario described the escapades of three sailors on shore leave as they meet up now with one girl and now with another. In *On the Town,* the three sailors have twenty-four hours leave in New York City. During that time they roam about the city, and, in the process, each meets the girl of his heart. Ozzie finds an anthropology student; Chip, a female taxi driver; and Gaby, a young lady, Ivy, whose picture he espied in the subway publicized as "Miss Turnstiles," and whom he finally locates in a Carnegie Hall studio after a frantic search.

Breezily paced by George Abbott's surehanded direction, *On the Town* proved, as Lewis Nichols said of it, "one of the freshest musicals to come into town in a long time." From opening to final curtain, the breathless excitement, irreverence, and energy of youth enlivened the whole production. As for Bernstein's score, ballads like "Lonely Town" and "Lucky to Be Me," comedy numbers like "I Get Carried Away" and the extended orchestral sequences used as background music for ballet episodes all revealed unmistakably that the composer had as significant a place on Broadway as he had in Carnegie Hall.

Wonderful Town came almost a decade later, on February 25, 1953. Starring Rosalind Russell in one of her most exuberant stage performances, *Wonderful Town* generated so much power, possessed such an unrelenting momentum, and was paced with such breathless speed that audiences were left limp.

Here, as in the earlier Bernstein musical, the "town" is New York. Based on *My Sister Eileen* (stories by Ruth McKenney which had been made into a successful non-musical stage play), *Wonderful Town* described the quixotic adventures of Eileen and Ruth, two sisters come from Ohio to settle in New York's Greenwich Village. Ruth, a hard-boiled and sophisticated young lady, wants to become a writer; Eileen, with a baby face and a schoolgirl naivete to match, has aspirations for the stage. The assortment of picaresque characters with which they surround themselves in their basement apartment is the guarantee that their life would run no normal course. But though disaster is an omnipresent possibility, Ruth and Eileen work out their destinies to their full satisfaction, both in their professional and personal lives.

In Leonard Bernstein, said Brooks Atkinson in his review, "they have the perfect composer for this sort of work—a modern with a sense of humor and a gift of melody. . . . He writes with wit, scope and variety." His now wide gamut of popular-song expression could pass from the sultry and the sentimental ("A Quiet Girl" and "Never Felt that Way"), and from the nostalgic ("Ohio") to wit, parody and broad satire ("One Hundred Easy Ways" and "Story Vignettes").

Both *On the Town* and *Wonderful Town* were musical comedies. Bernstein's transition to the musical play was made with *Candide,* in 1956, a musical stage adaptation of the famous Voltaire satire of the same name. *Candide* was a box-office disaster; but both Lillian Hellman's text and Leonard

Bernstein's music were far better than its feeble run of seventy-three performances would suggest. Someday *Candide* will be revived and will be appreciated for its charm, brilliance, grace, and salty wit. Meanwhile, its overture has become a staple in the symphonic repertory.

The disappointment and frustration that accompanied the sad fate of *Candide* were thoroughly dissipated with the critical and public reaction to Bernstein's next musical play, *West Side Story,* which opened at the Winter Garden on September 26, 1957, where it remained for 734 performances. A national tour followed, after which the company returned to the Winter Garden for still another extended run. *West Side Story* toured Israel, Africa, and the Near East in 1961; was produced with outstanding success in several European capitals; and in 1968 was included in the regular repertory of the renowned Volksoper in Vienna. The motion-picture adaptation released in 1961 (starring Natalie Wood and Richard Beymer) was a box-office and artistic success of the first magnitude, grossing over twenty-five million dollars, and capturing the Academy Award.

Its success was well earned, for *West Side Story* is one of our musical theatre's proudest achievements to date, a landmark.

The idea to adapt the theme of Shakespeare's *Romeo and Juliet* for modern New York City, to describe the conflict of two teen-age gangs in terms of the struggle between the Capulets and the Montagues in old Verona, was born with Jerome Robbins, the choreographer. Arthur Laurents then wrote the text, and Stephen Sondheim the lyrics for Bernstein's songs. Jerome Robbins devised the choreography which became the dominant element in the production and helped induce an altogether new concept in musical playwriting. Climactic points in the drama are achieved through ballet; the ballet (no less than the story, the characterizations, and the music) points up the social problem that complicates the lives of hero and heroine. And in Bernstein's music we find fixed the tensions, bitterness, and hate created by this social problem.

West Side Story is essentially the love story of Tony and Maria in New York's West Side, a story placed in front of the ominous background of a life-and-death struggle between two teen-age gangs. Tony is a member of the Jets, a group dedicated to keep Puerto Ricans out of their territory. Maria is the sister of the leader of the opposing Sharks, a Puerto Rican gang. Though they thus belong to opposing sides, Tony and Maria manage to carry on their tender romance secretly, and then to improvise a mock marriage for themselves in a bridal shop, a marriage they themselves consider the real thing. But this love affair is doomed, even as was that of Romeo and Juliet in Shakespeare's Verona. In a gang war, Tony kills Maria's brother. Then he himself is murdered by an avenging Shark.

Rarely has our musical theatre, traditionally so devoted to escapism, concerned itself with a tragedy like this, and more rarely still has it developed tragedy with such vivid realism. Nevertheless, as Brooks Atkinson pointed out in his review, *West Side Story* managed to draw beauty out of ugliness. "For it has a searching point of view. . . . Everything . . . is of a piece. Everything contributes to the total impression of wildness, ecstasy, and anguish."

Wildness, ecstasy, and anguish can be found in Bernstein's remarkable score. The wildness appears in his extraordinary ballet music, some of the most ambitious symphonic writing he had as yet attempted for the popular theatre. The ecstasy and the anguish are in turns encountered in songs like "Maria," "I Feel Pretty," "Somewhere," and "Tonight."

"There are passages worthy of grand opera," said John McClain, while Walter Kerr maintained that "by the magic of good music . . . is built up moments of theatrical beauty."

In 1966, Bernstein announced that at the conclusion of the 1968–1969 season he would retire as the music director of the New York Philharmonic. "A time is arriving in my life when I must concentrate on composition." He was thinking not only of the concert hall but also of the Broadway theatre which is also close to his heart. After *West Side Story,* Bernstein had been involved in an effort to make a musical out of Thornton Wilder's play, *The Skin of Our Teeth,* which had received the Pulitzer Prize in 1943. About a half a year was spent on this project by Bernstein and his collaborators before they decided to scrap it because they were not satisfied with the results. But the anguish that attended such a defeat could hardly dampen the kind of enthusiasm Bernstein has for the musical stage, certainly, not permanently. Bernstein is still a musical force in the theatre to be reckoned with strongly. Whether he turns to musical comedy or musical play, once he begins to direct a good deal more of his enormous energies and talents to composition, he will have much to say about the directions which our musical theatre will take in the future.

INDEX

INDEX

INDEX

INDEX

INDEX